Political Religion beyond Totalitarianism

Also by Joost Augusteijn

REGION AND STATE IN NINETEENTH-CENTURY EUROPE: Nation-building, Regional Identities and Separatism (*ed. with Eric Storm*)

FROM PUBLIC DEFIANCE TO GUERRILLA WARFARE: The Experience of Ordinary Volunteers in the Irish War of Independence, 1916–1921

THE MEMOIRS OF JOHN M. REGAN, A CATHOLIC OFFICER IN THE RIC AND RUC, 1909–1948 (*ed.*)

PATRICK PEARSE: The Making of a Revolutionary

THE IRISH REVOLUTION, 1913–1923 (*ed.*)

IRELAND IN THE 1930s: New Perspectives (*ed.*)

IRISH HISTORY: A Research Yearbook (1) (*ed. with Mary-Ann Lyons*)

IRISH HISTORY: A Research Yearbook (2) (*ed. with Mary-Ann Lyons and Deirdre Macmahon*)

Also by Patrick Dassen

THE MANY FACES OF EVOLUTION IN EUROPE, c. 1860–1914 (*ed. with M. Kemperink*)

DE ONTTOVERING VAN DE WERELD. Max Weber en het probleem van de moderniteit in Duitsland, 1890–1920

GEGIJZELD DOOR HET VERLEDEN. Van de Historikerstreit tot het Sloterdijk-debat (*ed. with Ton Nijhuis*)

DUITSERS ALS SLACHTOFFERS. Het einde van een taboe? (*ed. with Krijn Thijs and Ton Nijhuis*)

VAN DE BARRICADEN NAAR DE LOOPGRAVEN. Oorlog en samenleving in Europa, 1789–1918 (*ed. with Petra Groen*)

Also by Maartje Janse

DE AFSCHAFFERS. Publieke opinie, organisatie en politiek in Nederland, 1840–1880

DE GEEST VAN JAN SALIE. Nederland in verval?

Political Religion beyond Totalitarianism

The Sacralization of Politics in the Age of Democracy

Edited by

Joost Augusteijn
Lecturer in European History, Leiden University, The Netherlands

Patrick Dassen
Lecturer in European History, Leiden University, The Netherlands

and

Maartje Janse
Postdoctoral Researcher, Leiden University, The Netherlands

First published 2013 by
PALGRAVE MACMILLAN

Palgrave Macmillan in the UK is an imprint of Macmillan Publishers Limited,
registered in England, company number 785998, of Houndmills, Basingstoke,
Hampshire RG21 6XS.

Palgrave Macmillan in the US is a division of St Martin's Press LLC,
175 Fifth Avenue, New York, NY 10010.

Palgrave Macmillan is the global academic imprint of the above companies
and has companies and representatives throughout the world.

Palgrave® and Macmillan® are registered trademarks in the United States,
the United Kingdom, Europe and other countries.

ISBN 978–1–137–29171–4

This book is printed on paper suitable for recycling and made from fully
managed and sustained forest sources. Logging, pulping and manufacturing
processes are expected to conform to the environmental regulations of the
country of origin.

A catalogue record for this book is available from the British Library.

A catalog record for this book is available from the Library of Congress.

10   9   8   7   6   5   4   3   2   1
22 21 20 19 18 17 16 15 14 13

Printed and bound in Great Britain by
CPI Antony Rowe, Chippenham and Eastbourne

Contents

List of Illustrations and Plates

All pictures courtesy of the International Institute of Social History in Amsterdam unless otherwise indicated.

Illustrations

Plates

Note: Every effort has been made to trace copyright holders and to obtain their permission for the use of copyright material. The publisher apologizes for any errors or omissions in the above list and would be grateful if notified of any corrections that should be incorporated in future reprints or editions of this book.

Notes on Contributors

Joost Augusteijn is a lecturer at Leiden University. He has previously held posts at the University of Amsterdam, Trinity College, Dublin and Queens University Belfast, and has taught at the College of William and Mary. He is the author of *From Public Defiance to Guerrilla Warfare: The Experience of Ordinary Volunteers in the Irish War of Independence 1916–1921* (1996), and *Patrick Pearse: The Making of a Revolutionary* (2010), as well as the editor of several volumes on Irish history and beyond.

Eduard van de Bilt has a PhD in History from Cornell. He teaches American History at Leiden University and the University of Amsterdam, and specializes in American intellectual history. He is co-editor of several books on American history and the author of *Becoming John Adams: The Making of a Great American in Leiden, 1780–1782* (2005), *Demasqué van een Democratie* (2002) and, together with Joke Kardux, *Newcomers in an Old City: The American Pilgrims in Leiden, 1609–1620* (1998) and *Obama in Historisch Perspectief* (2009).

Dennis Bos is a lecturer in Dutch History at Leiden University. He has published on the history of the early socialist movement in the nineteenth century and is currently finishing a book on the socialist mythology surrounding the Paris Commune of 1871.

Patrick Dassen lectures at Leiden University where he specializes in German history, 1870–1945. He has previously held posts at the University of Amsterdam, the University of Groningen and the Germany Institute Amsterdam. He is the author of a monograph on Max Weber, *De onttovering van de wereld: Max Weber en het probleem van de moderniteit in Duitsland, 1890–1920* (1999), and co-editor of several volumes, including *The Many Faces of Evolution in Europe, c. 1860–1914* (2005).

Adam Fairclough holds the Raymond and Beverly Sackler Chair of American History and Culture at Leiden University. He is the author of *To Redeem the Soul of America: The Southern Christian Leadership and Martin Luther King, Jr.* (1987), *Race and Democracy: The Civil Rights Struggle in Louisiana, 1915–1972* (1995), *Better Day Coming: Blacks and Equality, 1890–2000* (2001) and *A Class of Their Own: Black Teachers in the Segregated South* (2007). He edited *The Star Creek Papers: Washington Parish and the Lynching of Jerome Wilson* (1997). He is currently writing a history of Reconstruction in the town and parish of Natchitoches, Louisiana.

Jolijn Groothuizen is a research masters student at Leiden University. She is also a high school teacher in history and has held several student-assistant positions at Leiden University. She is the author of 'Tot hier en niet verder' in the journal *De Negentiende Eeuw*.

Maartje Janse is a postdoctoral researcher at the Institute of History of Leiden University. She specializes in nineteenth-century European and American political culture. Her publications include *De Afschaffers. Publieke opinie, organisatie en politiek in Nederland, 1840–1880* (2007). Her current research focuses on the impact on politics of early nineteenth-century mass organizations against, for instance, slavery and temperance.

Henk Kern is a lecturer at Leiden University and teaches in the departments of History and Russian Studies. He has published the monograph *Denken over Rusland. Europese beschouwingen over de Grote Hervormingen, 1861–1881* (2008) and several articles on Russian and Soviet history.

Herman Paul is a lecturer in historiography and historical theory at Leiden University. He also holds a special chair in secularization studies at the University of Groningen. Among his recent publications are *Hayden White: The Historical Imagination* (2011), *Het moeras van de geschiedenis: Nederlandse debatten over historisme* (2012) and the co-edited volume, *Hermeneutics and the Humanities: Dialogues with Hans-Georg Gadamer* (2012).

Eric Storm is a lecturer at Leiden University. He began as a specialist on Spanish intellectual history but during the last few years he has primarily studied processes of nation-building and regional identity creation from a comparative perspective. This has resulted in the publication of *El descubrimiento del Greco: Nacionalismo y arte moderno, 1860–1914* (2011) and *The Culture of Regionalism: Art, Architecture and International Exhibitions in France, Germany and Spain, 1890–1939* (2010).

Henk te Velde is a professor of history at Leiden University. Until 2005 he was professor of history at the University of Groningen where he also graduated. During short research stays he was a visiting fellow and visiting professor at Oxford (St Edmund Hall), Berlin (ZVGE) and Paris (Science Po). He has written a number of books about Dutch political history and many articles in the field of comparative history of political culture.

Adriaan van Veldhuizen is a lecturer at Leiden University, where he is currently completing his PhD in the Dutch history department. He studied both history and philosophy at Groningen University. He specializes in the history of political culture and the philosophy of history.

Acknowledgements

This volume is the product of sustained academic debate among members of the Research Theme Group 'Political Culture and National Identity' (PCNI) at the Institute for History, Leiden University. The central conclusion arising from these discussions was the contention that modern politics necessarily assumes religious forms and content. The group subsequently organized a series of lectures around this theme 'Political Religion in the Western World, c. 1800–2000'. The extent to which this 'sacralization of politics' can be identified in different countries and political systems was analysed in a series of case studies covering various European countries and the United States. We also invited Emilio Gentile (Sapienza University of Rome), whose book *Politics as Religion* (2006) had inspired us to start our debate. We express our gratitude to Professor Gentile for the interesting discussion he held with us and for his inspiring lecture to our students.

These experiences convinced us that as a group we had something substantial to add to the debate on the 'Religion of Politics'. The results can be found in the combination of theoretical engagement and empirical case studies presented in this volume, which we hope in turn will be a springboard to further exploration by graduate students and scholars alike.

Finally, we wish to thank the Institute for History of Leiden University and the staff of Palgrave Macmillan, without whose assistance this volume would not have been completed.

The Editors, June 2012

Introduction:
Politics and Religion

Joost Augusteijn, Patrick Dassen and Maartje Janse

One of the major consequences of the rise of democracy at the end of the eighteenth century has been that popular consent has become a necessary factor in obtaining political legitimacy. Initially the people came to participate in politics indirectly. Facilitated by a growing space for public debate, a greater appreciation of public opinion and more powerful parliaments, ordinary people began to speak out and to organize themselves. Over time popular influence became more direct through the formation of modern political parties and a gradual extension of the franchise.

Authorities of several, partly new, nation-states reacted to this potential breaking up of the polity with increasing attempts to 'nationalize' the masses by creating a sense of loyalty and unity among their citizens. In order to mobilize the population, political parties and state authorities, particularly from the 1870s onwards, put ever more emphasis on providing attractive political messages. Of course, the promise of improvement in material circumstances was very important – higher wages, better housing and so forth – but an immaterial message, a narrative about community, meaning and hope for a better world, proved to be a strong mobilizing instrument as well.

Any agent in modern politics, be it states, parties, politicians, pressure groups or newspapers, simply had to appeal to the masses and win their hearts and minds. This was done through messages that often used religious forms and language, providing meaning, coherence, identity, myths, rituals and a clear distinction between 'good' and 'evil'. While in many Western countries church and state were formally separated, ambitious political agents offered narratives which gave their adherents a feeling of belonging and a sense of meaning. Increasingly politics came to resemble belief systems which claimed to explain the purpose

1

of human existence, thus creating what has been termed a 'secular religion'. Veneration and sacralization became a characteristic of all forms of modern politics: of democracies, political leaders, the nation, the people, the Aryan race and so on. Modern politics, it can be argued, has its own 'holy scriptures' (the American Constitution [1787], the *Communist Manifesto* [1848] or *Mein Kampf* [1925–26]), its own prophets (Karl Marx, Adam Smith or Abraham Lincoln) and its own martyrs (Martin Luther King, Horst Wessel or Mahatma Gandhi). In the Western world, since the late eighteenth century, people thus often came to experience 'politics as religion'.[1] Since politics obtained this religious dimension due to the need to mobilize the masses, the 'sacralization of politics' is not a unique, atypical phenomenon but lies at the heart of modern politics.

Although the importance of the sacralization of politics was already recognized by Jean-Jacques Rousseau in the eighteenth century,[2] the (historiographical) problem is that the phenomenon has, since the 1930s, been studied almost exclusively by researchers of totalitarian regimes. They used the concept of 'political religion' when referring to the religious elements of totalitarian states, in juxtaposition with the more generally defined concept of civil religion that Rousseau had coined. As a result, the overarching phenomenon of sacralization of politics became mainly applied to the regimes of Communist Soviet Union, Fascist Italy and Nazi Germany. Because of the obvious religious dimension of totalitarian politics, this is not very surprising. For example, the propaganda movie *Triumph des Willens* (1935) by Leni Riefenstahl on the Nazis' Nuremberg *Reichsparteitag* in 1934 is a classic example of 'political liturgy', an almost perfect 'ideal type' in the Weberian sense. The movie is about hope for the future (after a very difficult period), the unity of the German people and the subordination of the individual to the collective, about sacrifice and martyrdom (the fallen heroes in Hitler's failed coup in November 1923) and, not in the least of course, about Hitler as the 'Messiah' of the German people. These elements, together with the underlying threat of force, formed the core by which the Nazi regime maintained its hold on German society and represented political religion in its almost purest form.

Many contemporaries had an eye for this religious dimension of the totalitarian regimes of inter-war Europe. From the 1930s the expression 'political religion' appeared in the writings of, among others, the young French sociologist Raymond Aron and the German theologian Hans-Joachim Schoeps.[3] Perhaps the phenomenon found its clearest representation in *Die politische Religionen* by the Austrian philosopher

Eric Voegelin in 1938. Though the author used a long-term perspective, even including the reign of the Egyptian pharaohs, his book culminated in the modern political religions of his age, for which the 'sacralization of the collectivity' was, in his view, central. The book also had a clear political message: according to Voegelin, who was forced to flee Vienna because of the *Anschluss*, it was precisely what he called the *religious* side of Nazism which made this regime so dangerous.[4]

After the Second World War it took a while before interest in the role of a 'secular religion' was renewed. In the first decades after 1945 it was instead the concept of 'totalitarianism' that dominated research and debate, with Hannah Arendt's *The Origins of Totalitarianism* (1951) playing an influential role. In this classic study she showed the similarities between the totalitarian systems of Nazism and Stalinism, emphasizing the lawlessness and terror of both regimes. In the long run this centrality of terror and the spreading of fear could not, however, explain the functioning of Stalinism and Nazism. In order to understand the attraction and success of totalitarian regimes, scholars were forced to pay more attention to the popular *belief* in these systems instead of their coercive qualities. In 1982 the French sociologist Jean-Pierre Sironneau, for example, took up the concept of political religion again in a study of Communism and Nazism in which he tried to show that both ideologies had an affinity with the traditional dimensions of religious experience, like ritualized behaviour. Furthermore, he stressed that political religions could assume positive functions of religion, such as social integration.[5] In this way it was made clear that these regimes fulfilled an essential function for their citizens and that they were not simply forced or manipulated into following their leaders but might have done so voluntarily. This phenomenon could be termed the 'democratic' side of totalitarianism.

The interest in political religion has resurfaced only in the last two decades. An important sign of this revival was the publication of the three-volume set of papers on totalitarianism and political religion, edited by Hans Maier (1996, 1997, 2003),[6] later translated into English. In the context of this volume, however, it is important to note that the study of the sacralization of politics was still very much connected to *totalitarian* regimes and rarely if ever in relation to democratic regimes. This pattern was reinforced by the launching of the prominent journal *Totalitarian Movements and Political Religions* in Britain in 2000. This journal (in 2011 relaunched as *Politics, Religion & Ideology*) explicitly provides a forum for the 'exploration of the politics of illiberal ideologies, both religious and secular'. So, although the focus has now been broadened by paying attention not only to radical politics but also to *religious* movements (in relation, of course, to the radicalization within Islam at the end of the twentieth century), the core of the journal is still about *illiberal* ideologies.[7] This same limitation is visible in the influential *Earthly Powers* (2005) and *Sacred Causes* (2007)[8] by Michael Burleigh (not coincidentally one of the founding editors of *Totalitarian Movements*) as well as in the volume *Fascism, Totalitarianism and Political Religion* (2005) edited by Roger Griffin[9] and *Beyond Totalitarianism: Stalinism and Nazism Compared* (2009), edited by Sheila Fitzpatrick and Michael Geyer.[10]

After the fall of the last totalitarian regimes in Eastern Europe and the apparent victory of the liberal democratic system, democracy lost its distinguishing features and has itself slowly come under scrutiny. Developments in new 'democracies' such as Russia and most recently in North African countries following the Arab Spring as well as the apparent neo-imperialist aspects of Western foreign policy (e.g. in Iraq) have fuelled doubts about the inevitability of the superiority and rationality of the Western democratic system.

Following suggestions put forward in the late 1960s by the sociologist Robert Bellah in relation to American politics,[11] Emilio Gentile was the first to study systematically the proposition that a sacralization of politics was an essential feature of mass politics,[12] concluding that in principle all political systems or concepts including democracies could be sacralized. To retain the distinction which had been established between democratic and totalitarian forms of politics, he reformulated the older concepts of 'political religion' and 'civil religion' as two ideal types. Although he states that all political systems 'in reality' offer hybrid combinations of these two extremes and that 'a civil religion can become as intolerant as a political religion', he nevertheless argues that there are 'substantial differences between the civil religions of democratic regimes and the political religions of totalitarian regimes', thus still maintaining the older dichotomy. In his thinking a civil religion does not identify with any particular ideology, party or religion but is above them. It tolerates individual autonomy in relation to the sacralized collectivity and elicits spontaneous consent. In contrast, a political religion is exclusive and does not accept the coexistence of other ideologies or movements. It demands compliance and denies individual autonomy while sanctioning the use of violence against its enemies.[13]

Despite these recent developments, research on 'politics as religion' has thus far been focused almost exclusively on totalitarian, illiberal states. This can at least partly be explained by moral and political concerns. The horrors of the Second World War exposed the incredible suffering the totalitarian regimes had caused. The sacralization of politics they had practised, which had ultimately led to a war of destruction, ethnic cleansings and genocide therefore came to be regarded as a degeneration of 'normal' politics. In this view the leaders of the totalitarian regimes had been able to get the support of their populations by propaganda and manipulation, by transforming their politics into a 'religion' slavishly followed by their citizens. Diametrically opposed to the political religion of the totalitarian regimes – the evil, as embodied by the dictators Hitler and Stalin – stood the politics of Western liberal democracy: prudent, moderate, sober and 'rational', unstained by emotional, let alone religious, aspects, which were then seen as something negative. Because after 1945 the future of vulnerable Western democracy was at stake, charismatic leaders, emotions and the mobilization of the masses were very much distrusted. This politically inspired analysis strengthened the contrast between the 'evil' totalitarian, illiberal regimes and the 'good' Western liberal democracy.[14] Although some question marks have been raised over the viability of seeing the Western democratic system as free from religious aspects, this dichotomy has broadly survived until today.

In the light of recent historiographical developments this strict dichotomy between 'bad totalitarianism' and 'good democracy' can, however, no longer be maintained. An important historiographical trend in the past two decades has been the challenging of traditional polarities. One of the most striking examples has been offered by sociologist Michael Mann in *The Dark Side of Democracy: Explaining Ethnic Cleansing* (2005).[15] He argues that episodes of ethnic cleansing, which have often been brushed aside as historical aberrations, are directly linked to processes of modernization and democratization. When in nationalist discourse the *demos* (the people) is increasingly identified with the *ethnos* (ethnicity), minorities are excluded and in some cases dehumanized, which can lead to ethnic cleansing. Mann shows that even American presidents Thomas Jefferson (around 1800) and Theodore Roosevelt (around 1900) spoke of the justified and inevitable extermination of the Native Americans.[16] In Mann's own words, 'Murderous ethnic cleansing has been a central problem of our civilization, our modernity, our conceptions of progress, and our attempts to introduce democracy in Europe and the colonies. It is our dark side.'[17] The fact that Hitler and Himmler could refer to the American genocide of Native Americans as a commendable example spurs us on as historians to take a critical look at our democratic heritage.[18]

A related development is illustrated by the evolution of populism research. As stated above, democracy was idealized as an ideology in its own right, especially after 1945. However, in practice liberal democracy has always contained internal contradictions. Whenever, for instance, a populist movement became successful, it was treated as a pathological symptom, requiring sociological explanation. However, as Margaret Canovan argues in an important essay, if we want to understand the workings of democracy, we should not locate populism outside the boundaries of democracy but rather study it as an illustration of the 'inescapable ambiguity' of democracy.[19] Where Mann spoke of the 'dark side of democracy', Canovan discusses the 'two faces of democracy', referring to what she calls the redemptive (idealistic) side and the pragmatic (practical) side of politics, arguing that populism thrives on the tension between the two.[20]

Both Mann and Canovan point to a duplicity in democracy, one that we are rediscovering now that the post-Second World War glorification of democracy has waned, and the optimism regarding the establishment of new stable democracies after the fall of Communism, most aptly represented by Francis Fukuyama's *The End of History and the Last Man* (1992), has turned into pessimism. Recent wars fought in the name of democracy have also stained its image. We now realize more than ever that democracy is not just a rational, ideal form of politics but also contains non-rational elements.[21] This perspective links up directly with a new direction in democracy studies, in which democratic ideals and practices are historicized and understood as a tradition rather than a given.[22] Despite their fundamental differences, democratic as well as totalitarian politics need and use emotions, irrational beliefs, charismatic leaders, symbols, coercion and even forms of violence, otherwise they could not function.

The second historiographical current that impacts on our research perspective when questioning the totalitarianism–democracy dichotomy in relation to the sacralization of politics is the shift in political history of the last decades. Traditionally, this form of history writing was mainly concerned with state institutions, biographies of politicians and the history of political ideas. A broader perspective developed in the 1970s, incorporating a new interest in the importance of popular politics and later of the worldview of ordinary people. This development grew out of a 'cultural turn' in traditional political history, which started paying more attention to language, religion, rituals and symbols in everyday politics, and a kind of 'political turn' by cultural historians, who took on board Michel Foucault's claim that power relations are everywhere and that every human interaction reveals political struggles over authority, legitimacy and power.[23] The result was that political leaders and the ideology they propagated lost their central place in the universe of political history, while the experience of ordinary people and the meanings they attributed to political life and political traditions gained prominence.

In the context of this volume, these developments have resulted in two central aims. First we want to reassess the role of the sacralization of politics in democratic systems. By taking this aspect of democratic systems seriously we want to show that creating a secular religion is an essential element of modern mass politics and that the division of religion and politics into separate spheres that was dominant in twentieth-century sociology cannot be maintained. A second, connected aim is that we want to reappraise the role of ordinary people in the process of the sacralization of politics. Whereas a political religion had been previously predominantly understood as having been forced upon the masses by manipulative totalitarian leaders, we now want to investigate how and why ordinary people seem to crave and create secular religions themselves in all types of political systems. This bottom-up instead of top-down perspective on politics also constitutes a new research approach in this field.

Our objective in studying the sacralization of politics is to understand the workings of modern democratic mass politics and the role of ordinary people in this process. This requires that regimes beyond those of Nazi Germany, Communist Russia and Fascist Italy be included in this volume. The wide range of case studies represented – from Ireland, Spain and the Netherlands to the United States, Imperial Germany and Russia – for the first time takes the sacralization of politics in the Western world as the starting point for a transnational perspective. Its broad basis, including smaller countries which have not played a central role in the shaping of the modern world, also allows for a more sophisticated analysis of the sacralization process.

Structure of This Volume

The various contributions to this volume are grouped around a number of themes. After a more programmatic and transnational first part, we present the chapters in thematic clusters, bringing case studies on similar issues together as much as possible. Thus a definitional first part is followed by sections on Religion and Democracy, Socialism, Nationalism and Religion and Revolution. Part I contains two chapters which take a more general look at the relationship between religion and politics. In the first chapter Herman Paul discusses the use of the term 'religion' to describe phenomena which are not conventionally associated with religion. He poses the question, What is religious about the 'political religion' identified in this volume? In the search for an answer he considers whether political religion must be understood as an *analogical* or *essentialist* notion: Does political religion resemble traditional religions or does it meet the definitional requirements of a religion? On the basis of Wittgenstein's notion of family resemblances he ultimately concludes that all definitions of religion are based on the identification of analogies, thus saving historians the difficult task of determining what constitutes the essence of religion. In the second chapter Henk te Velde discusses the use of religious language in democratic politics to show that it refers to the hopes and dreams of the people. To explain the existing association between secular religions and totalitarianism he starts off by discussing how the definition of the concept of political religion became an important means of the defence of post-war liberal democracy against totalitarian politics. He then focuses on the way people referred to what they described as a 'conversion' to democratic socialism around 1900. Drawing on autobiographies he provides insight into the important functions of party politics for the shaping of personal and group identities. He concludes by showing the relevance of this insight for the current debate on populism, defining it as a controversial but essential part of democracy itself, instead of a threat to it.

The relationship between religion and democratic politics is central to the second part. Maartje Janse's contribution deals with early nineteenth-century Irish, British and American reform movements. National organizations like those calling for the abolition of slavery or Catholic emancipation succeeded in mobilizing hundreds of thousands of people in their campaigns. She argues that their mobilizing and disciplining methods were deeply rooted in the religious world, and that for large groups of people at this time politics and religion were intimately connected. Critics, however, argued that this mingling of religion and politics would lead from despotism and mind-control to a form of political religion. In the fourth chapter Eduard van de Bilt discusses one specific case where religion and politics were directly connected, the anti-slavery novel *Uncle Tom's Cabin* by Harriet Beecher Stowe. He shows that religion motivated Stowe but that this breaching of the 'wall of separation between church and state' led neither to ignoring the world of politics nor to a sacralization of politics. Her Christian conviction forced her into the realm of politics but at the same time meant that politics could never be sacralized.

Part III deals with the religious aspects of socialism. In a visual essay Jolijn Groothuizen and Dennis Bos make clear why socialism is so often seen as the prime example of a secular religion. In its use of images socialism displays almost all of the features of a traditional religion. In the sixth chapter Adriaan van Veldhuizen deals with the sacralization of the history of the socialist party itself, in this case the nineteenth-century Dutch Social Democratic Party (SDAP), to show that the sacralization of politics was not limited to totalitarianism nor to a state. He shows how the socialist promise of a better future was supported by a sacralization of the movement's past, both crucial elements in tying its members to the party. This celebration of socialism's history can be found in propaganda, memoirs, biographies, plays and songs, and was often initiated not by the party but by individual members themselves.

The fourth section deals with the connection between nationalism and the sacralization of politics in three diverse contributions. Joost Augusteijn explores the proposition that nationalism functions essentially as a political religion because all forms of nationalism submerge the individual's interests to the nation's will. He thereby challenges the traditional distinction between an inclusive form of political nationalism, which allows everyone to join its ranks regardless of their background, and an exclusivist cultural form, which accepts only people with certain characteristics. He does this through a study of the thinking of various Irish nationalists from the nineteenth and early twentieth centuries. Patrick Dassen shows in his chapter how at the beginning of the First World War the German nation, as a secular entity, was sacralized by the German intellectual and cultural elite. The German nation at first sight seemed to assume the religious function of social integration and the feeling of 'belonging together'. However, soon after the armed conflict began, the war turned out to be a divisive element: nationalism not only integrated but more importantly also deeply polarized the German people. The German nation was therefore no longer able to function as a sacralized entity and elevate the people as a whole. In the final chapter of this section Adam Fairclough investigates the notion of the United States as the archetype of a civil religion. He uses Lincoln's famous phrase (1862) that the United States is 'the last best hope on earth' for democracy to highlight the notion of American exceptionalism, that the United States was not only uniquely fitted to teach liberty and democracy to other peoples but also had a providential mission to do so, which lies at the heart of American civil religion. The chapter goes on to argue that the nationalistic belief in American exceptionalism is so potent that Lincoln's phrase has led many historians to misconceive fundamentally America's role in the development of democracy and that civil religion should therefore be redefined.

The final section looks at the sacralization of politics in times of conflict. In the tenth chapter Henk Kern re-evaluates the role of political religion as an instrument of a ruthless totalitarian regime to subdue the population. He does this by exploring the way the people interpreted the events of the Russian Revolution and how traditional religious images and beliefs served to give meaning to what happened. In this way the social and cultural environment of the new regime forced the atheistic leadership of the Communist Party to accept the development of a political religion in Soviet society. In his contribution Eric Storm describes how the anticlericalism in Spain as it developed during the first decades of the twentieth century came to a violent outburst during the Spanish Civil War (1936–39). After an historical overview of European anticlericalism since the end of the eighteenth century, Storm makes clear that the anticlerical 'belief in unbelief' contained strong religious elements and culminated in a kind of ritual catharsis and iconoclastic fury in the Republican zone during the Civil War, which clearly was not coordinated from above but was pushed from below.

Given the virtual absence in current historiography of case studies on the role of the sacralization of politics in democratic society and the lack of serious consideration of the role of the people in its emergence, this volume hopes to provide a fresh impulse to the further study of the sacralization of politics as well as the functioning of totalitarian and democratic regimes. We are convinced that the new perspectives presented here will be useful to all those interested in the complex relationship between people, parties, governments and states, and we hope that it will inspire further research in this field.

Notes

1. This is also the title of the seminal work by Emilio Gentile, *Politics as Religion*, trans. George Staunton (Princeton, NJ and Oxford, 2006). See for the 'religions of politics' as modern phenomena, xvi–xix, 141ff.
2. Gentile, *Politics as Religion*, 1–2.
3. For a good historiographical overview see Philippe Burrin, 'Political Religion: The Relevance of a Concept', *History and Memory* 9/1–2 (1997), 321–49; David D. Roberts, '"Political Religion" and the Totalitarian Departures of Inter-War Europe: On the Uses and Disadvantages of an Analytical Category', *Contemporary European History* 18/4 (2009), 381–414.

4. On Voegelin see Dietmar Herz, 'Die politische Religionen im Werk Voegelins', in Hans Maier and Michael Schäfer (eds), *'Totalitarismus' und 'Politische Religionen'. Konzepte des Diktaturvergleichs*, vol. 1 (Paderborn, 1996), 191–210.

5. Jean-Pierre Sironneau, *Sécularisation et religions politiques* (The Hague, 1982). See also George L. Mosse, *The Nationalization of the Masses* (New York, 1975); Emilio Gentile, *The Sacralization of Politics in Fascist Italy* (Cambridge, 1996).

6. Hans Maier (ed.), *'Totalitarismus' und 'Politische Religionen'. Konzepte des Diktaturvergleichs*, 3 vols (Paderborn et al., 1996, 1997, 2003).

7. In the mission statement we read, *'Totalitarian Movements and Political Religions* will scrutinize all attempts to totally refashion mankind and society, whether these hailed from the Left or the Right which, unusually, will receive equal consideration. Although its primary focus will be on the authoritarian and totalitarian politics of the twentieth century, the journal will also provide a forum for the wider discussion of the politics and faith of salvation in general, from the first stirrings of millenarian longings in the Middle Ages to the fundamentalist creeds of the present, together with examination of their inexorably catastrophic consequences' (http://gulib. georgetown.edu/newjour/t/msg02629.html, retrieved May 2012).

8. Michael Burleigh, *Earthly Powers: The Clash of Religion and Politics in Europe from the French Revolution to the Great War* (New York, 2005), and idem, *Sacred Causes: Religion and Politics from the European Dictators to Al Qaida* (New York, 2007).

9. Roger Griffin (ed.), *Fascism, Totalitarianism and Political Religion* (London and New York, 2005).

10. Sheila Fitzpatrick and Michael Geyer (eds), *Beyond Totalitarianism: Stalinism and Nazism Compared* (Cambridge, 2009).

11. Robert Bellah, 'Civil Religion in America', *Daedalus* 97/1 (1967), 1–21. See also Robert Bellah, *The Broken Covenant: American Civil Religion in Time of Trial* (New York, 1975).

12. Roger Griffin, '"Religious Politics": A Concept Comes of Age', *Leidschrift Historisch Tijdschrift* 26/2 (2011), 7–18 (11).

13. Gentile, *Politics as Religion*, xv, 139–40.

14. Griffin, 'Religious Politics', 9.

15. Michael Mann, *The Dark Side of Democracy: Explaining Ethnic Cleansing* (Cambridge, 2005).

16. Mann, *The Dark Side*, ix.

17. Ibid.

18. Ibid., 98, ix.

19. Margaret Canovan, 'Trust the People! Populism and the Two Faces of Democracy', *Political Studies* 47/1 (1999), 2–16 (16).

20. Canovan, 'Trust the People!', 8–14.

21. See for an introduction, Jeff Goodwin, James M. Jasper and Francesca Polletta, 'Introduction: Why Emotions Matter', in idem (eds), *Passionate Politics: Emotions and Social Movements* (Chicago, 2001), 1–24.

22. See Jeffrey Stout, *Democracy and Tradition* (Princeton, NJ and Oxford, 2004).

23. For an excellent analysis see Susan Pedersen, 'What Is Political History Now?', in David Cannadine (ed.), *What Is History Now?* (Basingstoke, 2002), 36–56.

Part I
Definition

Religion and Politics:
In Search of Resemblances

Herman Paul

As unlikely as it would have sounded a generation ago, historians of modern Europe have rediscovered religion.[1] Apart from being increasingly attentive to the various social, cultural and intellectual roles played by its so-called 'traditional religions' (Judaism, Christianity and Islam),[2] growing numbers of historians employ 'religion' as a key concept in the study of phenomena not conventionally associated with religion. Thus we hear about the 'religion of nature' practiced by eighteenth-century travellers and writers who perceived an unspoiled wood or wilderness as reaching beyond itself[3] or about the 'religion of history' professed by those nineteenth-century historicists who believed that historical inquiry would tell them who they were by showing where they came from.[4] We are told about a 'religion of science' that made its appearance among nineteenth-century scientific entrepreneurs and, in rather different form, entered school books in the atheistic German Democratic Republic.[5] Likewise, in the field of political history, we find scholars discussing 'liberal religion', the 'religion of socialism' and, most notably, 'political religion'.[6] Perhaps Stanley Fish was right after all to predict a couple of years ago that religion would succeed 'high theory and the triumvirate of race, gender and class as the centre of intellectual energy in the academy'.[7]

Yet, amidst all this creative employment of the term religion, one cannot help but wonder, What does religion mean? How exalted must one's language be or how sublime one's feelings of wonder and awe for such to count as religious? What is religious about the 'political religion' that contributors to this volume detect in totalitarian and even democratic political regimes? In this chapter, I try to respond to the last of these questions (while briefly addressing the other ones along the way). After a brief overview of how political religion entered scholarly discourse in the 1920s and 1930s, I focus on the frequently raised but rarely answered question whether political religion must be understood as an *analogical* or an *essentialist* notion. In more practical terms, Was Fascism a political religion because it *resembled* traditional religions such as Italian Catholicism, at least in certain crucial respects, or rather because the Fascist movement *itself* met the definitional requirements of religion?[8] Based on Ludwig Wittgenstein's notion of 'family resemblances', I argue that this is a falsely construed dilemma. Given that every attempt to specify what religion 'is' draws on what religions 'look like', there is no escape from analogical reasoning. Accordingly, historians can be spared the difficult task of identifying the essence of (political) religion. They are better advised to specify, with some degree of precision, which political and religious ideas, rituals or practices they perceive as resembling each other.

This does not only hold for political religion, the subject matter of this volume, but also for such scholarly constructs as 'religion of science' and 'religion of history'. In all of these cases, historians have to ponder whether or how they can employ the term religion, analogously or otherwise, in realms outside synagogue, church and mosque.

Political Religion: A Brief History

Although the genealogy of 'political religion' can be traced back to at least the seventeenth century,[9] the expression gained wide currency only in the Interbellum, after the establishment of a Communist regime in Russia and the emergence of Fascism in Italy and National Socialism in Germany. Worried about the totalitarian aspirations of these new regimes, great numbers of philosophers, theologians and political scientists almost simultaneously began to speak about 'political religion', a term they used to refer to the religious aspirations that the political realms under Lenin, Mussolini and Hitler began to display. The German Jewish philosopher of religion, Hans-Joachim Schoeps, for example, observed that Hitler presented himself as a messiah, although 'not as a king of peace and even less as an anointed of the Lord'. He noted that *Mein Kampf* served as a catechism of the new religion, that Horst Wessel was its principal martyr and that Jewish citizens such as Schoeps himself were increasingly regarded as heretics deserving excommunication or death.[10]

Whereas Schoeps highlighted the similarities between the political liturgies of the Nazi movement and those known from such 'traditional' religions as Judaism, Christianity and Islam, other scholars employed the term political religion to indicate a relocation of religion in the modern era. A case in point is Eric Voegelin's famous 1938 book, *Die politische Religionen*, which argued that 'inner-worldly religions' (*innerweltliche Religionen*) such as nationalism and socialism increasingly occupied places previously reserved to 'trans-worldly religions' (*überweltliche Religionen*). Whereas in the Middle Ages God had served as the most real being – what philosophers called the *ens realissimum* – this most real being was increasingly identified with such secular things as nature, science, the state or the nation. So, in Voegelin's view, people have a religion as soon as they elevate something, either in or outside the world of human affairs, to the status of most real being. 'Wherever a reality discloses itself in the religious experience as sacred, it becomes the most real, a *realissimum*.'[11] This, in turn, suggests that, for Voegelin, political religions, understood as those inner-worldly religions which treat the state or nation as most real, were not twentieth-century inventions. Attempts to sacralize the state had already been made by Niccolò Machiavelli and Thomas Hobbes. Accordingly, what the Communist, Fascist and Nazi regimes brought to light were rather the consequences of a gradual centuries-long process in which God had increasingly been replaced by Leviathan (the sea monster that in Hobbes's philosophy had lent its name to the secular state).[12]

Other examples besides Schoeps or Voegelin can easily be found. However, the story of how an interwar generation of scholars came to interpret the Lenin, Mussolini and Hitler regimes in terms of political religions has been told so often recently that it does not need to be recounted here.[13] For the purpose of this chapter, though, two things must be noted. One is that Schoeps's and Voegelin's generation did not at all agree on what exactly was religious about political religion. For them as for us, 'the crux of the problem is how religion itself is defined'.[14] Was Communism a political religion because its symbolic repertoire was *indebted* to the Orthodox Church? Did Nazism qualify as a 'disguised religion' because of its striking *similarities* with Christian religion, as Schoeps and, more famously, Carl Christian Bry pointed out?[15] Must the term political religion be reserved to those political regimes that displayed certain *functional equivalences* with traditional religions, as the French philosopher Raymond Aron argued in the early 1940s?[16] Or is religion rather an *anthropological* category and does the *homo religiosus* manifest itself as easily in congress or parliament as in synagogues, churches and mosques? Indeed, if 'political religion' in the interwar period denoted an extraordinary kind of interaction between the realms of politics and religion, as perceived by contemporaries, both the nature of that interaction and the defining features of the individual realms were open to debate.

Second, in spite of their conceptual divergences, all these authors agreed that political religion was a dangerous phenomenon which had to be analysed carefully in order to be opposed effectively. Almost without exception, they warned against the exclusive pretensions of the new religions – 'I am Adolf, thy Hitler; thou shalt have no other gods before me'[17] – and voiced their concerns about a politicization of society. Of course, the religious and ideological beliefs underlying these worries also varied. Whereas some humanist authors explained that the dignity and freedom of the individual became endangered, a more conservative author such as Voegelin argued that humanism was part of the problem, given that 'the secularization of life that accompanied the doctrine of humanitarianism' could be regarded as 'the soil in which such an anti-Christian religious movement as National Socialism was able to prosper'.[18]

This example illustrates, moreover, that for at least some authors, political religion was more than an analytical tool for understanding the quasi-religious aspirations of totalitarian regimes. What lent a special aura of gravitas to Voegelin's analysis was that the emergence of political religions was said to signal not only the weakened position of traditional religions but also the (politically) destructive consequences of the secularization process. In its most succinct formulation, the argument was that the death of God inevitably causes the birth of new gods, illustrated most dramatically in the political religions of the 1930s. If Western societies no longer worship the true God, they will turn the state, their leaders or some abstract ideal into an object worthy of worship. Along such lines, then, the concept of political religion could easily be assimilated in such secularization narratives as offered by Carl Schmitt, Jacques Maritain, Karl Löwith and their likes.[19]

What Is Religious about Political Religion?

This twofold heritage has loomed over the study of political religion ever since. In the post-Second World War period, the term political religion remained by and large reserved for totalitarian regimes, including especially German Nazism, Italian Fascism and Soviet Communism. Even though such scholars as Klaus Vondung, George L. Mosse and Jean-Pierre Sironneau increasingly came to prefer detached historical analysis over prophetic warning, they followed Schoeps's and Voegelin's examples by treating 'religion', 'cults' and 'liturgies' as features that could help explain the attractiveness of Hitler's or Mussolini's political styles.[20] Intentionally or not, this linkage of political religion with totalitarian politics reinforced the stereotypical idea that religion in the political sphere is a recipe for violence.[21] Only recently have historians come to argue that a sacralization of politics also occurs in non-totalitarian contexts and that political religion is therefore not necessarily as evil as Voegelin *cum suis* assumed.

Given that this move beyond the totalitarian is discussed in several of the chapters that follow, I should like to focus here on the second issue that students of political religion have inherited from their predecessors in the interwar period: the question of what exactly constitutes political religion. Can Mussolini's Fascism be considered a political religion because it met certain definitional requirements? Or does the religious terminology suggest itself because Fascist myths and rituals resembled those known from, for example, the Christian tradition? Just as students in the interwar period found themselves disagreeing on whether Fascism *was* a religion or merely *looked like* one, more recent generations of scholars have been struggling with definitional matters. While some have focused on *resemblances* between political styles and religious practices, others have advanced the more ambitious claim that Nazism and Fascism *as such* can be classified as religions.

Philippe Burrin offers an example of the first strategy when he argues for a textured, context-sensitive analysis of how political regimes 'use the religious culture of their society in order to elevate the political to a supreme and all-encompassing sphere, thereby establishing an absolute mission and authority'.[22] Although the second half of this sentence seems to contain a crypto-essentialist definition (with 'absolute mission' and 'absolute authority' serving as key religious features), the Swiss historian explains at some length that this is not his aim. He is rather interested in processes of how political regimes borrow, appropriate and mobilize 'patterns, symbols, rituals, attitudes and kinds of behavior molded by their society's religious culture'.[23] What he suggests is that historians can speak about political religion only when they specify with some degree of precision what political leaders at a given time and place derive from 'traditional' religions in their region, country or empire and why they do so. In other words, what matters for Burrin is not whether or not Soviet Communism can be classified as religious but what kind of symbols, ideas or practices Communist leaders or propagandists in the Soviet Union took from, most likely, the Orthodox Church. Who engaged in such processes of borrowing, at what time, for which purposes and with what effects? To what extent did Soviet Communism begin to 'resemble' Orthodox Christianity by appropriating some of its features?

While Burrin opts for what could be called an *analogical* approach to political religion, others claim that political systems themselves can become religious in nature. Vivid illustrations of this *essentialist* approach can be found in Emilio Gentile's influential study, *Politics as Religion*. In a historiographical survey, the Italian historian discusses no fewer than four classic essentialist definitions of religion. One of these is the so-called *crowd manipulation* definition, developed in the early twentieth century by Gaetano Mosca. This view equates religion with 'myths, symbols and rituals that are consciously adopted for propagandistic and demagogic reasons'.[24] In so far as this amounts to a definition, it focuses on the instrumental use that can be made of religion more than on what religion essentially is. Gentile therefore turns to what he calls a *fideistic* definition, derived from Gustave Le Bon.[25] This sees religion as expressing an 'irrepressible' human desire to submit oneself to a higher entity and to worship such an entity through rituals and festivals. Unlike the crowd manipulation definition, which highlights the strategic exploitation of religion, the fideistic approach 'accepts that myths and rituals can also be the spontaneous expression of the masses, produced by their need for faith and beliefs'.[26] Third, Gentile presents a *functionalist* theory of religion such as developed by Émile Durkheim, which differs from the fideistic one by highlighting the social bonds that religious sentiments create. For Durkheim, God is nothing but society writ large. 'Religious beliefs express the unity and identity of a collectivity, while rituals are forms of action that serve to evoke, maintain and renew the unity and identity of a social group through their reference to sacred entities, which can be objects, animals, persons or ideas.'[27] Finally, Gentile invokes Rudolf Otto, author of *Das Heilige* (1917), who equated religion with a 'numinous experience of the sacred', an enthralling feeling of 'absolute dependency' or a mystical experience of an 'immense, mysterious, and majestic power'.[28] Whereas Durkheim emphasized collective aspects of religion, this fourth definition seems to focus entirely on individuals and their personal inexpressible experiences of the divine.

Although Gentile argues that none of these early twentieth-century theories of religion 'can be sufficient in itself to explain the sacralization of politics', he seems open to the possibility of combining them: 'A religion of politics, like any other religion, can contain *crowd manipulation* features, can fulfil the functions of social cohesion and the legitimization of power, can satisfy the religious sentiment of the masses, and can be the genuine expression of a numinous experience.'[29] If these are all essentialist approaches to religion, so, too, is Gentile's own definition.[30]

In Gentile's view, a political movement or regime becomes religious as soon as it

1 consecrates the primacy of a *secular collective entity* by placing it at the centre of a set of beliefs and myths that define the meaning and the ultimate purpose of the social existence and prescribe the principles for discriminating between good and evil;
2 formalizes this concept in an ethical and social *code of commandments* that binds the individual to the sacralized entity and imposes loyalty, devotion and even willingness to lay down one's life;
3 considers its followers to be the *community of the elect* and interprets its political action as a *messianic function* to fulfil a mission of benefit to all humanity;
4 creates a *political liturgy* for the adoration of the sacralized collective entity through the cult of the person who embodies it, and through the mythical and symbolic representation of its *sacred history* – a regular ritual evocation of events and deeds performed over a period of time by the community of the elect.[31]

For Gentile, then, the question is not, as it is for Burrin, to what extent and in what ways political regimes resemble traditional religions; his question is rather whether or not regimes become religious by doing the same things as traditional religions do. Whereas Burrin prefers an analogical approach, Gentile opts for an essentialist one. Historians may wonder, then, with whom to side. Which of these definitional approaches is to be preferred? Or can they perhaps be combined?

Religion: A Matter of Family Resemblances

The two alternatives are perhaps not as mutually exclusive as they appear at first sight, for to what extent would it be possible to develop an essentialist definition of (political) religion that is not, in one way or another, indebted to particular manifestations of what is conventionally classified as religion? Isn't there, in other words, an analogical element to every definition of religion? Doesn't every attempt to specify the 'is' necessarily draw on what 'looks like'? The four classic essentialist definitions mentioned in the previous section offer some cases in point. Durkheim's view of religion as an essentially societal phenomenon, for example, was clearly indebted to the author's close experience with various forms of religious patriotism developed in *fin de siècle* France by Catholic, Protestant and Jewish intellectuals.[32] Likewise, Otto's equation of religion with numinous experience drew heavily on a mode of liberal Protestant theology for which the nineteenth-century German theologian Friedrich Schleiermacher, hailed by Otto as 'the Church Father of modern Protestantism', had laid the foundation stones.[33]

If essentialist definitions of religion tend to be modelled, at least partly, on ideas or practices that are conventionally known as religious, then it comes as no surprise that essentialist definitions, precisely to the extent that they draw on such resemblances, also can exclude ideas or practices that its adherents would not hesitate to classify as religious. To give only one example, in 1893, at the famous World's Parliament of Religions in Chicago, quite a few Buddhist and Hindu leaders felt rather embarrassed by the 'common religious discourse' that the parliament tried to develop. When asked what kind of proofs they could offer for the existence of God or how their theologies dealt with sin and evil, they could answer only that these were typically Christian questions, which reflected Christian-inspired assumptions on the proper ingredients of a religious worldview. The essentialist approach turned out to be an analogical one in disguise. Unsurprisingly, then, the Parliament had to conclude that common ground among its participants was hard to establish.[34]

These examples do not necessarily suggest that *das Wesen der Religion* – the holy grail of nineteenth-century religious studies – does not exist.[35] Rather, I take them to illustrate a conceptual flaw in the dichotomy between essentialist and analogical definitions of (political) religion. Given that such definitions never emerge in a vacuum, they are likely to bear the stamp of one or more traditional religions. Because scholarship is always, consciously or unconsciously, informed by historical contexts, it would be naive to assume that an essentialist definition of religion is one that avoids all comparison with what is historically known as religion. Gentile's definition is a case in point: 'community of the elect' and 'code of commandments' are phrases derived from Jewish and Christian sources. In spite of the essentialist tones, the definition contains important analogical elements. More in general, it may be hard to think of anyone defining 'the essence of religion' without attempting to take on board at least some of those traditions that have previously been classified as religious. Accordingly, it would be false to present essentialist and analogical approaches to political religion ('Fascism was a religion' vs 'Fascism looked like early twentieth-century Italian Catholicism') as mutually exclusive.

Perhaps no one has made this point more forcefully than the Austrian-British philosopher Ludwig Wittgenstein. His philosophy of language was premised on the assumption that language usage is a common enterprise: private languages do not exist. Wittgenstein was therefore utterly sceptical of the idea that language users can invent non-contextual definitions or create a-historical meanings. For a linguistic utterance to be comprehensible, argued Wittgenstein, it must resonate at least to some degree with what is familiar to its receivers. Even though language users can, for various reasons, try to be original or attempt to stretch the limits of their existing language games, unintelligibility awaits them if they push too hard or try to dissociate themselves too much from other language users. Accordingly, what is central to Wittgenstein's philosophy is the actual usage of language or the acts of communication in which language users are involved when they utter a sentence. Language users – including, of course, scholars in search of a proper definition of (political) religion – are situated in historical contexts (language games) in which words have acquired certain meanings and grammar rules have been established for making meaningful connections between them. Given that no one can escape such contexts, it is not possible to propose definitions that avoid analogies with what is historically known.

In Wittgenstein's view, then, the dilemma between essentialist and comparative definitions of political religion is a false one. Confronted with the question whether Mussolini's Fascism 'was' or merely 'looked like' a religion, he would have answered that definitions are a matter of 'family resemblances'. Such family resemblances are analogies on the basis of which we classify certain objects as belonging together, even if these objects do not share a number of common characteristics. Think, for example, of board games, card games and ball games: why do we classify all these activities under the rubric 'games'?

> Don't say: 'There *must* be something common, or they would not be called "games"' – but *look and see* whether there is anything common to all. – For if you look at them you will not see something that is common to *all*, but similarities, relationships and a whole series of them at that.[36]

For Wittgenstein, family resemblances denote 'a complicated network of similarities' or a set of objects that are seen as belonging together, not by virtue of certain shared 'essences' but because of overlapping features.[37] Applied to the theme of this chapter, what counts as religion does not depend on a shared number of 'religion-making characteristics' (ritual practices, worship of a divine being, a body of scriptures and so forth) but on a certain degree of resemblance to what is traditionally known as religion.[38]

Such a Wittgensteinian approach, I note in passing, is not uncommon among students of religion. In *The Oxford Dictionary of World Religions*, for example, John Bowker explicitly invokes the notion of family resemblances when he observes, 'We can recognize a religion when we see one because we know what the many characteristics of religion are; but we would not expect to find any religion which exhibited all the characteristics without exception.'[39] Already in the 1970s, one of the world's most famous students of religion, Ninian Smart, advocated such a family-resemblance-type of definition, primarily because he did not believe in firm boundaries between 'religion as traditionally conceived' and 'phenomena which bear enough likeness to a religion as traditionally conceived to make them important to the student of religion' (Chinese Maoism serving as one of his examples).[40] According to Peter Byrne, such explorations beyond the realm of the familiar are precisely what make the study of religion relevant to larger groups of humanities scholars:

> Family resemblance allows for the open-endedness of a concept such as religion, thus recognizing that in the course of applying it away from its original context of use we are testing how far it can be modified to take into account new phenomena which bear real and important analogies with the paradigms to which it was once tied.[41]

Unsurprisingly, these Wittgenstein-inspired approaches to religion have not been spared criticism.[42] Timothy Fitzgerald, for example, argues that the idiom of family resemblances is too vague for scholars who prefer unequivocal definitions. If the boundaries between religion and non-religion cannot neatly be drawn (as Wittgenstein himself did not hesitate to emphasize), what then distinguishes religion from, say, ideology, worldview or 'symbolic systems in general'?[43] Besides, the family metaphor has been said to be misleading to the extent that it suggests genetic relationships between members of a group that religions sometimes, but certainly not always, have. 'What Wittgenstein ought to have said', Nicholas Griffin therefore suggests, 'is not, "family resemblance" but "resemblance like the physical resemblance between members of the same family"'.[44] None of these critics, however, has challenged Wittgenstein's most significant point: that whenever we speak about religion, we do so in the mode of analogy. Classifying an object as religious is not to claim that this object meets a certain set of definitional requirements. It rather amounts to saying that it resembles something previously labelled as religious. On Wittgensteinian premises, there is no escape from analogical reasoning.

Comparing Religion and Politics

Three conclusions follow from this. In the first place, Wittgenstein's notion of family resemblances has the great advantage of saving historians the difficult task of determining what the essence of religion is – a task that not even students of religion have managed to accomplish satisfactorily. It allows historians to speak about religion in a non-essentialist, that is, analogical manner. So, despite its philosophical appearance, the notion of family resemblances actually spares historians a difficult foray into definitional matters. It does not require them to prove that 'religions of politics' share a common essence with 'traditional religions'. For this reason, the notion of family resemblances may well be described as a rather 'historian-friendly' idea.

Second, if this Wittgensteinian approach invites historians to investigate resemblances between political practices and those traditionally classified as religious, it goes without saying that this procedure yields illuminating results only as long as historians specify what they understand traditional religions to be and thereby manage to avoid such stereotypical prejudices as that religion is 'false consciousness' or the 'opium of the people'. Insightful comparisons between politics and religion are unlikely to follow from biased, one-sided or tendentious accounts of religion. It may be helpful to recall in this context a warning issued in 2007 by Stanley Stowers, an American scholar of religion, in a review of recent literature on political religion. In reference to Gentile and others, Stowers observed that scholars of political religion often rely on so-called symbolist concepts of religion. They treat religion 'as an essentially expressive phenomenon in that it concerns belief, meaning and the symbolic in contrast to science, economics and politics which concern "pragmatic" activities that accomplish work in the world'. If these scholars study the use, exploitation or instrumentalization of religion in the hands of political authorities, they often contrast an 'inward' domain of meaning with an 'outward' domain of power and legislation. Yet, by doing so, they draw on a nineteenth-century tradition that few scholars of religion would be prepared to defend. In Stowers's formulation, 'The form/content, instrumental/expressive, and sacralization/profanation distinctions derive largely from the romantic tradition and belong to a class of theories about religion commonly designated as symbolist.'[45]

The four early twentieth-century definitions of religion mentioned in the previous section indeed fall neatly into this symbolist category. They all focus on the meaning of human existence as experienced, voluntarily (Le Bon) or involuntarily (Mosca), by individuals (Otto) or collectivities (Durkheim), through myths, symbols and rituals. What these four approaches have in common is the idea that religion provides *meaning* rather than, for instance, knowledge, power or life-forms (another Wittgensteinian term). They emphasize the symbolic aspects of religion at the cost of, especially, its social and political aspects.[46] Counterintuitive as it may sound, even Durkheim, despite his overarching interest in the social glue of religion, limited himself to the symbolic arsenal of Jewish and Christian religions (their myths, rituals and symbols), thereby neglecting their more tangible faith practices (welfare work and community-building, for example) as well as the communities created by those practices. In other words, even Durkheim's notion of religion was symbolist in so far as the French sociologist was more interested in how societies appropriate religious symbols in creating and maintaining social cohesion than in the social and political manifestations of Judaism and Christianity themselves.[47] In so far as Gentile treats religion as a matter of *'beliefs, myths, rituals, and symbols that interpret and define the meaning and end of human existence'*, he also draws expressly on this symbolist tradition.[48]

How, then, can historians correct this definitional one-sidedness without falling into the essentialist pitfall? How can they avoid a symbolist essentialism without offering another type of essentialism? This brings us to the third and perhaps most important implication of Wittgenstein's approach. If it is resemblances rather than essences that count, then historians should engage in comparative practices. They should compare religion and politics, as specifically as possible, and inquire in what respects a political phenomenon resembles a religious one. Basically, this can take two forms.[49] First, historians can apply themselves to the study of (political, religious) transfer.[50] When they suspect a religious element in, for example, socialist martyr cults or funerary practices, they do not need to reach for the dictionary (s.v. 'religion') or consult a study on political religion, but have to ask themselves, Where does this religious element come from? From which religious sources could these socialists have tapped? What did they know, what did they need, what did they use and how did they adapt these religious practices to their own ideas or purposes? Along the lines sketched by Burrin, then, scholars of political religion can study processes of appropriation, borrowing and adaption.

A second comparative practice in which historians can engage is the study of resemblances between phenomena that are not causally connected through processes of transfer. As we saw above, Wittgenstein's metaphor of family resemblances did not depend on genetic kinship between family members but, in Griffin's formulation, 'physical resemblance between members of the same family'. Accordingly, political slogans or hero-worship do not need to be derived from traditional religious practices in order to be classified as religious. Just as it made sense for Christian missionaries in West Africa to identify certain rites of passages that they encountered in what would become Ghana and Côte d'Ivoire as religious, simply because these rites resembled Catholic rituals without being derived from them, so historians can highlight similarities between socialist funerary rites and Christian memory cultures by employing the vocabulary of (political) religion. However, given that a maximum degree of clarity about units of comparison is a first requirement for all comparative history,[51] historians will also in this case need to pay a great deal of attention to what exactly they refer to when they classify a political style or argument as religious. If it is resemblances that count, then it is not religion as such but particular religions in particular manifestations, at particular times and places that offer reference material for historians speaking about political religion. Again, the question is not whether or not a political phenomenon is religious but what kind of resemblances to what kind of things conventionally classified as religious prompt the religious analogy.

Conclusion

In sum, on Wittgensteinian grounds, historians do not need to choose between essentialist and analogical conceptions of religion; that is, between the views that political religion 'is' a religion or 'looks like' religion as traditionally known. Wittgenstein's notion of family resemblances effectively eliminates this very distinction by arguing that there is no escape from analogical reasoning: what a religion 'is' always depends on what it 'looks like'. This is why Burrin rightly emphasizes the element of comparison in any study of political religion. Regardless whether such comparisons are focused on invention of tradition, attribution of exceptional value to a person or group, or ritualization that helps create imagined communities, in all cases the attribution of religious elements to political behaviour is a matter of discerning family resemblances.

However, if attribution of the word 'religious' depends on resemblances rather than on shared essences, then historians cannot afford to speak loosely about 'political religion' every time they come across political leaders who are hailed as saviours or ethnic groups that consider themselves as chosen peoples. As in all comparative history, the quality of the argument is positively related to the specificity of the case studies. This implies that little has been said by describing Hitler and Mussolini as religious figures. What matters is rather the resemblance between their political practices and some specific features of specific religious traditions. If political religion (or, for that matter, the religion of history or religion of science) is a matter of family resemblance, then historians will have to spell out which family members they perceive as resembling each other.

Although, or perhaps because, this exercise has lost most of the political urgency that it once held for Voegelin and Schoeps, the study of such family resemblances is an important step towards recognizing that politics and religion may be less distinct than assumed in much of our inherited language. It may contribute to critical scrutiny of those conventions of linguistic classification that cause us to assume, often unreflectively, that religion and politics are separate domains of reality. By forcing us to consider politics in terms of religion, or vice versa, the religious analogy discussed in this chapter may help explore the possibility that religion and politics, rather than being distinct spheres of reality, are in fact dimensions that can be detected in almost any form of human behaviour. Seen in this light, a volume exploring political religion may not only testify to the observation that historians of modern Europe are rediscovering religion as an important subject of study, but also contribute to a reassessment of what we understand religion and politics to be.

Notes

1. I should like to thank Emilio Gentile for his illuminating response to an earlier version of this chapter.
2. Thomas Albert Howard, 'Commentary: A "Religious Turn" in Modern European Historiography?', *Church History* 75/1 (2006), 156–62. See also 'The Persistence of Religion in Modern Europe', theme issue of *The Journal of Modern History* 82/2 (2010).
3. Jack Fruchtman, Jr, *Thomas Paine and the Religion of Nature* (Baltimore, MD and London, 1993); John Gatta, *Making Nature Sacred: Literature, Religion, and Environment in America from the Puritans to the Present* (Oxford, 2004).
4. Wolfgang Hardtwig, 'Geschichtsreligion, Wissenschaft als Arbeit, Objektivität: Der Historismus in neuer Sicht', *Historische Zeitschrift* 252 (1991), 1–32; Philipp Müller, 'Geschichtsreligion in der historischen Erzählung: Jules Michelets Geschichte der Französischen Revolution', in Martin Baumeister, Moritz Föllmer and Philipp Müller (eds), *Die Kunst der Geschichte: Historiographie, Ästhetik, Erzählung* (Göttingen, 2009), 169–88.

5. Angela Matyssek, 'Die Wissenschaft als Religion, das Präparat als Reliquie: Rudolf Virchow und das Pathologische Museum der Friedrich-Wilhelms-Universität zu Berlin', in Anke te Heesen and E.C. Spary (eds), *Sammeln als Wissen: Das Sammeln und seine wissenschaftsgeschichtliche Bedeutung*, 2nd edn (Göttingen, 2001), 142–68; Thomas Schmidt-Lux, *Wissenschaft als Religion: Szientismus im ostdeutschen Säkularisierungsprozess* (Würzburg, 2008).

6. Joseph M. Siry, *Unity Temple: Frank Lloyd Wright and Architecture for Liberal Religion* (Cambridge, 1996); Stephen Yeo, 'A New Life: The Religion of Socialism in Britain, 1883–1896', *History Workshop* 4/1 (1977), 5–56.

7. Stanley Fish, 'One University Under God?', *The Chronicle of Higher Education*, 7 January 2005.

8. That this is more than just an academic terminological issue is illustrated by the recent Swedish government's decision to acknowledge 'Kopimism' (an online community devoted to ideals of information sharing) as a religious organization. See 'Sweden Recognizes New File-Sharing Religion Kopimism', online at http://www.bbc.com/news/technology-16424659 (retrieved April 2012).

9. Hans Otto Seitschek, 'Frühe Verwendungen des Begriffs "politische Religion": Campanella, Clasen, Wieland', in Hans Maier (ed.), *'Totalitarismus' und 'Politische Religionen': Konzepte des Diktaturvergleichs*, vol. 3 (Paderborn, 2003), 109–20.

10. [Hans-Joachim Schoeps,] 'Der Nationalsozialismus als verkappte Religion', *Eltheto* 93 (1939), 93–8 (93, 94). Unless indicated otherwise, all translations are mine.

11. Eric Voegelin, 'The Political Religions' (1938), in *The Collected Works of Eric Voegelin*, ed. Manfred Henningsen, vol. 5 (Columbia, MO and London, 2000), 19–75 (32).

12. Voegelin's concept of political religion has been discussed extensively. See, e.g., Dietmar Herz, 'Der Begriff der "politischen Religionen" im Denken Eric Voegelins', in Maier (ed.), *'Totalitarismus' und 'Politische Religionen'*, vol. 1, 191–209; Hans Otto Seitschek, 'Die Deutung des Totalitarismus als Religion', in Maier (ed.), *'Totalitarismus' und 'politische Religionen'*, vol. 3, 129–77 (129–49); Michael Ley, 'Zur Theorie des politischen Religionen: Der Nationalismus als Paradigma politischer Religiosität', in Michael Ley, Heinrich Neisser and Gilbert Weiss (eds), *Politische Religion? Politik, Religion und Anthropologie im Werk von Eric Voegelin* (Munich, 2003), 77–85.

13. For an overview, see Philippe Burrin, 'Political Religion: The Relevance of a Concept', *History and Memory* 9 (1997), 321–49; Peter Schöttler, 'Das Konzept der politischen Religionen bei Lucie Varga und Franz Borkenau', in Michael Ley and Julius H. Schoeps (eds), *Der Nationalsozialismus als politische Religion* (Bodenheim, 1997), 186–205; David D. Roberts, '"Political Religion" and the Totalitarian Departures of Inter-War Europe: On the Uses and Disadvantages of an Analytical Category', *Contemporary European History* 18/4 (2009), 381–414.

14. Burrin, 'Political Religion', 325.

15. Carl Christian Bry, *Verkappte Religionen* (Gotha, 1924).

16. Raymond Aron, 'L'avenir des religions séculières' (1944), in idem, *Chroniques de guerre: la France libre, 1940–1945*, ed. Christian Bachelier (Paris, 1990), 925–48 (926).

30   Herman Paul

17. [Schoeps,] 'Nationalsozialismus', 94.
18. Voegelin, 'Political Religions', 24.
19. Carl Schmitt, *Politische Theologie: Vier Kapitel zur Lehre von der Souveränität* (Munich and Leipzig, 1922); Jacques Maritain, *Humanisme intégral: problèmes temporels et spirituels d'une nouvelle chrétienté* (Paris, 1937); Karl Löwith, *Meaning in History: The Theological Implications of the Philosophy of History* (Chicago, 1949).
20. Klaus Vondung, *Magie und Manipulation: Ideologischer Kult und politische Religion des Nationalsozialismus* (Göttingen, 1971); George L. Mosse, *The Nationalization of the Masses: Political Symbolism and Mass Movements in Germany from the Napoleonic Wars through the Third Reich* (New York, 1975); Jean-Pierre Sironneau, *Sécularisation et religions politiques* (The Hague et al., 1982). See also Hans-Jochen Gamm, *Der braune Kult: das Dritte Reich und seine Ersatzreligion: Ein Beitrag zur politischen Bildung* (Hamburg, 1962); Friedrich Heer, *Der Glaube des Adolf Hitler: Anatomie einer politischen Religiosität* (Munich, Esslingen, 1968).
21. William T. Cavanaugh, *The Myth of Religious Violence: Secular Ideology and the Roots of Modern Conflict* (New York, 2009).
22. Burrin, 'Political Religion', 330.
23. Ibid., 331.
24. Emilio Gentile, *Politics as Religion*, trans. George Staunton (Princeton, NJ and Oxford, 2006), 4.
25. The word 'fideistic' strikes me as infelicitous, given that fideism conventionally refers to 'the doctrine that all or some knowledge depends on faith or revelation' (*The Concise Oxford Dictionary of Current English*, ed. Della Thompson, 9th edn [Oxford, 1995], 500). Accordingly, a fideistic view of religion would be one contending that only the Tanakh, the Bible or the Qur'an can tell what religion is. 'Fideism' might perhaps better be described as a *psychological* definition of religion.
26. Gentile, *Politics as Religion*, 7–8.
27. Ibid., 8.
28. Ibid., 10.
29. Ibid., 145.
30. Yet, as Roger Griffin's observes, Gentile's notion of religion is a rather multifaceted one: 'it embodies a multi-point perspective in which terms are used in a complementary way to form a cluster or conceptual "constellation"'. Roger Griffin, 'A New Constellation? Emilio Gentile's Theory of Political Religion and Its Implications for the Human Sciences', as quoted in Ines Prodöhl, 'Die politische Religionen als Kategorie der neuesten Geschichte', online at http://hsozkult.geschichte.hu-berlin.de/tagungsberichte/id=355 (retrieved April 2012).
31. Gentile, *Politics as Religion*, 138–9.
32. Ivan Strenski, *Durkheim and the Jews of France* (Chicago and London, 1997), 16–52.
33. Todd A. Gooch, *The Numinous and Modernity: An Interpretation of Rudolf Otto's Philosophy of Religion* (Berlin and New York, 2000), 189, 211.
34. Richard Hughes Seager, *The World's Parliament of Religions: The East/West Encounter, Chicago 1893* (Bloomington, 1995), 44, 50.

35. On the nineteenth-century quest for this grail, see Karl-Heinz Menke, *Die Frage nach dem Wesen des Christentums: Eine theologiegeschichtliche Analyse* (Paderborn, 2005).
36. Ludwig Wittgenstein, *Philosophical Investigations*, trans. G.E.M. Anscombe (Oxford, 1953), 31e (§66).
37. Ibid., 32e (§66).
38. I borrow the expression 'religion-making characteristics' from William P. Alston, 'Religion', in Paul Edwards (ed.), *The Encyclopedia of Philosophy*, vol. 7 (New York, 1967), 140–5.
39. John Bowker, 'Religion', in idem (ed.), *The Oxford Dictionary of World Religions* (Oxford, 1997), xv–xxiv (xxiv).
40. Ninian Smart, *The Science of Religion and the Sociology of Knowledge: Some Methodological Questions* (Princeton, NJ, 1973), 16.
41. Peter Byrne, *Natural Religion and the Nature of Religion: The Legacy of Deism* (London, New York, 1989), 221.
42. A variety of problems associated with Wittgenstein's approach are discussed in Benson Saler, *Conceptualizing Religion: Immanent Anthropologists, Transcendent Natives, and Unbounded Categories* (Leiden, New York and Cologne, 1993), esp. 158–96.
43. Timothy Fitzgerald, 'Religion, Philosophy and Family Resemblances', *Religion* 26/3 (1996), 215–36 (216).
44. Nicholas Griffin, 'Wittgenstein, Universals and Family Resemblances', *Canadian Journal of Philosophy* 3/4 (1974), 635–51 (637).
45. Stanley Stowers, 'The Concepts of "Religion", "Political Religion" and the Study of Nazism', *Journal of Contemporary History* 42/1 (2007), 9–24 (11).
46. If Christianity in ancient Rome had served merely as a meaning-providing system of rituals and myths, then Diocletian would surely not have taken the trouble to persecute the Christians, to sack their churches and to burn their holy books. Diocletian's edicts against the Christians make sense only if we recognize, as did the emperor, that a twofold political claim was inherent to Christian religion. First, Christians professed God, rather than the Roman emperor, as their real *dominus*. Their claim that God rules the world and that accordingly all worldly power must be derived from God was a straightforward political statement. Second, by welcoming women, slaves and foreigners into their congregations, Christians created political communities of their own. Their rituals and symbols constituted communities that were political in so far as they posed a threat or offered an alternative to the existing political order. Such political aspects of religion are easily overlooked as long as religion is treated merely as a source of meaning. See, among other titles, Oliver O'Donovan, *The Desire of the Nations: Rediscovering the Roots of Political Theology* (Cambridge, 1996); Bernd Wannenwetsch, *Political Worship: Ethics for Christian Citizens*, trans. Margaret Kohl (Oxford, 2004); Christoph Stumpf and Holger Zaborowski (eds), *Church as Politeia: The Political Self-Understanding of Christianity* (Berlin, New York, 2004).
47. Strenski, *Durkheim and the Jews of France*, 16–52.
48. Gentile, *Politics as Religion*, xiv.
49. In practice, these two forms are often intermingled, especially in what is nowadays called 'entangled histories'. See Michael Werner and Bénédicte

Zimmermann, 'Beyond Comparison: *Histoire Croisée* and the Challenge of Reflexivity', *History and Theory* 45/1 (2006), 30–50.

50. Henk te Velde, 'Political Transfer: An Introduction', *European Review of History* 12/2 (2005), 205–21.

51. Chris Lorenz, 'Comparative Historiography: Problems and Perspectives', *History and Theory* 38/1 (1999), 25–39; Stefan Berger, 'Comparative History', in Stefan Berger, Heiko Feldner and Kevin Passmore (eds), *Writing History: Theory and Practice* (London, 2003), 161–79.

The Religious Side of Democracy: Early Socialism, Twenty-first-century Populism and the Sacralization of Politics

Henk te Velde

Cultural analysis is a product of its time. The concept of political religion acquired its current meaning in studies of totalitarian politics in the interwar period. Its perhaps most classic text is *Politische Religionen* by Eric Voegelin (1938). Voegelin offered a number of historical examples of political religion but would not have written his essay had he not experienced Hitler's Germany: in 1938, the Anschluss caused Voegelin to flee from Vienna where he worked and to emigrate to the United States. In this sense the concept of political religion originated as a weapon in the fight against National Socialism. Even were it part of a scholarly analysis, it had a clear political message: the religious aspect of Nazi politics was perhaps the most prominent sign of its dangerous nature.

The combination of political religion and totalitarian politics forced itself on many observers of Nazi Germany. Seen from scholarly as well as political perspectives it was useful and convincing to link these two things together, and after the Second World War the crisis of democracy of the interwar years was overcome by stressing that a sober liberal democracy was the only real alternative to totalitarianism. The dichotomy of liberal democracy and totalitarianism was equated with a dichotomy between liberal democracy and political religion. Critics of totalitarian politics noticed that their enemies transformed politics into a kind of religion, and after the Second World War this view resulted in a clear-cut, though sometimes implicit, model of politics. This split has helped us discern and interpret important aspects of totalitarian politics and has drawn our attention to the very dangerous sides of political religion.

However, this dichotomy does not do justice to the ambiguities of modern democracy, especially to the ways people are politically mobilized. The study of political religion has had a preference for an analysis of the politics of the (totalitarian) state and has often ignored the religious aspects of (democratic) political movements. Even if recent interpretations of political religion tend to acknowledge that there are also democratic variants of this phenomenon, they often continue to build on the ideas of the 1930s and thus also continue the pattern of dichotomous reasoning, as illustrated by Emilio Gentile's distinction between (largely evil) political and (mainly benevolent) civil religion.[1] If one's purpose is to understand totalitarianism, one should keep the dichotomy. If, however, the purpose of one's research is to understand all aspects of democratic political mobilization, a study of the sacralization of politics or the religious aspects of politics is needed that does not start by considering it to be the opposite of democracy. Of course, this is not to say that there are no real differences between totalitarianism and democracy but rather that the instruments chosen to study political religion will at least partly determine what will be found and that the choice of perspective is crucial.

This contribution will discuss the examples of 'conversion' in early democratic socialism around 1900 (the main case being Germany), and of religious language in contemporary populism (in the Netherlands and elsewhere). Both examples will demonstrate that religious language was also used in a democratic political context. This sort of language has served, I will argue, to express that politics is not only about administration but also about the hopes and dreams of the people. This higher meaning has more often than not been expressed in religious terms, and, moreover, in phrases that could resemble the language of political religion in its totalitarian form. However, it is not as such a marker of totalitarian politics but rather an indication of the ambiguities of modern democratic politics. I will start by saying a few words about the way the concept of political religion became an important means of the defence of post-war liberal democracy against totalitarian politics of any kind. This is a crucial starting point because it shows that this use of the concept was a product of its age. As I will argue, it is useful to broaden the perspective and to use the occurrence of religious language to ponder the functions of (democratic) politics. Of course, my interpretation is also a product of its age and a contribution to a contemporary debate, and I will conclude by pointing out the relevance of this position for the current debate about populism.

Political Religion in Post-war Historiography

The Second World War had been a fight against evil, and the evil had taken on a religious guise. The enemy was National Socialism but also totalitarianism in general. Religious terms were used not only in the analysis of the Fascist opponents of liberal democracy in the 1930s but also in order to demonstrate the pernicious nature of Communism and other forms of 'totalitarian democracy', in the famous phrase coined by Jacob Talmon (1916–80). Talmon was a Jewish historian of Polish descent who distinguished two forms of democracy, 'liberal' and 'totalitarian'. Talmon characterizes this second form in the introduction of his *The Origins of Totalitarian Democracy* (1952) also as 'Messianic democracy', 'Totalitarian Messianism' and 'political Messianism'. According to Talmon, totalitarian democracy originated in the French Revolution and resulted among other things in totalitarian Russian Communism. Talmon localizes 'the birth of the modern secular religion, not merely as a system of ideas, but as a passionate faith', in the work of Jean-Jacques Rousseau, and he is interested in 'the thrill of fulfilment experienced by the believers in a modern Messianic movement, which makes them experience submission as deliverance'. He is studying a state of mind 'best compared to the set of attitudes engendered by a religion' and to an 'eschatological revolutionary current'.[2]

Religious terms were common in the analysis of communist totalitarianism, both in scholarly and essayistic work. *The God That Failed*, a collection of memories of ex-communists published in 1949, was an emotional analysis of the totalitarian party experience. Six ex-communist writers (or at least fellow-travellers) wrote about their experiences. They tried to explain the attraction the Communist Party once had had for them. Most of them, including those from Catholic countries such as André Gide, the French author, used the word 'conversion' when they gave a description of what membership meant to the party militants. 'Our concern was to study the state of mind of the Communist convert', they said, 'and the atmosphere of the [interwar] period [...] when conversion was so common'. Typically one of them wrote, 'For me to join the Party of Proletarian Revolution was not just a matter of signing up with a political organization; it meant a conversion, a complete dedication.' But with hindsight they described their conversion experience as 'infatuation' or 'addiction'. The book is an impressive and even moving testimony of the destructive power of totalitarian politics, and the inevitable conclusion seems to be that religious forms of politics are totalitarian and totalitarian politics are religious. The use of religious language seems to be a sure sign that the boundaries of normal democratic politics have been crossed and dangerous territory entered.[3]

This view resembles the analysis of a political scientist of the period. In 1951 the French political scientist Maurice Duvergier wrote *Les parties politiques,* a standard work about political parties, perhaps the first of its kind after Robert Michels's *Political Parties: A Sociological Study of the Oligarchical Tendencies of Modern Democracy* (German original of 1911). Duvergier drew a line between ordinary democratic parties and sectarian communist or fascist parties which were totalitarian not only in their political ambitions but also in their total claim on the life of their adherents. The totalitarian parties resembled religious orders because the individual was merged into and subordinated to the group. There was only one Party, written with a capital P – according to Duvergier a sign of its 'sacralization'. This party was the object of a 'culte'. It was literally 'sacré', in the sense of being transcendent, superior and beyond criticism, Duvergier says, with a reference to Émile Durkheim, the French sociologist of religion. Participation and the mutual bonds in this party take on 'une nature véritablement religieuse'. As in nascent religions and monastic orders, the individuals fuse into a community that transcends them. Duvergier uses the word 'conversion' to describe the joining of this type of party, which he analyses dispassionately, though his preferences are clear.[4]

Duvergier's scheme has the virtue of clarity. But do such simple dividing lines between democratic and totalitarian parties really exist? After the totalitarian experience it has become difficult not to feel suspicion when religious language is used in connection with politics, but it is important to realize that an intense political experience is not in itself totalitarian or even dangerous. It is certainly ambiguous, to say the least, but it is not necessarily evil. Duvergier mentions in passing that the early phase of social democratic parties more or less resembled the quasi-religious totalitarian style of the communists, that is, of their most embittered enemies. He does not pay much attention to this long-gone phase and goes on to define only totalitarian politics as religious.

The Religious Aspect of Party Politics

At first glance, Duvergier's analysis seems to have been in line with the self-image of social democrats. Even before the First World War the famous revisionist German social democrat Eduard Bernstein had published a small book with the title *Von der Sekte zur Partei: Die deutsche Sozialdemokratie einst und jetzt.* When it still was a utopian movement it was either anti-political – with the revolutionary ambition to destroy existing politics altogether – or apolitical – living in its own world, without participation in elections. It was a 'sect', not a 'political party'.[5]

Bernstein did, of course, not give an innocent description of the development of the party but made a contribution to the struggle within the party. Also, when social democrats looked back on the history of their party, they tended to describe its first phase as an unruly and undisciplined period, a kind of 'puberty'. Now they were mature, balanced, and sober, not an unbalanced sect. In short, they were on their way to becoming administrators. That was not how socialist parties had started. At first they had been a party of outsiders, outsiders to such an extent that they had not even been sure they wanted to enter formal politics. The religious language was connected to this phase. It signified that their movement was more than ordinary politics: it was a 'faith', with a 'Messiah' and so on. Terms such as sects, churches and religion had been already used by a number of observers such as the early political scientists Vilfredo Pareto and Gaetano Mosca, who described the new phenomenon of the mass party, and the mass psychologist Gustave le Bon.[6] For them these were rather derogatory terms. This reaction testified to the critical way in which they considered modern political organizations, which were not supposed to be part of politics proper. This analysis was not confined to socialist parties but was used for modern political parties in general. One of the first and most famous analyses of this curious new thing was Moseï Ostrogorski's description of the 'caucus' in the United States and in British liberalism in particular. He concluded that the modern party was 'a sort of *integral* association' and

> was founded on theological and ecclesiastical conceptions; the grouping of the members of a party exactly resembled that of the adherents of a Church; the principles or the programme of the party constituted a creed invested, like the creed of a Church, with the sanction of orthodoxy or heterodoxy. The adhesion had to be undivided, one could not differ from the party on any article of its faith any more than one can choose between the dogmas of a religion. Like the Church, which takes charge of all the spiritual needs of man, the party demanded the whole citizen.[7]

Ostrogorski did not like the new organizations, and he used the comparison with religion and churches to show the pressure they put on their members and the lack of real and open discussion they demonstrated. A couple of decades later another critic of modern mass democracy, the jurist and political philosopher Carl Schmitt, used words like 'total' and 'totalization' in order to convey the meaning the modern party had for its members, and to characterize the 'complete cultural program' it offered.[8]

If only their critics had used religious comparisons, this could have been disposed of as an enemy strategy. Members of modern parties, however, also used religious language themselves in order to describe their experiences.[9] One of the most common features of the democratic 'new politics' of the late nineteenth and early twentieth centuries was the worship of 'charismatic' leaders, in the expression borrowed from theology by Max Weber. Figures as diverse as socialist leaders in various countries, the liberal William Gladstone in Britain, the orthodox Protestant Abraham Kuyper in the Netherlands, or even the dissident Catholic leader Karl Lueger in Vienna, belonged to this category.[10] They used religious language themselves and were 'worshipped' in the same language.

Religious language was used abundantly, but one case stood out as the prime example of the modern party: the German Social Democratic Party. Socialist parties were internationally not necessarily the first modern parties – in the Netherlands the Orthodox Protestant Party was the first in 1879, and Ostrogorski studied first and foremost the liberal Birmingham caucus of the late 1870s – but socialist parties were internationally the most common, and the German party impressed commentators by its sheer magnitude and the full cultural programme its members received. It has often been used as the prime example of the democratic mass party of the sort that existed in Europe roughly between the end of the nineteenth century and the 1960s, used to bridge the gap between state and society, and give a certain stability to political relations. In general social democratic parties presented the most obvious cases of the modern political party, and especially in its first phase before the First World War the German social democracy was seen as a model to be followed by socialists everywhere. The most important analysis of a modern mass party, by Robert Michels (1911), was devoted to this party – and used many religious words, such as apostles, martyrs, prophets and sects.[11]

The Conversion to Socialism

At first German socialists hesitated over whether they wanted to join parliamentary politics at all.[12] This was, of course, a difficult position for a party in parliament, but it illustrates that social democrats wanted to introduce a new, more serious form of politics, which gave a sense of purpose and a new identity to its followers. Because it provided its militants with a sense of identity and mission, the essentially rational socialist politics acquired a religious flavour.

Bernstein tried to downplay this side of socialism. Socialism used to be a quasi-religious sect, but it was a real – perhaps almost ordinary – political party now. Many of his fellow party militants would not have agreed. Religious language was everywhere.[13] In the 1860s the German socialist leader Ferdinand Lassalle had already referred to the early Christian community of the first century as a source of inspiration, and half a century later the same reference could still be found.[14] In the 1870s the German socialist theorist Joseph Dietzgen wrote a number of popular essays in which he described socialism as something that was becoming 'religious', 'which means something that takes hold of the whole heart, mind and soul of those who believe'.[15] And in the early twentieth century many books and articles were published in which socialists recalled how they had become members of the Party 20 or 40 years earlier. In particular in Germany scores of autobiographies appeared, 'and always the title was: How I became a Social Democrat!'[16]

Almost invariably they recounted their 'conversion'. Internationally the most famous example of this type of literature was the *Autobiography of a Working Woman* (1909) by the Austrian socialist Adelheid Popp. The original version of her book was published in German and prefaced by the socialist leader August Bebel; the English version received an additional preface by James Ramsay MacDonald, the English Labour leader. Many of these autobiographies contained a chapter or at least a few pages about what was described as the 'turning point' or the 'inner change' brought about by the conversion to Socialism. To convey their emotions they often used the biblical expression 'the scales fell from my eyes', which is the expression used in the Acts of the Apostles to describe the conversion of St Paul.[17] The phrasing became a bit of a cliché, even to the point where it was sometimes added afterwards. Paul Göhre, a clergyman turned socialist, edited a few autobiographies by workers. One of them did not contain a single word about the conversion to socialism, so Göhre asked the writer how he had become a socialist. And then, of course, he got what he wanted: in the countryside the writer had received the 'seed of Socialism' and 'the scales fell from his eyes'.[18]

In the first decades of the twentieth century the socialist conversion stories constituted their own literary genre, with their own conventions and stereotypes. The stories about heroes and martyrs of the early days of the party were meant to keep the fire burning in the now established Party, especially among young workers who had not personally experienced its history. In the preface of one of the accounts, the author said that his life story should serve to kindle the fighting spirit of young comrades and the readiness to make sacrifices. Most of the autobiographies had the same structure. They consisted of a dark period before and a happy period after joining the Party. In the dark period many authors did not know much about socialism and had been told that socialists were horrible people for whom nothing was sacred and who wanted to destroy or divide everything. Through this story the authors stressed the distance that separated the bourgeois world from the socialist community. In order to reach the socialist community, a boundary had to be crossed, and the conversion presented the checkpoint and the border crossing. Precisely because a border had to be crossed, the moment of conversion was so important, even if it was partly symbolic. The authors did not hide that the conversion itself was not an intellectual process. Many of them had gone to a socialist mass meeting and been struck by what they heard and by the atmosphere; they perhaps went once more, surprised themselves by taking the floor, and were overcome by the feeling that this was what they had been looking for. In most cases the ground had been prepared by friends or sometimes by books, but careful study of the socialist ideology followed only after they had joined the Party. Thus, mass meetings were of crucial importance for the actual conversion, though most socialists valued written media more highly because compared to the continuous influence of newspapers and books, which served to cement a permanent loyalty to the movement, mass meetings were rather random occurrences.[19]

Most of the stories were written decades after the event, and the authors wanted to show the change in their identity, which significantly had taken place when most were susceptible adolescents; their stories contained elements of a classic *Bildungsroman*, telling the story of the development of an identity. Most conversion stories tend to be stories about identity, and this is certainly true in the case of the socialist conversions. An extreme example is offered by the agitator Johann Most, who wrote around 1900 that he had become a human being only by joining socialism. Socialism had provided him with a purpose in life; henceforth only the great mission and the movement counted, the private person was not relevant anymore.[20] This fervency testifies to what conversion meant in the socialist case. It was joining a group outside bourgeois society and joining a separate world which gave a whole new meaning to one's personal identity. The group was more important than the individual, whose life should be devoted to the efforts of the group. In contrast to classic parliamentarianism, where politicians of different views had shared a common bourgeois culture, politics now meant joining a separate group with clear boundaries. 'For the worker the party means something different than for the bourgeois. For the worker the party is more.'[21]

The authors did not hide that their conversions resulted from a long and sometimes painful process. But now they had seen the light and the truth was theirs. It is important to notice that their stories were written in hindsight. The description of the 'conversion' served, at least partly, as a rhetorical device to separate the unclear initial phase of the awakening of political consciousness from the unshakeable certainty that resulted from joining the party. Often a socialist ideology did not precede the formation of socialist parties but was in fact partly a result of this process. In the life of the individual activist the free debates of mass meetings only gradually developed into the fixed ideology of the established party.[22] In the process the militant transformed from a relatively independently thinking activist into a party bureaucrat or a faithful follower of the party line. Looking back the conversion stories served to mark the transition of the writer from the first stage to the second.

'Let me tell you how I developed from a Saul to a Paul', a Socialist veteran told the readers of a Socialist youth review (he wanted to show 'wie ich aus einem Saulus zu einem Paulus wurde'). This had been a difficult process, and he had had a lot of trouble in finding the socialist truth. However, according to him many of his readers were in a much more favourable position. They were, as it were, 'born into' socialism because many of them had socialist parents and had from the very beginning been raised as socialists.[23] This is an interesting remark. These stories were not meant as an encouragement to their readers to experience a conversion themselves. On the contrary, the readers had to rely on the successful search for the socialist truth of the older generation. Socialism had become an established party which had formed its own tradition with heroes, martyrs and stories that made sense of its previous suffering, as Adriaan van Veldhuizen shows in his contribution to this volume. If the party of the initial phase could be compared to a religious sect, with its dramatic conversions, then the established party was (also according to contemporary observers)[24] more like a church, with its traditions which were passed down from one generation to the next and with a kind of loyalty that resembled that of a family. Seen from the perspective of the established party, politics was a disciplined, well-organized activity which involved the possession and defence of the truth and a lifelong loyalty. The conversion was the moment when the struggle for the truth was ended. The conversion stories served as a legitimization of the established Socialist Party.

The stories contain many elements of the classic accounts of religious conversions; for example, the link between adolescence and conversion, the conversion as a way to give a new purpose to life and the division of life into three episodes: the period before and the period after the conversion, and the conversion itself. Some of the most dramatic stories were written by somewhat emotional people who sometimes went through a series of conversions, first to revivalist Protestantism and then to socialism. These elements served political purposes. The stories were not about individual salvation nor about the hereafter but about the importance of the socialist community, and they all tried to demonstrate that the conversion itself was perhaps an emotional and radical change, but the end was the rational almost scientific truth of socialism. In this sense the stories had at least two goals. The first one was to demonstrate the gap between bourgeois society and the Socialist Party, and the existence of the socialist community as an almost separate world. As historian Philippe Burrin has written, 'a "political religion" dimension tends to increase in a political group along with its propensity to form a kind of counter-society', including in democratic politics.[25] To cross that gap required a leap, and the conversion was that leap. Second, once the initial step had been taken, so the stories argued, it became clear that the socialist perspective presented the only rational and legitimate way to consider society. After the emotional upheaval of the first leap or step, socialist politics were at the same time a matter of faith and an essentially rational matter. The element of faith was used to keep the fire burning within the movement, but in debates with adversaries rational arguments were all-important.

The social democratic conversion stories laid bare an ambiguity in democratic politics. The message of the conversion to totalitarian Communism presented by the post-war collection *The God That Failed* is clear: religion and politics should be separate domains, and once people start talking about conversion, they leave the field of democratic politics and enter a totalitarian pseudo-religion. This is one way to see things. But it could be argued that, particularly during a certain phase, democratic politics needed clear-cut differences between opposing groups. Before the advent of modern mass parties, of which the Socialist Party was the prime example, politics used to be a matter of notables who did not agree on everything but nevertheless belonged to the same more or less homogeneous social milieu. It was precisely by opposing this milieu that socialism succeeded in mobilizing new social groups and thus eventually furthering democracy. Instead of playing down differences with their adversaries, they had to dramatize them in order to appeal to their potential voters. It was 'us' against 'them', and 'we' had to stick together and build a New Jerusalem. This meant that politics were not just a matter of parliaments and laws but a matter of personal identity; the choice for socialism was the choice for a community and a lifestyle. The religious metaphor of conversion captured two things that the socialists liked to convey: the strong personal involvement of the party militant and the gap between the socialist and other parties.

This experience was not confined to the German party. In the inter-war years British observers looked back on the history of the Labour Party. Labour had been something different, a romantic and even heroic enterprise. Now it was becoming a party like the other parties. The early Labour movement, and especially the Independent Labour Party, was seen as more akin perhaps to a religious sect than to a parliamentary party. Ramsay MacDonald (who became the first Labour PM) described Socialism as his religion, and his colleague Snowden says in his auto-biography that the socialist 'movement was something new in politics. It was politics inspired by idealism and religious fervour'. Snowden exclaims, 'Oh that the Socialist movement of today could recapture the spiritual exaltation and religious faith of those early days!'[26] Labour politicians also wrote in their memoirs about their conversion: 'my conversion to socialism [...] was not [...] the result of an intellectual process, but rather a sort of emotional transmutation'.[27] Early socialist meetings were often described as revivalist gatherings, and joining the socialists was like joining a new community or a new family; socialists sometimes even 'made their declaration of faith by rising in the meeting and telling of their conversion'.[28]

The topos of the conversion was probably strongest in Germany, but it could also be found in other countries such as the Netherlands. Socialists talked about their 'rebirth'. A volume with conversion stories was issued,[29] and Dutch socialist leaders used just as much religious language as their German counterparts. The early socialist leader Domela Nieuwenhuis often compared himself to Christ and his journey to the Via Dolorosa. And the always exciting comparison with Moses appeared in the memoirs of another leader, Pieter Jelles Troelstra. He was so convincing that others adopted the image in their own memoirs and used it after Troelstra's death, even quoting passages from the Bible: 'And there arose not a prophet since in Israel like unto Moses' (Deut. 34:10).[30]

Political Religion and the 'Meaning' of Politics

In his contribution to this volume Herman Paul remarks that the concept of political religion uses a definition of religion that relates only to 'meaning'. This is indeed a reduction of the many aspects of religion. 'Religion is identified with everything that produces meaning and connection', Philippe Burrin writes about political religion,[31] but perhaps this is what authors working on *political* religion have been mainly interested in. There is also much material to suggest that this is what socialists wanted to say when they used religious language. When a new German review was started in the early 1920s that would write about socialist culture, it was explained that the 'religious communities' had previously 'determined the meaning of life'. Now it was the turn for socialism to take over this function.[32]

Some literature on aspects of political religion seems to suggest that it is akin to theatre. This is the direction George Mosse takes in his *Nationalization of the Masses* when he describes the 'new [mass] politics' as an attempt 'to transform political action into a drama'. Mosse is primarily interested in the staging, the *mise en scène*, of the 'nationalization of the masses'.[33] He uses expressions such as political religion (once) and secular religion (twice), cult, community of faith and sacred, but it is significant that the theological word he uses most is 'liturgy', a word expressing the top-down rules of the 'play' of the formal religious service, as it were.[34]

However, Mosse does not imply that this type of politics is a mere show but that its aesthetic effects resulted in the fusion of the individual into a larger whole, which according to Maurice Duvergier was typical for totalitarian 'religious' parties. Mosse stresses the 'active public participation' and the 'reality' of the magic.[35] This he has in common with, for instance, Gentile, who argues that political religion should be taken seriously as something more than just propaganda expedients or political devices. Gentile is rather critical of the likes of Mosca who present political religions (in the case of Mosca not fascism but rather early socialism) as crowd manipulation.[36]

The study of political religion re-emerged in the 1990s as a relevant type of analysis of totalitarianism because it had something to say about the real effects of this type of politics, not only about propaganda. Totalitarian political religions gave their supporters a sense of purpose and meaning. However, this function has of course not been confined to totalitarian politics. The modern political party, of which the social democrats were the prime example, also provided its adherents and members with a sense of meaning, a 'feeling of belonging and a sense of identification' and even a 'social identity and destiny'.[37] Seen from this perspective the clear line between sober, democratic politics, on the one hand, and immoderate and totalitarian political religion, on the other, that was drawn in the post-war period and that has dominated the study of political religions, does not exist. One could even provocatively argue that democratic politics potentially offer a more fruitful field for studying the power of the religious aspect of politics or the sacralization of politics than totalitarianism does. Totalitarian politics may be based on political religion, but, more or less by definition, it is also based on state violence. The whole point of the study of political religion is that this side of totalitarian politics and the use of religious language and symbols that it involves should be taken seriously and not reduced to simple 'crowd manipulation'. On the other hand, however, hardly anyone would deny its strongly manipulative side. In the final analysis, therefore, it has proven hard to avoid the impression that political religion is still about 'top-down total domination' after all. The alternative, the study of totalitarianism, 'as a novel mode of collective action', sounds appealing but also seems to point in the direction of democratic politics, which involves free collective action.[38] Early social democracy is a more convincing example as a voluntary way of using religious aspects of politics. Even if it is clear that this was partly the result of just copying elements of traditional religion in a still very religious environment,[39] this is not the whole story. The vocabulary was used to express the new form of politics socialism offered. In particular the conversion stories show that more than (outward) ritual and symbolism were involved. Conversion was a shattering personal experience as well as an expression of the coherence of the group, and it thus had an important political meaning.

Populism and the 'Redemptive' Side of Democracy

If we want to understand the ambiguities of modern democracy, it is probably more fruitful to concentrate on the tensions within (liberal) democracy than to try to separate it absolutely from a totalitarian counterpart. Such an analysis could perhaps help us to understand the problems facing democracy in the twenty-first century, which are very different from the ones facing it in the interwar period. Today, one of the most discussed issues concerning European democracy is the challenge posed by populism. In many countries populist parties have received a lot of votes and are influencing government policies.

Apart from the issues they address, they have ways of mobilizing their voters that mainstream parties lack. They often criticize the rule of law – a crucial element of liberal democracy – when they see it as countering 'the will of the people', but they also reveal the problems of democracy.

One of the ways to analyse populism is to present it as a form of illiberal democracy that is akin to, or on the way to becoming, a sort of Jacobin 'totalitarian democracy', in short the opposite of liberal democracy. This is a way to demonstrate the (potential) danger of populism. However, if we are interested in the tensions within liberal democracy, another type of literature has recently become available, which does not present populism as a radical deviation or illness of democracy but rather as an extreme version of 'normal' politics and as a 'mirror' of democracy.[40] In an article about the 'two faces of democracy', which has become a modern classic, political philosopher Margaret Canovan tries to make sense of populism along these lines.[41] On the one hand, democracy is about administration, but, on the other, it is about the dreams of the people. Canovan provides a reinterpretation of Michael Oakeshott's distinction between 'the politics of scepticism' and 'the politics of faith', which has also been used in the study of political religion, and calls the two the 'pragmatic' and the 'redemptive' sides of democracy. Populism addresses this redemptive side, which is not by chance a religious word.

According to most definitions, populism comprises at least two elements: on the one hand, criticism of the allegedly closed and corrupted political and social elite, which should, on the other hand, be corrected by the wisdom of the unspoiled, more or less homogeneous, common people. The power of the elite is, according to many populists, often bolstered by a *complot* with a group of outsiders, and the elite uses the institutions of liberal democracy to hamper the execution of the will of the people. If they really wanted to, politicians could solve the problems of the common people.

If we conceive of populism in this way, we could see it as a controversial part of democracy instead of its opposite. It then becomes plausible to look for populist elements in democratic movements, such as early socialism – exactly at the time when the beginning of the history of populism as a word and a movement has often been situated.[42] The instance that made the most impression at that time was Gladstonian liberalism in Great Britain (which has also often been called populist in a loose way). This was a battle against the corrupted 'classes' by the virtuous 'masses' or 'the people' led by William Gladstone. 'The People's William' belonged to the political elite but sided with the common people. He argued rationally but presented his mission in a religious form, reminiscent of revivalist meetings, similar to popular evangelists of that time.[43] Religious language abounded. Gladstone compared his work to that of Moses, and for his adherents 'Gladstone was the political god'.[44] Gladstone, on the other hand, took the expression *Vox populi vox Dei* very seriously and almost literally.[45] He provided a 'combination of democratic politics and religious fervour under the leadership of a lay prophet'.[46]

Seen from this perspective another element of the religious dimension of early socialism becomes visible. Religious language was used not only to convey the 'meaning' of politics or the separation of their own counter-culture from official politics, but was also used to express the revivalist quality of socialist movements. This dynamic aspect is a common element in forms of populism, ranging from democratic Gladstonian liberalism to totalitarian populism in the interwar period, but also to populism today. The literature on political religion has been criticized for assuming that religion is essentially emotional or about a Pentecostal 'mobilization of emotional enthusiasm'.[47] This reduction of religion to emotion reflects, however, the paramount interest in this aspect of political religions, just as the reduction of religion to 'meaning' does.[48] As part of the post-war wave of fascination for the religious and fanatic side of mass movements, the American social psychologist Eric Hoffer wrote the famous and popular *The True Believer* (1951). The book mentions 'the brotherhood and the revivalist atmosphere of a rising movement'. The author says he is mainly interested in the 'revivalist phase of mass movements' – religious, socialist, fascist or otherwise. This was the phase 'dominated by the true believer – the man of fanatical faith who is ready to sacrifice his life for a holy cause'.[49]

As has become clear, not only opponents but also adherents of this type of movement described their relationship with politics in religious terms. Populism has often been connected to a revivalist phase of politics. This was true even for the short-lived Dutch populist movement of Pim Fortuyn in 2002. The Netherlands is one of the most secularized countries in the world, but both Fortuyn and his populist followers couched their experience in religious terms. This type of language boomed after his murder in May 2002. However, a number of years before his political success (which started only in the course of 2001) Fortuyn had already compared his political quest with the journey of Moses to the Promised Land and had written, 'I am ready. Are you? Let us go to the Promised Land!'[50] After his murder newspapers wrote about 'The Death of a Messiah', 'A Dutch Messiah', and 'Our Postmodern Prophet'.[51] Now it was time for his 'apostles'.[52]

Fortuyn's adherents also pictured their devotion in religious terms
and compared their emotions to those of the followers of 'Jomanda',
a Dutch female faith-healer.[53] When he was murdered, they erected
spontaneous memorial shrines in his honour. Ethnologists collected
the notes that were left at those places, and these also demonstrate
a religious idea of what had happened. 'Why should I still believe in
God? I believed in you! Love, Bianca', they wrote. Or: 'Serene Highness,
You were the source and the way! A creative fellow man with a message.
Called: A Messiah.'[54] After Fortuyn's death one commentator wrote that
the movement would have to turn from a sect into a church (from a
one-person enterprise into an organization with an elaborate ideology)
perhaps consciously echoing Bernstein's description of the development of the socialist party.[55] This did not happen. The movement
fell apart and was succeeded after a few years by the disciplined and
one-dimensional party of Geert Wilders.

Like other populist movements the Fortuyn movement tapped into
a sense of frustration with the current state of democracy. Its religious
language is a sign that in the long run a defence of the formal forms
of liberal democracy is a necessary but insufficient condition of a lively
democracy. Democracy is about not only administration but also the
dreams of the people. Religious language is, of course, not the same as a
full-blown political religion, certainly not in the terms of Gentile's definition where it is presented as first and foremost the cultural pendant of
totalitarianism. It could be argued that the examples used in the pages
above are merely instances of religious language in politics and not of
proper political religion at all. But that would miss the point that it would
be a pity to use the instruments of the illuminating approach of political
religion only for totalitarian regimes. As part of a totalitarian state, political religion is at its most dangerous, but aspects of it could also have a
strong democratic appeal. Even a sceptic such as Eric Hoffer alludes to
the function of revivalist (political) movements 'in the awakening and
renovation of stagnant societies'.[56] The promise of a better world, with all
the religious connotations involved, is the strength, the weakness and the
risk of democracy as we have known it since the nineteenth century.

Notes

1. The relevant literature is voluminous. For overviews see Hans Maier (ed.),
'Totalitarismus' und 'Politische Religionen'. Konzepte des Diktaturvergleichs, 3 vols
(Paderborn et al., 1996, 1997, 2003), and Emilio Gentile, *Politics as Religion*,
trans. George Staunton (Princeton, NJ and Oxford, 2006).

2. J.L. Talmon, *The Origins of Totalitarian Democracy* (London, 1961 [1952]), 1–13, 43.
3. Richard Crossman (ed.), *The God That Failed* (New York, 1954 [1949]), 2, 68, 99, 102.
4. Maurice Duvergier, *Les partis politiques* (Paris, 1951), 147–57.
5. Eduard Bernstein, *Von der Sekte zur Partei. Die deutsche Sozialdemokratie einst und jetzt* (Jena, 1911), 2. On p. 10 Bernstein quotes the famous nineteenth-century socialist leader Ferdinand Lassalle, who also distinguished between a 'religious sect' and a 'political party'.
6. Paolo Pombeni, *Introduction à l'histoire des partis politiques* (Paris, 1992), 164, 170–4; Gustave le Bon, *Psychologie du socialisme*, 5th edn (Paris, 1907), 93–111.
7. M. Ostrogorski, *Democracy and the Organization of Political Parties*, 2 vols (New York and London, 1922 [1902]), II, 615 and 620.
8. Quoted by Bernard Manin, *The Principles of Representative Government* (Cambridge, 1997), 215.
9. Gentile, *Politics as Religion*, 31; many examples can be found in Berthold Unfried and Christine Schindler (eds), *Riten, Mythen und Symbole. Die Arbeiterbewegung zwischen 'Zivilreligion' und Volkskultur* (Leipzig, 1999).
10. The argument of this paragraph can be found in more detail in Henk te Velde, 'Charismatic Leaders, Political Religion and Social Movements: Western Europe at the End of the Nineteenth Century', in Jan Willem Stutje (ed.), *Charismatic Leadership and Social Movements* (New York, 2012); cf. idem, 'Charismatic Leadership, c.1870–1914. A Comparative European Perspective', in Richard Toye and Julie Gottlieb (eds), *Making Reputations: Power, Persuasion and the Individual in Modern British Politics* (London and New York, 2005), 42–55.
11. Robert Michels, *Zur Soziologie des Parteiwesens in der modernen Demokratie* (Stuttgart, 1989 [1911]).
12. See in general Elfi Pracht, *Parlamentarismus und deutsche Sozialdemokratie 1867–1914* (Pfaffenweiler, 1990).
13. Wolfgang Hardtwig, 'Political Religion in Modern Germany: Reflections on Nationalism, Socialism, and National Socialism', *Bulletin of the German Historical Institute* 28 (2001), 10–11 and passim, which also contains references to older work; Unfried and Schindler (eds), *Riten, Mythen und Symbol*; Heiner Grote, *Sozialdemokratie und Religion* (Tübingen, 1968); Gottfried Korff, 'Politischer "Heiligenkult" im 19. und 20. Jahrhundert', *Zeitschrift für Volkskunde* 71 (1975), 202–20; Lucian Hölscher, *Weltgericht oder Revolution. Protestantische und sozialistische Zukunftsvorstellungen im deutschen Kaiserreich* (Stuttgart, 1989).
14. G. Niendorf, 'Aus der Jugendzeit', *Arbeiter-Jugend* 1 (1909), 250, comparing his faith in Social Democracy with the faith of the first Christians; Wilhelm Bock, *Im Dienste der Freiheit. Freud und Leid aus sechs Jahrzehnten Kampf und Aufstieg* (Berlin, 1927), 20, who presents the early Christian martyrs under Emperor Nero as examples for his Socialist comrades.
15. Josef Dietzgen, *Die Religion der Sozialdemokratie. Kanzelreden* (1870–75), in idem, *Sämtliche Schriften*, ed. Eugen Dietzgen, 3 vols (Wiesbaden, 1911), I, 95.
16. '[U]nd immer lautet der Titel: Wie ich Sozialdemokrat wurde!' Franz Diederich, 'Ein Buch Vorgeschichte des modernen Industriearbeiters in

Deutschland', *Die Neue Zeit* 21/2 (1903), 700. Cf. Bollenbeck, *Arbeiterlebenser innerungen*, 274–5.

17. Adelheid Popp, *Jugend einer Arbeiterin* (Berlin, 1977), 78; Wolfgang Emmerich, *Proletarische Lebensläufe. Autobiographische Dokumente zur Entstehung der Zweiten Kultur in Deutschland*, vol. I (Reinbek, 1974), 149, 280, 284, 374; 'Meine grosse Wandlung', 'den grossen inneren Wendepunkt' and 'scales falling from eyes' also in Andreas Scheu, *Umsturzkeime. Erlebnisse eines Kämpfers* (Vienna, 1923), 134; cf. an example quoted in Hölscher, *Weltgericht oder Revolution*, 273.

18. Franz Rehbein, *Das Leben eines Landarbeiters* (Hamburg, 1985), passim; the original edition by Paul Göhre was from 1911.

19. Cf. Jochen Loreck, *Wie man früher Sozialdemokrat wurde. Das Kommunikationsverhalten in der deutschen Arbeiterbewegung und die Konzeption der sozialistischen Parteipublizistik durch August Bebel* (Bonn and Bad Godesberg, 1977).

20. Johann Most, *Ein Sozialist in Deutschland*, ed. Dieter Kühn (München, 1974), 44.

21. A German Socialist journal in 1924, quoted by Stefan Berger, *The British Labour Party and the German Social Democrats, 1900–1931* (Oxford, 1994), 204.

22. Thomas Welskopp, *Das Banner der Brüderlichkeit. Die deutsche Sozialdemokratie vom Vormärz bis zum Sozialistengesetz* (Bonn, 2000), mainly part II.

23. M., 'Aus der Jugendzeit. Ein Bekenntnis', *Arbeiter-Jugend* 1 (1909), 235–6.

24. See, e.g., Sebastian Prüfer, 'Die frühe deutsche Sozialdemokratie 1863–1890 als Religion. Zur Problematik eines revitalisierten Konzepts', in Unfried and Schindler (eds), *Riten, Mythen und Symbole*, 38.

25. Philippe Burrin, 'Political Religion: The Relevance of a Concept', *History and Memory* 9/1–2 (1997), 321–49 (esp. 332); the same line in French in idem, 'Religion civile, religion politique, religion séculière', in Unfried and Schindler (eds), *Riten, Mythen und Symbole*, 27 (where political religion is used for socialism).

26. Philip Snowden, *Autobiography* (London, 1934), I, 71 and 63.

27. Quoted by Berger, *Labour Party and Social Democrats*, 206.

28. Quoted by Stephen Yeo, 'A New Life: The Religion of Socialism in Britain 1883–1896', *History Workshop* 4/1 (1977), 11.

29. J.H. Schaper, *Een halve eeuw strijd. Herinneringen*, vol. I (Groningen et al., 1933), 16 ('wedergeboorte'); J.F. Ankersmit, *Arbeiderslevens* (Amsterdam, c.1919) – probably a copy of the earlier German example.

30. Sam de Wolff, *Voor het land van belofte. Een terugblik op mijn leven* (Nijmegen, c.1976 [1954]), 161.

31. Burrin, 'Political Religion', 326.

32. Karl Mennicke, 'Sozialistische Lebensgestaltung', *Sozialistische Lebensgestaltung* 1 (1921), 5–6.

33. George Mosse, *The Nationalization of the Masses* (Ithaca and London, 1975), 8, 150.

34. Ibid., 'liturgy', 'liturgical' (9, 16, 74, 122, 135, 168, 181–2, 200, 208, 214); 'the Nazi cult and its essentially religious nature' (10); 'sacred' (50, 63); 'a community of faith' (115, 194); 'political religion' (207); 'a secular religion' (16, 214).

35. Ibid., 15, 60, 205.

36. Gentile, *Politics as Religion*, xxiii, 4–6.

37. Manin, *Representative Government*, 209, 211 (in a section about party government).
38. David D. Roberts, '"Political Religion" and the Totalitarian Departures of Inter-war Europe: On the Uses and Disadvantages of an Analytical Category', *Contemporary European History* 18/4 (2009), 412–14, who, among others, discusses the work by Gentile.
39. See, e.g., Unfried and Schindler (eds), *Riten, Mythen und Symbole*.
40. Cas Mudde, 'The Populist Radical Right: A Pathological Normalcy', *West European Politics* 33/6 (2010), 1167–86; Francisco Panizza (ed.), *Populism and the Mirror of Democracy* (London, 2005).
41. Margaret Canovan, 'Trust the People! Populism and the Two Faces of Democracy', *Political Studies* 47/1 (1999), 2–16.
42. Cf. Paul Taggart, *Populism* (Buckingham et al., 2000).
43. H.C.G. Matthew, *Gladstone 1875–1898* (Oxford, 1995), 58, 298 and passim.
44. Quoted by Eugenio F. Biagini, *Liberty, Retrenchment and Reform: Popular Liberalism in the Age of Gladstone, 1860–1880* (Cambridge, 1992), 392.
45. Richard Shannon, *Gladstone: Heroic Minister 1865–1898* (London et al., 1999), 172, 179 and passim.
46. Eugenio F. Biagini, *Gladstone* (Houndmills et al., 2000), 61.
47. Stanley Stowers, 'The Concepts of "Religion", "Political Religion" and the Study of Nazism', *Journal of Contemporary History* 42/1 (2007), 9–24 (esp. 18).
48. Cf. the routine combination of 'Gefühlspolitik' and 'glaubensähnliche Sinn-stiftung' as the elements of political religion in Berthold Unfried, 'Einleitung', in Unfried and Schindler (eds), *Riten, Mythen und Symbole*, 10.
49. Eric Hoffer, *The True Believer: Thoughts on the Nature of Mass Movements* (New York et al., 1966 [1951]), preface and 48. Cf. Tamir Bar-On, 'Understanding Political Conversion and Mimetic Rivalry', *Totalitarian Movements and Political Religions* 10/3–4 (2009), 241–64 (esp. 243).
50. Pim Fortuyn in the conclusion of his *De verweesde samenleving: een religieus-sociologisch traktaat* (Utrecht, 1995), 194.
51. *Trouw*, 8 May 2002; *NRC Handelsblad*, 11–12 and 21 May 2002. In digitized Dutch newspapers the combination 'Fortuyn and messiah' (*messias*) gives about 100 hits for 2002, including before his death.
52. *NRC Handelsblad*, 8 May 2002. The combination 'Fortuyn and apostles' gives about 30 hits.
53. Jutta Chorus and Menno de Galan, *In de ban van Fortuyn. Reconstructie van een politieke aardschok* (Amsterdam, 2002), 140.
54. Quoted by Peter Jan Margry, 'The Murder of Pim Fortuyn and Collective Emotions: Hype, Hysteria and Holiness in the Netherlands?', *Etnofoor. Antropologisch tijdschrift* 16/2 (2003), 102–27 (esp. 120–1).
55. J.A.A. van Doorn, 'De LPF op weg van sekte naar kerk', *Trouw*, 31 May 2002. Van Doorn was a sociologist who wrote about the history of German socialism and referred to Bernstein in the article, even if he did not quote his book or its title.
56. Hoffer, *True Believer*, 149.

Part II
Religion and Democracy

A Dangerous Type of Politics?
Politics and Religion in
Early Mass Organizations: The
Anglo-American World, *c.*1830

Maartje Janse

In both the United States and Britain, the participation of the common man and woman in politics increased dramatically in the early nineteenth century. Groups of disenfranchised citizens and members of religious and ethnic minorities started to organize and speak out in favour of reform. Slavery proved one of the most powerful issues, and antislavery movements in both countries were capable of mobilizing the masses and empowering men and women alike to take a political stance. For this reason, the development of the antislavery movement is valued today as an important step in the process of democratization in both the United States and Britain.

Some contemporary observers, however, were not at all excited about the new developments. Critics pointed out that political mass organizations such as antislavery societies posed a threat to political stability and democracy. One critic denounced the American Anti-Slavery Society (founded in 1833) as an 'anomaly' because of its hybrid character of being at once a religious and a political organization:

> The public, the Government, the world, have been taken by surprise. Here is an immense and powerful combination, that has suddenly leaped from the sphere of the religious world, brought with it a machinery which was manufactured in that sphere, seized upon affairs of State, usurped the business of State, and neither the public, nor the Government, seem yet to know which end, or how, head or tail, to take hold of the monster.[1]

This essay addresses the notion of the sacralization of politics from a different angle, thereby raising questions about the viability of the concept for the early nineteenth century. Towards the end of the nineteenth century, when the political domain had become dominant, the sacralization of politics could be observed and commented on. However, in the early nineteenth century for many people the religious domain was dominant, and when politics and religion became intertwined, this development was identified as a politicization of religion, rather than as sacralization of politics. In this sense, it could be argued that through focusing on the period around 1800, this case study mirrors the later process of the sacralization of politics.

This chapter goes back to a period in history in which politics was not yet a mass endeavour. Understanding the reasons why in the late eighteenth and early nineteenth centuries large groups of people were successfully mobilized and motivated to enlist in a political struggle gives us a better insight into the nature of mass politics. Based on case studies loosely selected from Irish, British and American reform movements, which reveal the widespread presence of this phenomenon, I argue that modern forms of mass politics were built upon a foundation of religious beliefs and practices, as early mass protests often centred around religious issues and religious constituencies were among the first groups to put forward political claims. Wherever the masses started participating in politics, religion and politics were intimately connected, even in countries where the separation of church and state had been formalized.

As the quote referring to the American Anti-Slavery Society as a 'monster' shows, the entrance of these religious movements into the political field did not go unnoticed or unchallenged by contemporary observers. In its second part, this chapter analyses the complaints of some of the early critics of mass political organizations, who argued that, exactly because of the major presence of religion, democratic mass politics harboured traits of totalitarian politics and were essentially antidemocratic. In the conclusion I will return to the issue of the relationship between religion and politics.

The Religious Roots of Mass Politics

The Democratization of Politics and Religion

The story of modern history is often told as a story of democratization. From the revolutionary era of the late eighteenth century onwards, the role of 'the people' in the political process increased dramatically. This expansion was based on the claim of popular sovereignty that now became broadly accepted: political decisions should represent the people's will. But how this 'will of the people' was to be expressed remained unclear. In theory, universal suffrage could be a solution. However, in post-revolutionary Europe this would not be put into practice until a century later. Even in France itself, where universal male suffrage was proclaimed in the direct aftermath of the Revolution, it was not implemented at the time. Instead, the franchise was extended only to those men who were thought financially and mentally independent enough to vote.[2] In the United States, where a relatively extensive franchise had emerged out of the Revolutionary Era, a major part of the population continued to be barred from the ballot, including women, and in many cases free blacks.[3]

Popular participation in nineteenth-century politics was thus only partly realized by the right to vote. Another, more indirect way in which the public could participate in the political process was through the notion of public opinion, understood as the outcome of public debate. Public opinion had no formal political status but was in the course of the nineteenth century increasingly taken into consideration in the political decision-making process, especially in Britain and the United States. Even though here too women and lower-ranking men remained in many ways excluded from public debate, politicians started taking the general public more seriously, if only to insure their re-election.[4]

It was another force, however, that shaped popular politics and facilitated modern democratic politics: mass organization. Some decades before the French Revolution, in Britain experiments with new and efficient forms of developing and expressing the will of the people were underway. According to some historians this was the reason why Britain did not experience a full-fledged revolution, unlike France or its former colony America. The national mass organization was one of the new elements in the protest repertoire developed by the pioneers of social movements in the decades around 1800. The organizers claimed that their organizations represented the people's will and often stressed that the official representation of the people in Parliament or in Congress was flawed. These first mass political organizations gave the disenfranchised an effective opportunity to exert extra-parliamentary pressure. For those officially excluded from the political process, organizing was more efficient than trying to influence public opinion as an individual. This does not imply that political organizations were vehicles for the disenfranchised only, as middle-class men who could vote often played leading roles in these associations.[5]

Parts of the population had, of course, been able to influence the political process before the advent of modern politics, for example in selecting local representatives. However, lower-class men and women often had only one means at their disposal to make their voices heard: violence. Spontaneous riots sometimes had a great impact. The French Revolution after all began with the storming of the Bastille, which became the most famous example of a riot ending a political system and transforming social relations. In modern politics the people developed new ways to pressure their government without the deployment of illegitimate means. As the following pages will show, these political innovations were deeply rooted in religious life.

The religious roots of mass politics have long been neglected in historiography. Twentieth-century historians have mostly been interested in secular social movements. Continental European historians have more often than not interpreted modern politics from the vantage point of the French Revolution, which was decidedly anticlerical and anti-religious in nature. By focusing on the theory of the separation of church and state they lost sight of the fact that in the United States and Britain, as well as to a lesser extent in continental Europe, religion still played a major role in politics. This role became even more important during the process of democratization, when the concerns of ordinary people – often deeply religious men and women – received more attention. More recently, the idea that the nineteenth century was an era of secularization has been challenged thoroughly, which has led to a re-establishment of the crucial role of religion in the shaping of social movements and modern politics.[6]

When studying the way politics and religion were interwoven in the early nineteenth century, it is crucial to take into account the fact that religion itself was changing shape and meaning around this time. A general 'democratization of Christianity' can be observed, especially within Protestantism. In the United States the authority of the clergy waned after disestablishment of the church. Once the clergy lost its firm hold on local societies, the importance of the church as an institution diminished. As an alternative, new networks of religious communication developed. The rapid technological developments in print culture in particular provided communication channels for new types of religious leaders.[7]

Ordinary people could now become powerful actors on the religious scene. The new leaders who successfully challenged the authority of the clergy were upwardly mobile, populist and democratic. The evangelical revivals that infused religious life with enthusiasm thus sprang from a populist upsurge. They reinforced the notion that virtue and insight resided within ordinary people. These new populist leaders did everything they could to make a profound impact on their audience.

Paradoxically, as an unintended result of the attack on the clergy's authority, new religious demagogues would gain an unprecedented influence upon the religious constituencies. One of the main criticisms of the power shift involved in the growth of democratic mass culture was that the new, populist leaders could exercise a tyranny over the masses, unimagined by the old elites.[8]

What happened in the world of religion deeply impacted the emerging mass politics. The democratization of religion coincided with a democratization of the political world, in which popular protest increasingly shaped political decisions. As historical sociologist Peter Stamatov formulates it in an article on the transformation of popular politics in the Anglo-American world, 'The religious field provided two important causal factors for the trajectory of collective action: formal organisations and "participation identities" through which ordinary people engaged in popular politics.'[9] 'Participation identities' here refers to the identification of individuals with a group that tries to mobilize them as members and to which they respond positively – for instance when they engage in political protest as women or as members of their church, town, occupation or country.[10] In the case of the early political mass movements, people participated as members of their religious constituency.

The political mass organizations took their organizational and disciplining techniques from churches and religious organizations. The religious associations of the decades around 1800 had created new networks, new imagined communities or new 'religious constituencies', as Stamatov calls them. It was in the religious domain that ambitions started to grow and people started to realize the political potential of mass mobilization through mass organizations.[11] What has been said of the British evangelical revivals applies here too: in the religious mass organizations as well as in the revivals, 'some may have discerned, dimly and indistinctly, the enormous latent power of the people'.[12]

Mobilizing the Masses

Mobilization entailed that many people at once needed to become (emotionally) involved in an issue and had to be induced to protest and/ or act. Religious issues were pre-eminently suitable for propelling people into action. This meant that for many people, church politics or political protests to protect religious rights were their first experiences with political activism. In Britain and Ireland dissenting rights, Catholic emancipation and the abolition of slavery were among the most important religious issues that would bring about the first instances of mass political protest in the form of social movements producing mass petitions.[13]

Reform movements deeply impacted political life in both the United Kingdom and the United States. Ordinary people now felt empowered to judge and condemn political opinions as well as religious ones. By application of religious perspectives to politics, as well as through the use of religious practices to mobilize political protest, political life was deeply influenced by religious forms and ideas. Tocqueville observed that in the United States Christianity was firmly linked to democracy, and popular culture at large became 'manifestly Christian'.[14] Not surprisingly, in the United States religion and reform movements remained closely identified with each other during the first half of the nineteenth century. The surging revivalism and millennialism (the belief that the coming of Christ was near and repentance was needed) provided a fertile breeding ground for the belief that reform was needed to eradicate national sins and redeem the nation. Slavery, in particular, was seen as such a national sin that needed redemption through a nationwide antislavery crusade.[15]

Even in Britain, where the ties between church and state had never been completely broken, the established church had lost much influence and authority while dissenting churches grew rapidly. Inspired by evangelical revivals, reform organizations became important centres of democratic politics, just as they were in the United States. Antislavery, the most prominent of the mass political movements, gained momentum every time it was explicitly framed as a religious crusade, as a battle of good versus evil. This happened, for instance, in 1824, when Quaker Elizabeth Heyrick, in her influential *Immediate, Not Gradual Emancipation*, referred to the battle against slavery as a 'sacred duty' and even a '*holy war*'. She called upon abolitionists to act 'with more the spirit of Christian combatants, and less of worldly politicians'.[16] Heyrick's words radicalized parts of the British movement. Women, in particular, started organizing in dozens of antislavery societies across the country. The female associations were far more radical in their position on immediate abolition than their male counterparts because their religious beliefs forced the women involved to discard political expediency and demand what was right, no matter the consequences.[17]

However, for years the main antislavery society remained cautious. According to some, this reticence hampered the cause. George Stephens together with others initiated the Agency Anti-Slavery Committee because he believed it was 'self-evident, that if the religious world could be induced to enter upon the subject, severing it from all its political relations, and viewing it simply as a question between God and man, the battle was won'.[18] He was right. It was much easier to sway public opinion and gain people's cooperation by presenting them with the choice between right and wrong, sin and redemption, than by repeating parliamentary speeches. However, the religious framing of the issue of slavery was more than a mere propaganda device.[19] These young and combative antislavery advocates were 'more at home in the religious than the political sphere. To such minds, politics, like religion, was a matter of first principles.'[20] The Agency Anti-Slavery Society, which campaigned much more aggressively than the existing Antislavery Society, was extremely successful in influencing public opinion through an intensive campaign. The itinerant agents and the massive volume of tracts all carried the message that slavery was a national sin, and that the choice to be made was one between good and bad, sin and virtue.[21]

Mobilization of the masses in reform issues, however, should not be merely regarded as instances of religious enthusiasm spilling over from the religious field onto the political. Rather, modern mass politics were fundamentally shaped by religious practices and techniques, especially those of Methodism.[22] Henry Jephson, one of the first historians of mass politics, argued in 1892 that the political mass meetings, known in Britain as 'the platform', had grown out of the techniques of the Methodist revivals of John Wesley in the 1730s and 1740s. Wesley held open-air rallies that had a seemingly spontaneous character but were to some extent organized because of their massive scale, eventually involving crowds of 30,000 to 40,000 people.[23]

The 'impressive meetings [and] thrilling addresses' of the religious revivals, according to Jephson, 'awoke in people what can only be described as a new sense'. They empowered people. The experience of the revival 'afforded a suggestion if not an example, and a precedent for similar action in the sphere of politics'.[24] The religious mass meeting was transferred into the political domain, and in the second half of the eighteenth century, and especially in the nineteenth century, countless political mass meetings were organized, often in the open air, in which speeches were made and resolutions proposed, discussed and voted on, which were often published in newspapers or even presented to Parliament as petitions.

The platform was famously employed by the British Chartists in the first half of the nineteenth century, when they demanded an extension of the franchise along with other rights and freedoms. The mass meetings posed a threat to the authorities, who feared the peaceful gatherings could turn into violent rioting at any time – which they indeed sometimes did. However, mostly these mass meetings were (in Charles Tilly's terms) displays of worthiness, unity, numbers and commitment, which supported the claims of those excluded from political participation that they were responsible and reliable citizens and ready to be included in the system. The agitation was partly effective, and the Reform Bill of 1832 extended the franchise considerably.[25] The struggle for a further extension nevertheless continued, and the numbers attending the mass meetings kept increasing. The first photograph ever taken of a crowd was of the 10 April 1848 Chartist 'Monster Meeting' where 150,000 people gathered around the platform at Kennington Common in London (Fig. 1). It is no mere coincidence that this open-air mass meeting was held on the very spot where John Wesley had addressed his largest crowds over a century earlier.

Disciplining the Masses

Once the masses were successfully mobilized, their energy had to be transformed into political pressure. Organizing the masses into pressure groups was the most efficient way of disciplining people in their protests. Voluntary associations, more than social movements in general, offered a strict hierarchical structure, which made it possible

Figure 1   The first picture ever taken of a crowd was taken 10 April 1848 at the Chartist 'Monster Meeting'.

for leaders to influence and discipline members. Anything that could discredit the cause and damage the reputation of the organization (such as the use of violence or quarrels about tactics) was often effectively suppressed. Displaying unity in the struggle was considered so important that individual dissent was often ignored. Leaders asked for the trust and loyalty of their members and for a mandate to decide the right course of action.

Much as the political mobilization of the masses was deeply influenced by religious practices, the disciplining of the masses was inspired by examples from religious life. Among the religious institutions that served as a blueprint for political organizers, the churches were the first and foremost example. Churches had been effective at organizing and disciplining institutions for ages, and even though many were losing some of their control over local communities, their structures were still in place. Both in Britain and the United States their function was partly taken over by religious benevolent organizations, which, like churches, were organized locally but united at a national level. Sunday school societies, missionary societies, Bible societies and religious tract societies were remarkably successful in focusing reform energy: with membership numbers and annual revenues that astounded contemporaries, they were among the first mass organizations. It was through observing the success of the religious mass organizations that people started to understand the power of organizing.[26]

The Irish Catholic Association (1823–29) offers a remarkable example of such disciplining of the masses along religious lines. Ireland had been part of the United Kingdom since 1801, but politically, most Irish were second-rate citizens. The aim of the Catholic Association was to end the exclusion of Catholics from public office. It would turn out to be the first mass organization to count among its subscribers members of the poor working classes. To achieve this, the Catholic Association employed several innovative techniques.

The first-year membership numbers were somewhat disappointing until the association's leader Daniel O'Connell, influenced by the examples of the French and American revolutions, came up with a new tactic. He transformed the Dublin-based elite group into a nationwide popular organization by proposing that every Catholic in Ireland could become an associate member of the Catholic Association by subscribing just a penny a month.[27] O'Connell also utilized the organizational structure of the Catholic Church to mobilize and discipline the Irish into loyal members. He made the parish the organizational unit of the association and the parish priests its agents.[28] The willingness of the Catholic clergy to participate in this struggle for democratization and civil rights is remarkable. Unlike in continental European Catholic countries, Irish Catholicism was not aligned with the powers of the *ancien régime* against forces of democratization. In response to the suffering of the Irish people under British oppression and economic distress, the Catholic clergy became democratically inclined and sided with the people. This alone had a profound impact on people's perception of the cause.

> A sort of religious sanction was thus communicated imperceptibly to a cause, which to those not immediately engaged in its promotion appeared purely and altogether political: the very principle upon which the exclusion had originally been founded was religious; and the late crude efforts at proselytism by the opposite church had enhanced not a little this conviction in the mind of a large mass of the population, that the whole struggle was religious.[29]

Because the participation identity of the protesters had been proven to be religious, the protesters could be mobilized and disciplined much more effectively along existing religious lines.

The success of this approach was astounding. In addition to ten thousand full members, in a short while, over three million associate members could be counted in a total population of seven million people. This resulted in a weekly income of over £2000, a staggering amount of money at that time. This high degree of disciplining meant that the members could be efficiently and swiftly mobilized. When the Catholic Association called for simultaneous meetings, over two-thirds of the Irish parishes held them (often after Sunday mass), resulting in 859 petitions. This display of power deeply worried the British authorities. They took seriously O'Connell's claims that he would not be able to contain the masses much longer and that revolution would be inevitable if the government did not give in to the demands of the Catholic Association. The demonstrated strength of the Association was an important factor in the decision made in 1829 to grant Catholics full rights of citizenship.[30]

Criticism of Mass Politics

In the United States of America a network of religious organizations, comparable to that of Britain, had developed in the first decades of the nineteenth century. Such groups as the American Board of Commissioners for Foreign Missions (1810), the American Bible Society (1816), the American Colonisation Society (1816), the American Sunday

School Union (1824) and the American Tract Society (1825) proved that 'Concentrated action is powerful action.'[31] Inspired by evangelical revivalism, these organizations aimed at a renewed Christianization of their country (and the world at large in the case of the missions). The massive numbers of auxiliaries, members, publications distributed or of funds raised were published widely, serving as a quantitative measure of their success.[32] They were even more successful than their British counterparts, according to some historians due to the relative lack of institutional context, resulting from the weak central state.[33]

The second quarter of the nineteenth century witnessed a transformation in reform practices. In the late 1820s, a new generation of reform movements developed a successful repertoire of action to engage in politics, which made them a force to be reckoned with. They built on the organizational techniques of earlier religious mass organizations.[34] The movement for Sabbath Observance, for example, demonstrated how a national organization (the General Union for the Promotion of the Christian Sabbath, 1828–32) could orchestrate a nationwide campaign through the use of massive amounts of printed material efficiently distributed by the postal system, resulting in mass petitions. Organizational skills developed in the religious sphere were now used in the political domain. The antislavery movement, which was quickly radicalizing in the 1830s, became the most visible example of this development.[35]

Critics expressed concern over these new types of organizations and argued that their ability to mobilize and discipline the masses posed a threat to the democratic system. Their criticism concerned two main points: the influence of religion in politics and the power these new organizations and their leaders held over the masses. The mobilizing techniques were thought to undermine a person's reason, and the evangelicals were therefore accused of acting as 'dictators to the consciences of thousands'.[36] The denunciations of the large and powerful religious institutions that had become known as the 'Benevolent Empire', as well as of those mixing religion with politics, were embedded in a broad denunciation of evangelical revivalism and its effects on society, 'a substantial body of protest and critique' that has until recently received insufficient scholarly attention.[37]

Following the broader criticism of evangelical revivals, participation in mass organizations was explained in terms of mass hysteria by, among others, Unitarian minister William Ellery Channing, in 1829:

> Whoever knows anything of human nature, knows the effect of excitement in a crowd. When systematically prolonged and urged onward, it subverts deliberation and self-control. The individual is

lost in the mass, and borne away as in a whirlwind. The prevalent emotion, be it love or hatred, terror or enthusiasm, masters every mind, which is not fortified by a rare energy, or secured by a rare insensibility.[38]

Where rational individual judgment disappeared, the masses would compliantly follow a few leaders.[39] This would eventually harm democracy. As Channing wrote,

Associations [...] accumulate power in a few hands [...]. In a large institution, a few men rule, a few do everything; and if the institution happens to be directed to objects about which conflict and controversy exist, a few are able to excite in the mass strong and bitter passions, and by these to obtain an immense ascendency. Through such an association, [...] a few leaders can send their voices and spirit far and wide, and, where great funds are accumulated, can league a host of instruments [... This] will gradually but surely encroach on freedom of thought, of speech, and of the press.[40]

It has been claimed that Channing on this occasion 'formulated the Iron Law of Oligarchy'.[41] Although sociologist Robert Michels would do so almost a century later, stipulating that even democratic organizations necessarily will become undemocratic because of the workings of the internal hierarchy and the demand for efficiency of the organization,[42] it was Channing who recognized this anti-democratic tendency at the core of democratic organizations long before Michels. Both the disciplining of the masses and the effectuation of a successful campaign called for efficient leadership, which, if necessary, sacrificed critical debate and the rights of individual members in order to further the great cause. In the great crusades against evil, the ends sanctified the means.

Channing even went so far as to suggest that these mass organizations functioned as the Spanish inquisition had in early modern Europe. Another critic, denouncing the radical methods of the New York Magdalen Society (aimed at battling prostitution), included in his anonymous pamphlet an illustration of a man being tortured. 'Remember the awful Inquisition', it said, and: 'this would be the result of Orthodoxy, were all orthodox plans to succeed' (Fig. 2).[43]

In a context of growing anti-Catholic sentiments, the critics (mainly Protestant ministers) warned the public that these mass organizations were 'foreign' to Protestantism and repeatedly invoked the spectre of Jesuitism. In 1836 Calvin Colton, a Protestant minister turned

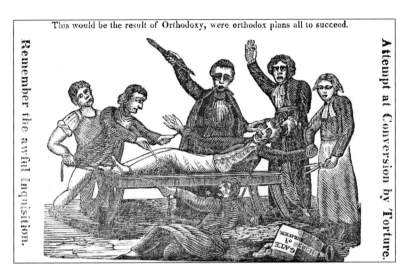

Figure 2 Adversaries of modern reform organizations believed they were forcing religion and reform upon the people and depicted them as infringing upon the freedoms of individuals.

journalist and a prominent critic of both antislavery and temperance movements, made this point in *Protestant Jesuitism*. In it he argued against the extremely successful temperance organizations (in 1832, a million people were said to have signed the temperance pledge). Colton denounced 'The arrogance, dictatorial airs, and tyranny, assumed by this society over the public, and over individuals.'[44] In *Abolition a Sedition*, his scathing critique of the national antislavery organization, published in 1838, he went so far as to call its president Gerrit Smith a 'Dictator General'.[45]

Colton considered the combination of religious mobilization and skilful disciplining extremely dangerous. He stressed that the antislavery movement's roots were religious, in motivation as well as organizing forms:

Consequently, the Abolition movement, which, as before remarked, originated in religious sentiment, which was prompted and is still sustained principally by religious men, and which borrowed the model of its organization from the action of the religious world, by instituting an exact copy, the moment it entered the field, was transformed into a political body from the very nature of the work it had undertaken, notwithstanding it was, and still is, actuated by religious sentiment. It is nevertheless political, and it is all the more dangerous, because religion is in it – not Christianity.[46]

The author asserted that the success of the antislavery movement sprang from the surprise effect of its 'perfectly anomalous character'. These new types of 'political crusade' – another reference to the Catholic roots of this type of politics – 'have thoroughly transcended the prescribed limits of Constitutional action, and entered a field untrodden before, in an unknown shape, that the public know not where to find them, or how to meet and take hold of them'.[47]

Because of the power the leaders held over the membership, a new, self-contained power structure was being introduced into the political system. Colton compared the Antislavery Society to a state within a state, an *imperium in imperio*. Abolitionists 'have erected a republic of their own, with a State machinery, and set themselves to change the government of the country'. It is 'an independent and powerful Commonwealth'. Because the constitution recognized only one government he declared the Antislavery Society to be an illegal, seditious organization, bound to lead the country to a revolution. Colton's prophecy that the antislavery crusade 'will dissolve the Union' turned out to be at least partly accurate: in the outbreak of the Civil War two decades later the controversy over slavery played an important role.[48]

Here we encounter a paradox: the mass organizations that are generally acknowledged for their important role in the democratization process – in terms of including the masses in the political decision-making process – are accused of despotism. Colton, Channing and other critics feared the tyranny of the majority as an effect of mass politics.[49]

We are persuaded that by an artful multiplication of societies [...] as cruel a persecution may be carried on in a free country as in a despotism. [...] it will be as perilous to think and speak with manly freedom, as if an inquisition were open before us. It is now discovered that the way to rule in this country, is by an array of numbers, which a prudent man will not like to face. Of consequence, all associations aiming or tending to establish sway by numbers, ought to be opposed. They create tyrants as effectually as standing armies.[50]

Channing even believed public opinion could no longer function properly in the political process because of the new mass organizations. Public opinion, he wrote, 'is in danger of becoming a steady, unrelenting tyrant, browbeating the timid, proscribing the resolute, silencing free speech, and virtually denying the dearest religious and civil rights'.[51]

Before Colton voiced his criticism, the idea of political mass organizations as a state within a state had been put forward in 1835 by French philosopher Alexis de Tocqueville in *Democracy in America*. In 1831–32 he travelled through the United States. When he wrote down his observations on the nature of American democracy, an important role was assigned to voluntary associations. Tocqueville had been impressed with the proliferation and vitality of associational life. Although he maintained that in general an unlimited freedom of association is dangerous because it could produce anarchy, he argued that this freedom functioned well in the United States, as it acted as a counterbalance against an even more dangerous phenomenon: the tyranny of the majority.[52]

However, like Channing, Tocqueville believed that seemingly democratic associations could themselves be despotic and tyrannical. Still, he attributed these characteristics more specifically to European political associations and idealized their American counterparts. This is why he was milder in his assertion of American political associations as an *imperium in imperio*:

> Americans have also established a government within associations; but it is, if I can express myself so, a civil government. Individual independence finds its part there: as in society, all men in it march at the same time toward the same goal; but each one is not required to march to it exactly on the same path. They make no sacrifice of their will and reason to it; but will and reason are applied in making a common undertaking succeed.[53]

In Europe, he believed, conditions were different. Whereas American political associations were civil, European ones had a military character. Tocqueville claimed that this was directly related to the presence or absence of democracy. Because in the United States the majority will was expressed through universal (white male) suffrage, political associations that challenged the government could not claim to represent a majority. Knowing that they voiced minority claims, their demeanour was peaceful and constructive. They petitioned, participated in public debates and tried to convince other citizens of their opinions, but always remained within legal confines. Tocqueville juxtaposed this 'civil' behaviour to the 'military' behaviour of European political organizations. Seemingly referring to French revolutionary associations, he asserted that European political associations claimed and believed that they represented the will of the majority, in the absence of universal suffrage. This idea emboldened them to use violence and break the law, which led them, according to Tocqueville,

> to introduce military habits and maxims within them: thus does one see them centralize the direction of their strength as much as they can and put the power of all in the hands of a very few. The members of these associations respond to the words of an order like soldiers on a campaign; they profess the dogma of passive obedience, or rather, in uniting, they have made the entire sacrifice of their judgment and their free will in a single stroke: thus there often reigns within these associations a tyranny more insupportable than that exercised in society in the name of the government that is attacked.[54]

It is important to note that, while Tocqueville was a very perceptive observer of American associational life, he also idealized it, and at the same time his information on European associational life was limited and prejudiced.[55] For the purpose of this article it is significant that he pointed out the tyrannical aspects of mass organization but at the same time stressed that mass organizations behaving 'civilly' could contribute to the stability of the political system.

Concluding Remarks

The innovative techniques of early political mass movements throughout the Anglo-American world were deeply rooted in religious traditions and practices. The early nineteenth-century mass movements gave rise to

> new fideistic relations between the masses and their leaders. The mass movements gave considerable impetus to the crystallization of secular entities into myths that were the core of their ideologies, and to political practices such as the all-absorbing dedication of the activist, which became a reason for and way of living.[56]

This development gave rise in turn to relentless criticism, which challenges our understanding of the early mass organizations. The American case study is especially interesting since historians of political religion point to the American Early Republic as an important example of tolerant and inclusive 'civil religion'. This is one of the two ideal types in the process of the sacralization of politics. Civil religion is supposed to be inclusive, tolerant and democratic, in contrast to political religion, which is exclusive, fundamentalist and totalitarian.[57]

However, as historian Emilio Gentile put it, 'The civil religion's accentuation of its nationalistic, racist, and imperialist tones tended to take on the characteristics of an intolerant and fundamentalist political religion that reserved full membership of the national community blessed by God to Americans of Anglo-Saxon stock.'[58] In that respect, mass movements can bear traits that evoke associations with totalitarianism. Critics of these organizations such as Colton and Channing, as well as the Southern slaveholders, agreed that the movements had intolerant, fanatic and despotic traits and would have disputed the tolerant and democratic nature of antislavery societies and the like. The violent antislavery mobs of the 1830s and 1840s as well as the Civil War itself testify to the intense contestation of slavery.

In their criticism of the sacralization of politics these nineteenth-century observers remind us of the more recent critics of totalitarianism who believed politics went wrong wherever religion raised its head. In both cases, religion was often equated with mass enthusiasm, sometimes even resulting in mass psychosis. Made most famous by *fin de siècle* pioneers of the field of crowd psychology, such as Gustave Le Bon, this criticism is actually older. It developed out of the criticism of the evangelical revivals, of early populist movements and of radical reform movements.[59] The underlying question is, What is the role of the individual in modern politics? Mobilizing the individual to support political ideas turned out to be much more difficult and inefficient than mobilizing the masses. In the increasing contestation for the hearts and minds of the people, techniques of mass politics, often borrowed from religious traditions, became more and more important.

According to critics, mass politics could function as a despotic system, exerting mind-control over the general public. While they certainly exaggerated this danger sometimes, they were right that the disciplining of the masses, necessary to build a strong political movement, often resulted in the oppression of individuals and was in some ways anti-democratic. This oppression was the unintended by-product of the inclusion of the masses into the political process in an orderly, disciplined and peaceful manner. This is not to claim that the early nineteenth-century mass organizations can be compared to the horrific totalitarian experiences of the twentieth century, but the question raised is significant: Can democratic mass politics operate without these despotic traits that derive from the necessary disciplining of the masses? For the time period and movements discussed in this essay, it seems that demonstrating unity was essential to the success of these movements, and disciplining individual members was the key to unity.

If one thing stands out, after this brief review of the birth of mass politics, it is that in the decades around 1800 politics and religion were much more intimately connected than one would assume based on the traditional views on the separation of church and state and the age of secularization. As I said earlier, to simply state that in the origins of mass politics we can see a clear case of the sacralization of politics would not do justice to the relationship between religion and politics in this era. Religious constituencies were among the first groups to participate in mass protests, often protesting against what they conceived of as religious issues with political implications. Around 1800 religious ideas and arguments, more than any other force, were capable of rallying support for a cause. This was the result of the central place people gave to religion in their lives.[60]

Mobilizing large groups of people turned out to be most effective in the case of mobilization on the basis of religious identity. In the antislavery crusade, for example, true mass mobilization was success-ful only after the issue of slavery was explicitly presented as a *religious* issue, with slavery as a national sin, and the antislavery movement as a sacred cause, trying to redeem the nation from God's wrath. In addi-tion to this, certain techniques for mobilizing the masses were derived from the religious field. One example discussed above is the tradition of 'the platform': religious mass meetings which inspired political mass meetings. The same is true for the organizational techniques used to discipline the masses once they had been mobilized. The first political mass organizations were built on the fundament of religious organi-zations. Churches and religious reform organizations had provided a well-developed infrastructure that political organizers could borrow from in their pioneering work.

Representatives of the establishment, who held on to a more narrowly defined perception of politics, felt understandably threatened by the broadening of the political debate by new (religious) issues, new (religious) arguments, new (religious) techniques and new (religious) constituencies. Seen from their perspective, the unwelcome newcom-ers were attacking the fundamental traits of political life and even, according to some, the very foundations of the state. That contempo-raries were worried about these developments indicates both that the religion-based political mobilization and disciplining of the masses were a novel phenomenon around 1830 and that much was at stake.

The question arises whether the politicization of religious issues, constituencies and forms as discussed in this contribution differs fundamentally from the process of the sacralization of politics as discussed throughout this volume. The notion of the sacralization of politics implies the idea that politics and religion are separate domains and fundamentally different from each other. Religion is often located in the realm of ideas and in the inner world of the individual, while politics refers to power relations and constitutes the outer world that individuals inhabit. The idea is that while in pre-modern societies religion and politics may have been mixed up, the separation of Church and State around 1800, and especially the professionalization of politics in the century that followed, have liberated politics from religion. As Stanley Stowers notes, this approach assumes that we can define 'inherently secular objects from the sphere of politics' and contrast these to 'certain emotional experiences' which are produced by religion.[61]

The separation of church and state had been established and accepted relatively early in the United States, with critics such as Channing and Colton defending the political order against those who wanted to tear down the walls between the spheres of religion and politics. The idea that politics and religion are distinct domains, however, is a historical construct, produced by the liberal notion of the separation of spheres.[62] Only after the broad acceptance of this idea of a separate political domain in the course of the nineteenth century could the emergence of religious forms and functions in politics come as a surprise and be seen as a threat to the 'proper' functioning of the political system.

When we accept that in the murky reality of lived historical experience these domains do not exist, that they are constructions and as such part of the discourse of political and religious legitimacy, we may not be so surprised to learn that politics and religion are often impossible to separate. In developing a clearer conception of the way politics functions, and of the relationship between politics and religion, we might do best to realize that just as the identities of individuals often consist of multiple layers, combining religious, political, gender, ethnic, national and local identities in one person, in the same vein certain popular movements can be political and religious at the same time.

Notes

1. [Calvin Colton,] *Abolition a Sedition, by a Northern Man* (Philadelphia, 1839), 29.
2. Patrick Gueniffey, 'Suffrage', in François Furet and Mona Ozouf (eds), *Dictionnaire critique de la révolution française* (Paris, 1988), 571–81; Alan S. Kahan,

Liberalism in Nineteenth-century Europe: The Political Culture of Limited Suffrage (Basingstoke and New York, 2003), 21–65.

3. Alexander Keyssar, *The Right to Vote: The Contested History of Democracy in the United States* (New York, 2000).

4. Keith Michael Baker, 'Representation Redefined', in idem, *Inventing the French Revolution: Essays on French Political Culture in the Eighteenth Century* (Cambridge, 1990), 224–51; Patricia Hollis, 'Pressure from without: An Introduction', in idem (ed.), *Pressure from without in Early Victorian England* (London, 1974), 1–26; John L. Brooke, 'Consent, Civil Society, and the Public Sphere in the Age of Revolution and the Early American Republic', in Jeffrey L. Pasley, Andrew W. Robertson and David Waldstreicher (eds), *Beyond the Founders: New Approaches to the Political History of the Early American Republic* (Chapel Hill, 2004), 207–50.

5. Eugene Charlton Black, *The Association: British Extraparliamentary Political Organisation 1769–1793* (Cambridge, MA, 1963); Charles Tilly, 'Britain Creates the Social Movement', in James E. Cronin and Jonathan Schneer (eds), *Social Conflict and the Political Order in Modern Britain* (London, 1982), 21–51.

6. See for an excellent historiographical critique, Peter Stamatov, 'The Religious Field and the Path-dependent Transformation of Popular Politics in the Anglo-American World, 1770–1840', *Theory and Society* 40/4 (2011), 437–73.

7. Nathan O. Hatch, *The Democratization of American Christianity* (New Haven and London, 1989), 125–8; Stamatov, 'The Religious Field'. For the Dutch case see Annemarie Houkes, *Christelijke vaderlanders: Godsdienst, burgerschap en de Nederlandse natie, 1850–1900* (Amsterdam, 2009).

8. Hatch, *Democratization of American Christianity*, 226, 16.

9. Stamatov, 'The Religious Field', 449.

10. For more on the concept, see Roger V. Gould, *Insurgent Identities: Class, Community, and Protest in Paris from 1848 to the Commune* (Chicago, 1995), 13–15.

11. Johann N. Neem, *Creating a Nation of Joiners: Democracy and Civil Society in Early National Massachusetts* (Cambridge, MA, 2008); Stamatov, 'The Religious Field'.

12. Henry Jephson, *The Platform: Its Rise and Progress*, vol. 1 (New York and London, 1892), 4.

13. Stamatov, 'The Religious Field', 443–7.

14. Hatch, *Democratization of American Christianity*, 209.

15. Robert H. Abzug, *Cosmos Crumbling: American Reform and the Religious Imagination* (New York and Oxford, 1994); Ronald G. Walters, *American Reformers, 1815–1860*, 2nd rev. edn (New York, 1997), 21–37.

16. Elizabeth Heyrick, *Immediate, Not Gradual Abolition, or, An Inquiry into the Shortest, Safest, and Most Effectual Means of Getting Rid of West Indian Slavery* (Boston, 1838 [1824]), 18 (original emphasis).

17. Clare Midgley, *Women against Slavery: The British Campaigns 1780–1870* (London and New York, 1992). Also see Eduard van de Bilt's chapter in this volume.

18. Cited in Howard Temperley, 'Antislavery', in Hollis (ed.), *Pressure from without*, 27–51, 30.

19. Ibid., 39–40.
20. Ibid., 40.
21. Ibid.
22. For a broader analysis of the impact of Methodist organizational models on political organizing, see Stamatov, 'The Religious Field', 451–4.
23. Jephson, *The Platform*, I, 5.
24. Ibid.
25. Charles Tilly, 'Introduction to Part II: Invention, Diffusion, and Transformation of the Social Movement Repertoire', *European Review of History* 12/2 (2005), 307–20; and idem, 'Britain Invents the Social Movement' for the relationship between the passing of the Reform Bill and the agitation in the years prior to passage.
26. Neem, *Creating a Nation of Joiners*.
27. Gillian M. Doherty and Tomás O'Riordan, 'The Campaign for Catholic Emancipation, 1823–1829', in Donnchadh Ó Corráin and Tomás O'Riordan (eds), *Ireland, 1815–70: Emancipation, Famine and Religion* (Dublin, 2011), 129–42, accessible through the Multitext project in Irish History, University College Cork, Ireland, http://multitext.ucc.ie/d (retrieved March 2011); Fergus O'Ferrall, *Catholic Emancipation: Daniel O'Connell and the Birth of Irish Democracy 1820–30* (Dublin, 1985).
28. O'Ferrall, *Catholic Emancipation*, 39–40, 61–3.
29. Thomas Wyse, *Historical Sketch of the Late Catholic Association of Ireland*, vol. 1 (London, 1829), 228–9.
30. Doherty and O'Riordan, 'Campaign'.
31. Peter J. Wosh, *Spreading the Word: The Bible Business in Nineteenth-century America* (Ithaca and London, 1994), 63.
32. Ibid.; Candy Gunther Brown, *The Word in the World: Evangelical Writing, Publishing, and Reading in America, 1789–1880* (Chapel Hill and London, 2004); David Paul Nord, *Faith in Reading: Religious Publishing and the Birth of Mass Media in America* (Oxford and New York, 2004); Judith Wellman, *Grass Roots Reform in the Burned-over District of Upstate New York* (New York and London, 2000); Neem, *Creating a Nation of Joiners*.
33. Michael P. Young, *Bearing Witness against Sin: The Evangelical Birth of the American Social Movement* (Chicago and London, 2006); Stamatov, 'The Religious Field'.
34. Neem, *Creating a Nation of Joiners*, 81–99.
35. Richard John, 'Taking Sabbatarianism Seriously: The Postal System, the Sabbath, and the Transformation of American Political Culture', *Journal of the Early Republic*, 10/4 (1990), 517–67; Bertram Wyatt-Brown, 'Prelude to Abolitionism: Sabbatarian Politics and the Rise of the Second Party System', *The Journal of American History* 58/2 (1971), 316–41.
36. Wyatt-Brown, 'Prelude to Abolitionism', 327.
37. James Bratt, 'Religious Anti-Revivalism in Antebellum America', *Journal of the Early Republic* 24/1 (2004), 65–106 (68).
38. William Ellery Channing, 'Remarks on the Disposition Which Now Prevails to Form Associations and to Accomplish All Objects by Organized Masses' (1829), *The Works of William E. Channing*, 6 vols (Boston, 1841), I, 281–332 (290).
39. See also Bratt, 'Religious Anti-Revivalism'; idem, 'From Revivalism to Anti-Revivalism to Whig Politics: The Strange Career of Calvin Colton', *Journal of Ecclesiastical History*, 52/1 (2001), 63–82.

40. Channing, 'Remarks', 298.
41. Frank Carpenter, 'William Ellery Channing', *Dictionary of Unitarian and Universalist Biography* (Unitarian Universalist Historical Society, 1999–2011). Available at http://www25-temp.uua.org/uuhs/duub/articles/williamellery channing.html (retrieved March 2011).
42. Robert Michels, *Zur Soziologie des Parteiwesens in der modernen Demokratie. Untersuchungen über die oligarchischen Tendenzen des Gruppenlebens* (Leipzig, 1911).
43. *Orthodox Bubbles, or a Review of the [...] New York Magdalen Society* (s.l., 1831).
44. [Calvin Colton,] *Protestant Jesuitism by a Protestant* (New York, 1836), 51.
45. [Colton,] *Abolition a Sedition*, 12.
46. Ibid., 30.
47. Ibid.
48. Ibid., 18, 4, 5.
49. On the debate on reform politics and the tyranny of the majority, see Kyle G. Volk, 'The Perils of "Pure Democracy": Minority Rights, Liquor Politics, and Popular Sovereignty in Antebellum America', *Journal of the Early Republic* 29/4 (2009), 641–79.
50. Channing, 'Remarks', 299.
51. Ibid., 300.
52. Alexis de Tocqueville, *Democracy in America*, ed. Harvey C. Mansfield and Delba Winthrop (Chicago and London, 2002), 182–4.
53. Ibid., 186.
54. Ibid., 185–6.
55. Stefan-Ludwig Hoffmann, *Civil Society: 1750–1914* (Basingstoke and New York, 2006), 1–6.
56. Emilio Gentile, *Politics as Religion*, trans. George Staunton (Princeton, NJ, 2006), 31.
57. Ibid., xi–xvi.
58. Ibid., 25.
59. Bratt, 'Religious Anti-Revivalism'; idem, 'From Revivalism to Anti-Revivalism'.
60. Hatch, *Democratization of American Christianity*, 184–9, 209.
61. Stanley Stowers, 'The Concepts of "Religion", "Political Religion" and the Study of Nazism', *Journal of Contemporary History*, 42/1 (2007), 9–24 (17).
62. Michael Walzer, 'Liberalism and the Art of Separation', *Political Theory*, 12/3 (1984), 315–30.

De-sanctifying Affairs of State: The Politics of Religion in Harriet Beecher Stowe's *Uncle Tom's Cabin* (1852)

Eduard van de Bilt

Introduction

This essay explores the relationship between politics and religion in Harriet Beecher Stowe's nineteenth-century antislavery novel *Uncle Tom's Cabin* (1852). More specifically, the article aims to show that although Stowe's novel breaches the 'wall of separation between church and state' written into the American constitution by demanding that Christian values determine government policies, her work 'sacralizes' the political realm only to a limited extent. *Uncle Tom's Cabin* does not condone the 'sacralization' of politics that, as Emilio Gentile's work on political religion points out, imbues political institutions and representatives with religious qualities: Stowe produced neither a political religion that can be denounced as totalitarian, nor the civil religion for which the United States has been presented as a model.[1] Whereas Gentile's work highlights the dangers of donning politicians and political institutions with a religious aura, Stowe's efforts to introduce religious values into the public sphere do not aim to imbue the political domain and its representatives with a religious halo. On the contrary, Stowe's distrust of, and distance from, politics bolster her religious qualms to consider anything earthly truly sacred. At the same time, Stowe undermines fears about the relationship between politics and religion best expressed by Hannah Arendt, who often complained that Christianity's two-world perspective undermined Christian political involvement.[2] Arendt was very much afraid that Christians would shy away from involvement in the public sphere of politics because they deemed this domain of relative importance compared to life after death. While Gentile warns that the intermingling of religion and politics occurs most prominently and dangerously in totalitarian regimes, Arendt, one of totalitarianism's most astute analysts, is afraid that Christianity's adherents are insufficiently interested in politics. If only because she would have refrained from going public with her antislavery novel without religious inspiration, Stowe's highly religious incursion into the public domain offers yet another perspective on the interrelationship of religion and politics next to Gentile's and Arendt's.

Although aiming to ground nineteenth-century American politics in Christian values, Stowe's *Uncle Tom's Cabin* never allows politics and religion to coincide fully. Stowe undoubtedly tried to make the United States' civil realm more 'sacred' than before, turning it into an object of devotion by making nationalist appeals part of her antislavery novel. The Christian convictions that fuelled her antislavery stance inevitably propelled her into politics: negating Arendt's fears, Stowe's was an involved, 'earthly' Christianity. But Stowe's religiously inspired civic engagement undermines chauvinistic political celebrations and, more importantly, does not condone the creation of a civil or political religion that attributes religious qualities to national political institutions and representatives. Too uninterested in everyday politics and its institutions and too much stamped by a separate-spheres theory that assigned politics to her male contemporaries, Stowe was also so much aware of the (Southern) church's support for, and justification of, the institution of slavery that she shied away from the sanctification of a political system and organization. Her Christian convictions, furthermore, may well have prevented her from assigning to religious faith so secular a function. Society and politics would always remain human, that is to say imperfect. Stowe's antislavery novel makes clear that religious politics is not a contradiction in terms, yet does not necessarily devolve into the sacralization of politics. As Emilio Gentile's work on political religion inadvertently indicates (he shows how Christians were among totalitarianism's most ardent opponents) and Stowe's work proves, though highly liable to become part of politics, religion itself at least partly prevents the two realms from coinciding: the very Christianity that Stowe aims to introduce into the public sphere of politics prevents her from 'sacralizing' politics. Religious politics not only differs substantively from political religion but may also contribute to the latter's undoing.

Activist Faith

As Stowe realized when writing *Uncle Tom's Cabin*, in the United States religion and politics were oddly separate yet intertwined. The country's constitution had officially institutionalized a separation of church and state and had added a clause defending the freedom of religion to the original text in 1791.[3] In a process that ended in the 1830s in Massachusetts, individual states had 'disestablished' religious denominations, no longer supporting 'state' churches with tax money – to the horror and disgust of Stowe's father Lyman Beecher, one of the United States' most prominent nineteenth-century preachers. As the first amendment to the constitution that guaranteed the freedom of religion argued, all Americans were free to exercise their own religious faith, without government support or interference. At the same time, however, religious convictions permeated politics. Highly contentious debates about Sunday mail delivery characterized American politics during the 1820s. More generally, in the decades before the American Civil War, campaigns against alcohol abuse and prostitution bore all the hallmarks of religious crusades. The same applies to other reform movements such as the efforts to end American slavery, to which Stowe and her family contributed significantly: applying Christian convictions to politics, churches, ministers and their flocks were at the core of these movements. Moreover, in a separate yet oddly similar application of Christian values to social and political debates, many antebellum American Christians relied on the Bible to justify and support the country's slave system. Despite the constitutional separation of church and state, American politics was stamped by American Christianity.[4]

The same odd relationship between faith and politics that pervades American society in general characterizes Harriet Beecher Stowe's antislavery novel. Though officially not even allowed to participate in America's democracy, Stowe became intricately involved in it due to her Christians convictions. While her religiously inspired antislavery novel could hardly remain apolitical, the extent to which its author aimed to 'sacralize' politics remains nevertheless ambiguous.

Religion propelled Harriet Beecher Stowe into the public domain. While *Uncle Tom's Cabin* was written in response to the 'Compromise of 1850', agreed to by Congress to arrange the admission into the United States of areas gained in its 1846–48 war against Mexico, changes in American Protestantism allowed Stowe to go public with her book in the first place. The Compromise of 1850 that Congress established stipulated how the newly conquered areas of California, New Mexico, Arizona, Nevada and Utah were to become part of the United States: as either free or slave states. It also adopted a strict version of the fugitive slave clause already written into the American constitution in 1787. The 'fugitive slave' clause of the compromise, which, in one of its provisions, forced northern officials to assist southerners in search of runaway slaves, infuriated northern public opinion to such an extent that someone like Stowe felt an almost religious urge to vent her anti-slavery position. She felt the more impelled to do so, however, because a few decades earlier the Second Great Awakening of the 1820s and 1830s had informed American Christians that they could earn their place in heaven by solving social problems and 'doing good' to fellow citizens. While Protestant orthodoxy had long maintained the value of tenets such as original sin and predestination, partly due to social and economic developments, notions of human free will and responsibil-ity crept into the Calvinist tradition in the United States. The religious revivals that swept the country in the first half of the nineteenth century created a more liberal Christianity conducive to activism: the human fate was no longer predicated on inscrutable decisions reached by an all-powerful God but on human efforts to improve the world.[5] Salvation lay no longer simply in God's hands. A reformed Christianity stimulated a series of reform movements among which the abolitionist attempt to rid the country of slavery was one of the most important. Politics and religion combined created the preconditions for the writing of *Uncle Tom's Cabin*.

In other respects as well, *Uncle Tom's Cabin* is stamped by the American Protestant tradition. As Sacvan Bercovitch argues, Stowe's antislavery novel fits generically into the tradition of 'the American Jeremiad', a genre based on the sermons of Puritan ministers who tried to stem the tide of Puritan declension by threatening New England set-tlers with hell and damnation the moment they did not live up to the Protestant promise and assuring them collective, communal bliss the moment they repented and tried to take care of their sins. The original, Puritan sermon transformed into a lament about American failings that increasingly took on chauvinist overtones: instead of emphasiz-ing transgressions, the jeremiad began to underscore the promise of national greatness. Moreover, even those highly critical of (aspects of) American society could not help expressing their censure within the confines of the jeremiad: in Bercovitch's book, nineteenth-century critical intellectuals and cultural figures such as Ralph Waldo Emerson and Herman Melville are tainted by the genre's increasing nationalism. Stowe cannot escape this fate either, at least not completely.[6] When, in her 'Concluding Remarks', she argues that 'Both North and South have been guilty before God' and that 'this Union [is] to be saved [...] by repentance', Stowe apparently in part verifies Bercovitch's perspective.[7] Trying to convince readers of the sins of slavery, *Uncle Tom's Cabin* holds out the promise of atonement and a glorious American future: as Bercovitch would have it, religion and chauvinism come together in Stowe's antislavery novel.

Uncle Tom's Cabin nevertheless approaches its readers in a more individual than national vein. Stowe aims to convince her readers of the evils of slavery by a personal appeal that, hopefully, induces each and every member of her audience to contribute to the abolitionist struggle. In the mode of pragmatic, 'can do' Christianity characteristic of the Second Great Awakening, Stowe appeals to all individual readers to start acting charitably toward their African American brothers and sisters and thus earn their place in heaven. In her 'Concluding Remarks', Stowe also asks, 'But, what can any individual do?' Her reply to the question informs readers that

> There is one thing that every individual can do, – they can see to it that *they feel right*. An atmosphere of sympathetic influence encircles every human being; and the man or woman who *feels* strongly, healthily and justly, on the great interests of humanity, is a constant benefactor to the human race.

Readers have to make sure that their sympathies are not 'swayed and perverted by the sophistries of worldly policy'.[8] Particularly the chapters describing Uncle Tom and little Eva (or Evangeline) show Stowe involved in delineating how true Christian values and attitudes, that is to say a life led in the pursuit of neighbourly love, create for the individual involved in the effort a seat next to God. Like so many other antebellum reformers, Stowe is first and foremost interested in individual salvation.[9] Only in her 'Concluding Remarks' does she engage in the nationalist rhetoric resembling Bercovitch's jeremiad, warning readers that a 'day of grace is yet held out to us'.[10]

According to Stowe, down-to-earth neighbourly love practised by individuals in face-to-face meetings with others will solve society's ills and guarantee blissful immortality for the individual do-gooders concerned. The highly sentimental chapters describing Evangeline's illness and death aim to show, for instance, the religious confidence of those who dedicate their lives to helping others. In contrast to the teachings of Stowe's stern father, Lyman Beecher, and earlier, orthodox Puritans, Evangeline dies happily, confident that she will go straight to heaven. When asked on her deathbed by her father what she sees, Evangeline refers to love, joy and peace, not at all exhibiting the anxiety about death usually expressed by representatives of traditional American

Calvinism. Little Eva conveys the kind of optimism that Protestants who believed in sinfulness and predestination hardly ever had. She knows that her Christian do-good mentality, which she even displayed in relation to the slaves her family owned, and self-effacing, charitable and humane treatment of African Americans as equals ensure her life after death. Having loved Jesus and transferred this love onto fellow human beings, she dies confident that she will enter God's kingdom of heaven. The liberal, or better perhaps, emotional, Christianity that guided her life turned her into a not only pious but also socially and, one may add, politically engaged person, who thus could face death and the coming of Christ self-assuredly.

Domestic Republicanism

Redefined Christianity and politics intersect on other levels of Stowe's *Uncle Tom's Cabin* as well. The same activist faith that guaranteed Evangeline a place next to God pushed a woman such as Stowe into the public domain that was officially not open to her. As historians have not failed to point out, according to the nineteenth-century domestic ideology women were expected to remain at home, taking care of their husbands and children, offering a safe haven from the nasty and aggressive worlds of economics and politics.[11] Being excluded from the public domain, women lacked the rights men had: they could not vote, for instance. At the same time, however, they were idealized as icons of respectability, as experts of morality: recognizing right from wrong, they represented the country's highest (Christian) values. The impact of this ideology on the status of women differed, however: whereas historians emphasized the negative consequences of this tradition at first, increasingly they explored its rather ambivalent nature. Together with a redefined Christianity that emphasized an activist attitude, the moral status of women in the domestic ideology undermined domesticity's major premises: intended to prevent women from entering the public domain, the ideology actually induced quite a few of them to seek a public role. Exactly because they gave voice to morality, women were society's best hope. They were better politicians than their official male counterparts because, unlike the latter, they would settle political issues on the basis of moral criteria. They would make sure that moral values were applied to politics. They were ideal reformers who would solve the problems besetting American society such as alcoholism, prostitution and slavery, as God's (and Christ's) nearest representatives on earth. The very Christianity that the domestic ideology occasionally invoked to keep women out of the public realm also propelled them into it. Long before the nineteenth amendment to the constitution would offer them the right to vote in 1920, women had a voice in the public domain: by portraying women as the representatives of morality, the domestic ideology that constrained them induced women such as Stowe to pass judgment on society and become actively engaged in reform movements.

A major contribution to, and defence of, the nineteenth-century tradition of domesticity, Stowe's antislavery novel enacts these tensions. It subverts the separate-spheres theory that it helps delineate. *Uncle Tom's Cabin* turns non-citizens into political role models. While deprived of the right to vote and prevented from participating in politics, women are exemplary citizens. Exactly because of their Christian values of fellow feeling and self-sacrifice, they indicate how the public realm can regain its former lustre. Problems such as slavery show how American society has degenerated. Only by re-institutionalizing the principles for which women stand can the American public domain be saved. Experienced as they are in pedagogical strategies that turn their children into decent adults, women know best how to turn individuals into self-effacing citizens. In a modestly framed but highly imperialist and ambitious agenda, *Uncle Tom's Cabin* claims that only women's Christian attitudes and convictions will restore America's republican tradition. Whereas representatives of republican ideology such as Alexis de Tocqueville claimed that only patrician politicians from his own aristocratic class (and their American 'counterparts' such as lawyers and judges) can sustain the republican tradition and channel its democratic forces, Stowe is convinced only women can do so.[12] For society to improve, women need to take over. *Uncle Tom's Cabin* quietly prods Stowe and fellow women to grab power; it opens up the public domain to those excluded from it and allows them to play a major role in it. In so doing, it also improves the quality of the public sphere. Even churches are democratized in the effort: as cultural historian David Reynolds shows, *Uncle Tom's Cabin* also signals the arrival of a new, female and democratic leadership in America's Protestant institutions, churches included.[13]

In other respects as well, Stowe's religiously inspired antislavery novel is radically democratic. It opens up American politics to more than female outsiders. Much has been said about the racialist aspects of Stowe's book.[14] As many critics have argued, in her depictions of African Americans Stowe relies very much on stereotypes. The happy-go-lucky Sambo, the merry mammy and the passive humble servant all make their appearance in *Uncle Tom's Cabin*. Topsy is depicted as a wild savage child. The only African American willing to defend his family against white atrocities and insults, George Harris, critics point out, is 'conveniently' sent off to Africa by the narrator at the end of the book, exhibiting Stowe's preference for the colonization project that many of her antislavery contemporaries likewise favoured.[15] Uncle Tom, the self-effacing, forgiving slave who even under the cruellest of masters is willing to turn the other cheek thanks to his Christian feelings, is the proverbial 'white man's negro'. According to critics, Stowe never favoured full equality between blacks and whites. These racialist aspects should, however, not obscure the radical nature of Stowe's book. In her address to the reader with which she ends the book, Stowe talks about reparations or financial compensation for African Americans because of their sufferings under the slave system, a radical gesture even today. Moreover, although often considered by critics too much of a 'white man's negro' because of his passivity, humility and modesty, Tom exhibits the very same features that Stowe idolizes in her 'heroic' women characters. Like Evangeline, Tom is the Christ-like figure willing to sacrifice his own self and as such the model citizen that Stowe hopes readers will emulate. The features critics object to are also part of Stowe's domestic women. Stowe is not only willing to allow African Americans a place in the public domain, but also puts one of them on a pedestal as a model citizen. As Reynolds also argues in his recent work on Stowe's novel, while several of her comments on African Americans 'Today [...] sound like racial stereotyping [...] in Stowe's day they were progressive. Most white Americans of the time considered blacks greatly inferior to whites.'[16]

Uncle Tom's Cabin is the more democratic because the criteria it sketches for a thriving public sphere and its suggestions for improving the quality of politics are, in a way, far from strict, and can be met by just anyone. In the debates about the public domain Stowe adopts a special position. Unlike many intellectuals discussing the preconditions and quality of the public realm, Stowe does not emphasize the relevance of rationality and the prerequisites of reason as the most decisive elements moulding the public domain.[17] Stowe believes in the presence of an innate moral sense prompted when we see others suffer. Paradoxically a disciple of Scottish enlightenment thinkers such as Adam Smith, Lord Kames, Francis Hutcheson and David Hume, who used John Locke's ideas about sense experience and its role in the formation of ideas to develop a 'moral sense' philosophy facilitating a moral society, the sentimental author of *Uncle Tom's Cabin* turns emotions (or sentiments) into the trigger mechanism that creates the Christian communities she advocates. Despite her efforts to rid American Protestantism of its notions of sin and predestination, Stowe follows Jonathan Edwards in emphasizing the importance of religious affections: affections and not rationality determine the quality of the public domain. As one Stowe scholar argues, persuaded 'that Americans had become deadened to the pain suffered by victims of heartless public policies because they thought in impersonal abstractions, authors like Stowe sought to restore feelings to dominant modes of cognition'.[18] Convinced that realistic renditions of people in pain create togetherness and communalities, Stowe, to facilitate this reinstatement of the emotions, turns *Uncle Tom's Cabin* into a meeting place of characters triggering identification, in a coming together that kindly and emphatically includes the reader. Vivid, real-life pictures and dialogues that focus on the suffering of slaves aim to undermine the sense of otherness that separates whites from blacks, or, for that matter, northerners from southerners. Unlike radical abolitionist William Lloyd Garrison, who during part of his abolitionist career dramatized the differences between North and South, Stowe refuses to think in terms of dichotomies. Inherently universal, her appeal to sentimentality and its power of sympathy not only corrects abstract reason but also undoes what in Stowe's perspective are artificial distinctions.[19] While providing Simon Legree (the novel's major villain) with northern ancestors, she depicts abolitionist Miss Ophelia as prejudiced: only face-to-face meetings with figures such as Topsy amend Miss Ophelia's rigid moral precepts and rather abstract, overly general notions about African Americans and allow her to engage in truly human interaction.[20] Since seeing others suffer enhances this interaction, *Uncle Tom's Cabin* abounds with depictions of people in distress. Because seeing and meeting others includes the ability to recognize affinities, in its efforts to transcend differences *Uncle Tom's Cabin* draws together the most diverse people and suggests an utterly open, democratic society. Anyone can lay claim to being Stowe's 'sensual' citizens, even, and emphatically so as little Eva shows, children, whose innocent gaze of empathy is particularly exemplary.

As other Stowe scholars have shown, the chapter 'In Which It Appears That a Senator Is but a Man' not only states concisely Stowe's prerequisites for a thriving public domain, but also conveys her criticism of other contributors to the debate about the public sphere. It depicts how Senator Bird, who in the state assembly is willing to support fugitive slave legislation, wittingly forfeits his political convictions when confronted with the real-life consequences of the legal system he advocates.

The senator who appeals to reason to resolve issues is shown the limitations of his approach. The instinctive, emotional response of womanly fellow feeling, imbued with a sense of morality, that his wife exhibits shoves aside political considerations and rational calculations. As the senator realizes as soon as he responds to his wife's query about his day's work in state politics, discussing the fugitive slave cause that was part of the day's political business with his wife is superfluous. Whereas the senator vainly advises his wife that 'we mustn't suffer our feelings to run away with our judgment', she on her part warns him against confiding in reasoning – 'especially reasoning on such subjects' as the fugitive slave law. Male logic is ineffectual and pathetic. Indifferent and harsh, male reason and ratiocination are not the proper foundation of a public sphere that can only thrive thanks to the womanly sense of morality anchored in feelings and eye-to-eye meetings. Eliza's appearance at his home induces the senator to help the escaped slave: face-to-face encounters prevail over abstract political notions. To explain the senator's conversion the narrator adds that the senator's

> idea of a fugitive was only an idea of the letters that spell the word, – or at the most, the image of a little newspaper picture of a man with a stick and bundle with 'Ran away from the subscriber' under it. The magic of the real presence of distress, – the imploring human eye, the frail, trembling human hand, the despairing appeal of helpless agony, – these he had never tried.[21]

The moment ideas confront real-life experiences, they are in need of correction; as soon as words made up of letters connect with the real presence of imploring eyes and trembling hands they lose their abstract nature. Far better than ideas and words, 'the imploring human eye, the frail, trembling human hand' elicit a response that triggers and sustains communities. Enacting her solutions to the problems of slavery and the public sphere, Stowe's chapter on the senator's humanity turns her into an early representative of a long line of thinkers defending face-to-face meetings as the first requirement, and model, for communal happiness.[22] At the same time, she corrects many colleagues in the debate about the public domain by emphasizing the relevance of emotions instead of reason.[23]

It is the absence of this compassionate, Christian power of sympathy that makes the American political system and its major documents and institutions of limited value in Stowe's opinion. As long as American politics is not pervaded by this 'womanly' power, politics and the public domain more generally will remain limited, diseased and unethical. Only when the female morality of the private sphere of the home pervades politics can politicians claim to be decent lawgivers. Whereas women's behaviour is based on the power of sympathy, male political action is driven by cold, rational opportunism; while a democratic openness to others and a fellow feeling stamp women's ideas and attitudes, egoistical and egotistical self-interest makes politicians tick. As Stowe notes, it is exactly this difference between the two realms of the home and politics that in her day makes for a poor public realm. The cold male rationality pervading the political domain is hardly conducive to the Christian community that Stowe is after. Only when men stop being 'politicians' will politics be saved.[24] 'True' politicians take women as their role models: becoming 'womanly', they transform politics, grounding its affairs and decisions in the very Christian morality that pervades the home. The moment these politicians become 'female', evils such as slavery will come to an end: as soon as politicians adopt the womanly features of compassion, love and self-sacrifice, the public sphere will be redeemed. As *Uncle Tom's Cabin* implicitly argues, only those who know how to run a household should be allowed to enter politics and pursue a political 'career'. 'True' politicians resemble the self-effacing women, who are beyond opportunism and Machiavellian games; a 'truly' democratic tradition is not interested in issues of power but aims to foster the face-to-face meetings and exchanges conducive to a civil society based on Christian values.

Different Worlds

Ideally, for Stowe, politics and religion are entwined. Recently, impelled by the religious right's political revival during the Reagan and Bush years, several historians and political scientists have warned against dissolving the gap between church and state in American politics.[25] Stowe adds a slightly different perspective to this debate, which mediates between the various voices that make up the discussion. According to Stowe, as long as politics is not suffused with Christian values, it will not prosper. Unlike the founding fathers of the American political tradition, she does not favour a separation of church and state: at least, she is convinced that religious values need to be part of politics. Her father Lyman fought hard but unsuccessfully to prevent the state of Connecticut from 'disestablishing' the Congregationalist church, no longer allowing ministers like him to be supported financially by state taxes. Though uninterested in re-establishing these pecuniary transactions between church and state, Stowe points to the spiritual and moral costs of a strict separation of religion and politics. Christian values cannot be relegated to the women's domain of the household without endangering the quality of society at large. A separation of church and state is detrimental to the representatives of the private as well as the public domains.[26] With the moral compass of the one no longer illuminating the affairs of the other, unrealized and imperfect potential permeates the two spheres and stamps everyone involved.

Stowe does not 'sacralize' politics, however. Far from launching the political or civil religions described by Gentile, she refuses to turn her redefined, 'womanly' politics into a sacred affair. It is exactly her modest view of politics, her refusal to attribute to it a certain religious halo, which makes Stowe so interesting in the debate about the relationship between church and state, or between religion and politics, in the United States.

Uncle Tom's Cabin treats politics rather disdainfully (the book's plea for humility notwithstanding), or, better perhaps, barely deigns to discuss it. In relation to the private sphere of the home and life after death, the public domain of politics dwarfs in importance. Stowe makes politics self-effacing and subservient. She aims to democratize politics by forcing it to sacrifice part of itself (its male part). Only after having shed its macho aspects can politics thrive: it needs to tone down its pretensions. Senator Bird is 'but a man' in his non-political capacity, as a Christian individual responding to the pain and needs of others. It is this emphasis on self-effacement that perhaps explains Stowe's ambivalent stance on such issues as women's voting rights (which *Uncle Tom's Cabin* does not discuss at all): whereas her sister Catherine vehemently rejected the woman's right to vote and her sister Isabella aggressively pursued it, Harriet took up a somewhat vague middle position in the debate about the issue.[27] Her 'politics' is not about aggressively asserting rights but donning disinterested Christian benevolence. The 'politicians' *Uncle Tom's Cabin* glorifies are modest but moral outsiders and non-politicians, and, as the subtitle to her book suggests, representatives of 'life among the lowly': women, children and slaves. True to the republican tradition of the American Revolution, Stowe never embraces professional politicians and their institutions as the mainstay of society. On the contrary, like George Washington and so many non-professional politicians, Stowe emphasizes the blessings of 'amateur' leaders, serving their country while sacrificing their self-interest – as women are wont to do anyway thanks to the domestic ideology.[28] *Uncle Tom's Cabin* advances the cause of non-politics. Its Christian values ensure that politics is not about power but the meekness of self-sacrificing individuals. The self-effacing figures that Stowe wants to goad into the centre of American politics partly dispense with and erode the political domain. When politicians are no longer macho men but gentle mothers, political affairs take on a completely different hue; when what matters is the virtuous citizen's willingness to engage in self-effacing action for the good of the community, political institutions such as parties become irrelevant.

Moreover, although the do-good efforts of these 'motherly' citizens are undoubtedly ethical and sanctifying, they do not automatically and necessarily create a 'sacred' society. Stowe is too much the Protestant to harbour a rosy and romantic perspective on the world: even an androgynous one does not simply consist of Evangeline and Uncle Tom look-alikes. The runaway slave George Harris, who at the end of her book moves to Liberia to spread the gospel, remarks about this endeavour,

> I go to *Liberia*, not as an Elysium of romance, but as to *a field of work*. I expect to work with both hands, – to work *hard*; to work against all sorts of difficulties and discouragements; and to work till I die. This is what I go for; and in this I am quite sure I shall not be disappointed.[29]

George's words can be said to represent the author's position as well: Christianizing the public domain remains hard work, even for those who are, in the jargon of American Calvinism, part of the elect (resembling Tom and Eva). The public domain is never so sanctified that it can forego labour. It will only be the ideal type announced in Stowe's novel in its pre- or postmillennial phase, at the end of time. The human and humane political domain generated by the values of Stowe's Christian women differs from the sacred one inhabited only by 'saints' such as little Eva and Tom. Most of *Uncle Tom's Cabin*'s 'regular' heroes remain human, with all of the weaknesses entailed: Stowe shows how, in the effort to escape slavery, George is, for instance, more than willing to resort to arms in self-defence.

The support that southern as well as northern churches offered the slave system must have increased Stowe's aversion to institutional politics and her awareness of the difficulties involved in the effort to domesticate the public sphere. Her desire to inject religious values into the public domain notwithstanding, the two realms of religion and politics were already intertwined, but in ways she deemed highly inappropriate: church ministers defended the institution of slavery with the help of arguments derived from the Bible. For Stowe, introducing religious values into the public domain implied eliminating this awkward association. Her campaign to bring politics and religion together partly involved its opposite: Christianizing politics included severing the despicable links uniting slavery, state institutions and church authorities. Because she realized the extent to which official church representatives justified the Southern states' slave system, Stowe's plea to Christianize the public domain never entailed an uncritical merger. Moreover, the intricate link between the institution of slavery and Protestant churches was another indication that the womanly public sphere she envisioned was an ideal type that was difficult to realize.

Republicanism and the sins of official Protestantism combined with domesticity to ensure that Stowe was never tempted to idealize the political domain. Exactly because as a woman she had such a low opinion of politics and such humble political aspirations, she may have been able to shy away from the sin of idolizing the public domain and its major institutions and representatives. Within a more down-to-earth perspective, one could add, exactly because she was a woman Stowe was not at all interested in politics: it represented a world that was alien to her.[30] Since Christian moral values were of prime importance, politics was of only relative relevance; because personal moral behaviour decided life after death, the games played in political institutions represented a diversion at best. The republican convictions that *Uncle Tom's Cabin* expresses go together with a Higher Law tradition, which proclaims Christian compassion and self-sacrifice to be more important than conventional male legislation, let alone the 1850 fugitive slave act.[31] In Stowe's perspective, even the 1787 founding document of the American political tradition fades in importance compared to this Higher Law tradition. The 'Godless constitution' and the system it established cannot function properly without the values coming out of a religious tradition.[32] Political institutions and documents are useless without the moral compass provided by Christianity. The anti-political aspects in the traditions of republicanism, domesticity and Protestantism combined prevent Stowe from idolizing institutions and representatives of secular power.

Ideally, politics is, in Stowe's perspective, irrelevant. Critics are right in accusing the author of *Uncle Tom's Cabin* of elitism.[33] As a woman convinced of the moral superiority of her own position, she abhors the give-and-take compromises that are part of democratic politics. Though aiming to persuade readers of the correctness of her perspective, she actually does not consider her views on slavery to be simply that: despite the book's friendly nature, Stowe is convinced that she represents the truth. More than the American constitution, *Uncle Tom's Cabin* has biblical status: Stowe wants to be a female Moses laying down the law. (It was in a way no coincidence that *Uncle Tom's Cabin* competed with the Bible in terms of sales numbers.) As French scholar Pierre Rosanvallon would have it, her politics of empathy, her notion of '*empathic representation*' of those victimized by society, corrects the failures of regular American democracy.[34] Stowe is the subject who knows, a prophet who ordains and bullies. That explains why she was offended by aspects of the reader response to her book. In contrast to what her own theories suggested, not all readers identified with the people in pain her novel portrayed. If Stowe ever believed that vivid pictures are sufficient to convince an audience, the Southern response to her book and complaints from African American readers about the black stereotypes on which she relies seem to prove sufficiently the weaknesses of her position. Her vivid depictions aimed to bolster the bonds between reader and author, and not to cause discontent. Apparently, empathy (or, as literary scholar Peter Brooks would have it, the 'transferential' relationship between author and reader) does not always work.[35] Building her campaign against slavery on sense experience and emotions, Stowe apparently failed to take into account that various readers will respond to her text differently. The hostile feelings that she evoked suggest the limitations and unpredictability of her emotional appeal. Not all readers decided to support the abolitionist movement immediately after finishing her novel. Particularly in the Southern press, she was accused of producing fictive accounts of the South's slave system. Because of these accusations of unreliability, Stowe felt compelled to publish *A Key to Uncle Tom's Cabin* a year after her bestselling novel appeared.[36] In the work, she presented as a true historian the sources that went into the making of her novel: not just abolitionist tracts and information but Southern newspaper clippings that offered the data and evidence that she had relied on in writing her antislavery text. A few years later, her second antislavery novel, *Dred*, explicitly discussed the status of writing and reading and reader-response issues.[37]

Stowe cannot have been totally surprised about this (lack of) response, however. Her own Christian convictions had made this type of reaction predictable. Her elitist streak not only comes to the fore in her disdain of politics but also shows in other respects. Despite the effort to distance herself from and rewrite the convictions of Puritan die-hard Jonathan Edwards, Stowe adopts parts of his beliefs. Her emphasis on the value of conversations and her pedagogical philosophy of equality notwithstanding, she harbours an anti-democratic ethos if only because she relies on Edwards's theory of the religious affections to define Evangeline's and Uncle Tom's position.[38] Edwards posits a kind of sixth sense, a spiritual indwelling that transforms the sense perceptions of regular human beings into a new view of the world permeated by the Holy Spirit. Truly religious people, the elect, sense the world differently, more perceptively, than natural people. Stowe adopts these ideas. Uncle Tom and Evangeline see and hear more than others: they can see Christ exactly because they believe in him so firmly. It is this special sense perception that distinguishes them from others: it is what turns them into the self-effacing Christians they are. While she was undoubtedly offended by the accusation that her work was unreliable, Stowe knew that not everyone resembled Evangeline and Tom. Following Edwards, she in a way distinguishes between spiritual or elect and natural readers. The distinction signals her awareness that the public domain does not simply consist of 'saints' and will hardly be transformed into a sacred realm effortlessly and overnight.

Her worries about the reader response to her book, however, also show her to be far more down-to-earth than the perspective on Christianity of intellectuals such as Hannah Arendt presumes. Despite her distance from ordinary politics, Stowe cannot be accused of focusing primarily on heaven instead of the slavery issue: she does not subordinate the discussion of slavery to the discussion about 'true' Protestant saints. In the debates about the public sphere, Arendt consistently warned against a two-world perspective, either in the shape of a Platonic tradition that proclaimed the world of ideas to be more important than the poor, worldly emanations it received here on earth or in the shape of a Christian tradition that considered action in the world of far less relevance than status in a life after death.[39] In one of her earliest works, Arendt tried to elaborate this perspective on Christianity by pointing out the ambiguities and contradictions in St Augustine's concept of neighbourly love.[40] Stowe, however, can hardly be said to remain uninvolved in the realm of action that Arendt favours. She wrote *Uncle Tom's Cabin* to induce people to act. (In *Dred*, the characters discuss the sermons of an incompetent minister at a revival meeting, whose words produce emotions but no more than that: his audience does not feel compelled to act at the end of the sermon.) While critics accuse Stowe of offering a weak foundation for the action she hopes to bring about, they can hardly deny that in *Uncle Tom's Cabin* action is one of her main concerns. Given the extensive debate about the status of action (or 'praxis') occurring in modern Western philosophy, for instance, the accusation appears somewhat gratuitous; intellectuals have been struggling to define action's preconditions for ages. Moreover, Stowe's theory of action is more intricate than many critics surmise. Stowe's emphasis on real-life meetings has been criticized as rather limited in its scope and effects: because they involve individual encounters, so the critics argue, their effect will be limited, conducive to individual salvation only. For dramatic social change more is needed than the face-to-face meetings of a few benevolent people.[41] This kind of criticism fails to take into account the status of Stowe's book: thanks to its sales figures, the multiplier effect of *Uncle Tom's Cabin* was enormous. Stowe's depictions of people in pain served as the substitute experience of real-life encounters. In combination with the sales numbers of her book these depictions ensured that quite a few readers experienced virtually what reality perhaps failed to offer: an acquaintance with slavery and slaves. As an effort to incite action, *Uncle Tom's Cabin* was more successful than similar efforts on the part of fellow abolitionists and representatives of other reform movements. The reception of her book in the United States and Europe proved as much.

Conclusion

Uncle Tom's Cabin shows how religious values (like values more generally) not only inform and stimulate political life but can also serve to protect politics against the very tendencies depicted as 'political religion' in the relationship between politics and religion. The emotional response to political problems such as slavery that Stowe wants to solicit does not aim to reinforce a political regime but to create identification with the victims of an oppressive political tradition. While the Christian values that Stowe wants to inject into the public domain are undoubtedly intended to improve politics, the sacred nature of this newly designed public domain nevertheless remains tenuous. Partly because of her outsider's perspective, Stowe is never in danger of inflating the political domain's relevance. Despite her strong Christian convictions and aversion to 'regular' politics, however, Stowe can hardly be said to remain uninvolved in the public realm of action that intellectuals such as Arendt deem so important either. Stowe wrote *Uncle Tom's Cabin* to incite Christian readers to act. Her audience was expected to be emotionally touched and, as a result, aggressively support the abolitionist movement. In the debate about the relationship between religion and politics Stowe is remarkable for never allowing politics to adopt a religious aura, yet never separating the two realms either.

94   *Eduard van de Bilt*

Notes

1. The phrase 'wall of separation between church and state' is from Thomas Jefferson's letter to the Danbury Baptist Association, 1 January 1802. Jefferson played a prominent role in the history of religious tolerance in the United States and was a strong advocate of the separation of church and state. Emilio Gentile discusses the dangers of political religion and civil religion in his *Politics as Religion* (Princeton and Oxford, 2006).
2. Arendt expresses her worries about two-world theorists who prevent people from engaging fully in the public domain in, for instance, the 'Prologue' to *The Human Condition* (Chicago, 1958).
3. The first amendment to the constitution, added in 1791, guarantees freedom of religion.
4. James Morone's *Hellfire Nation: The Politics of Sin in America* (New Haven and London, 2003) is one the books corroborating this perspective. As the dust jacket of the study indicates, 'The American Constitution firmly separates church and state. Yet religion lies at the heart of American politics. How did America become a nation with the soul of a church?'
5. Daniel Walker Howe, *What Has God Wrought: The Transformation of America, 1815–1848* (Oxford and New York, 2007); George McKenna, *The Puritan Origins of American Patriotism* (New Haven and London, 2007).
6. Sacvan Bercovitch, *The American Jeremiad* (Madison, 1978). Bercovitch refers to Stowe's antislavery novel in ch. 5, which delineates how the jeremiad became 'a ritual of consensus' (as the chapter is titled); Bercovitch, *The American Jeremiad*, nn. 174–5.
7. Harriet Beecher Stowe, *Uncle Tom's Cabin; or, Life among the Lowly* (New York, 1994 [1852]), 388.
8. Stowe, *Uncle Tom's Cabin*, 385; Stowe's italics.
9. Historians usually distinguish between the reform movements before the American Civil War and the Progressive Era of the end of the nineteenth and the beginning of the twentieth centuries by arguing that while the former were convinced that individuals were the cause of and solution to society's problems, the latter realized the impact of the environment on human behaviour and were interested in changing the social and economic circumstances that impacted human ideas and attitudes.
10. Stowe, *Uncle Tom's Cabin*, 388.
11. Kathryn Kish Sklar, *Catherine Beecher: A Study in Domesticity* (New Haven, 1973) offers one of the early and classic depictions of the domestic ideology (or theory of domesticity) and its separate-spheres aspects. A more recent contribution to the debates about domesticity is the 'No More Separate Spheres!' special issue of *American Literature* 70/3 (1998) edited by Cathy Davidson.
12. In terms of the specifics that Stowe provides in her depictions of, among others, Miss Ophelia, only those who can run a kitchen should be actively involved in the public domain. Alexis de Tocqueville's defence of the republican ideology can be found in, among other works, his classic two-volume study on the American political tradition, *Democracy in America* (1835, 1840); for a more general depiction of the republican ideology, see Bernard Bailyn, *The Ideological Origins of the American Revolution* (Cambridge, MA,

1967); J.G.A. Pocock, *The Machiavellian Moment: Florentine Political Thought and the Atlantic Republican Tradition* (Princeton, 1975); and Gordon Wood, *The Radicalism of the American Revolution* (New York, 1992).

13. Reynolds's *Mightier Than the Sword* moves beyond Nathan Hatch's *The Democratization of American Christianity* (New Haven and London, 1989) by emphasizing not just the new role of (male and occasionally African American) 'lay' preachers in American Christianity during the first half of the nineteenth century, but also of women. As he explicitly argues, theirs is not a 'feeble' but a strong and democratic Christianity; David Reynolds, *Mightier Than the Sword: Uncle Tom's Cabin and the Battle for America* (New York, 2011), especially 39–42, 45.

14. For the widespread accusation that Stowe depicts African Americans in highly stereotypical fashion, see, among others, James Baldwin, 'Everybody's Protest Novel', in *Notes of a Native Son*; reprinted in *James Baldwin: Collected Essays*, ed. Toni Morrison (New York, 1998), 11–18. J.C. Furnas, Donald Chaput, Addison Gayle Jr and Richard Yarborough have buttressed Baldwin's criticism.

15. The most famous example in this respect is Abraham Lincoln. See Eric Foner, *The Fiery Trial: Abraham Lincoln and American Slavery* (New York, 2010).

16. Reynolds, *Mightier Than the Sword*, 38.

17. Despite their efforts to come up with a democratic perspective that allows everyone access to the political realm, major participants in the debate about the public realm such as Jürgen Habermas, Richard Rorty and Hannah Arendt cannot help emphasizing criteria that are based on their own position as intellectuals, such as reasonable discussion and a reading culture. Stowe only partly does so.

18. Marianne Noble, 'The Ecstasies of Sentimental Wounding in *Uncle Tom's Cabin*', *The Yale Journal of Criticism* (1997), 10.2, 295.

19. Stowe's notion of empathy (or power of sympathy) contains, as Stowe scholars have noted, odd aspects. Whereas Stowe is convinced that empathy abets sensing the pain of others, critics point out that the power of sympathy easily degenerates into selfish projections and homogenizing gestures of otherness: in this perspective, Stowe's 'vision' falls victim to Foucault's gaze. They also note that empathy creates odd bedfellows by allowing women such as Stowe to identify with (features of) others they do not want to be associated with. Elizabeth Barnes comes up with this kind of criticism in *States of Sympathy: Seduction and Democracy in the American Novel* (New York, 1997). As Noble argues, Stowe's references to the slaves' bodily wounds had unintended consequences: 'The effort to provoke in readers an experience of intersubjective connectedness at the level of the body had the unanticipated effect of eroticizing the reading experience, and in so doing, it undermined its own effort to humanize the slaves, who were positioned as erotic objects of sympathy rather than subjects in their own right' ('The Ecstasies of Sentimental Wounding', 296).

20. Personal acquaintance, Stowe shows, supplements Ophelia's, and the reader's, abstract knowledge and moral precepts. Higher Law can only become real through face-to-face meetings.

21. Stowe, *Uncle Tom's Cabin*, 77.

22. John Dewey and Richard Rorty are among the prominent philosophers who follow in Stowe's footsteps and adopt many of her ideas. See Dewey,

The Public and Its Problems (Athens, OH, 1980 [1927]), and Rorty, *Contingency, Irony, and Solidarity* (Cambridge, 1989). For a critique of this position in the public sphere debates, see Walter Lippmann, *Public Opinion* (New Brunswick and London, 1991 [1922]), and Jeffrey Alexander, *The Civil Sphere* (Oxford and New York, 2006), 71–2.

23. Literary scholar Jane Tompkins, whose 'Sentimental Power: *Uncle Tom's Cabin* and the Politics of Literary History' contributed to the renewed interest in Stowe's work subsequently appealed for an 'emotional criticism' which responds to literature emotionally rather than rationally. Tompkins's plea appears an 'intellectually' more honest reaction to Stowe's 'philosophy' than the rather paradoxical effort to turn Stowe into an Enlightenment figure. Tompkins, 'Sentimental Power: *Uncle Tom's Cabin* and the Politics of Literary History', in idem, *Sensational Designs: The Cultural Work of American Fiction, 1790–1860* (New York and Oxford, 1985), 122–46. Her plea for emotional criticism can be found in her *A Life in School: What the Teacher Learned* (Cambridge, MA, 1996).

24. Several *Uncle Tom's Cabin* scholars refer to the chapter's relevance for a good understanding of Stowe's perspective.

25. The nature of their worries varies. Whereas R.L. Moore and Isaac Kramnick, for instance, criticize religious conservatives in the Republican Party for their attack on the American constitution in their *The Godless Constitution: The Case against Religious Correctness* (New York and London, 1996), a scholar such as Emilio Gentile warns against the 'sacralization' of politics that occurs when political leaders and institutions are invested with religious symbols. In what he calls a 'political religion', this 'sacralization' takes on a rather dangerous nature; but even a 'civil religion', in which democratic institutions are in a way 'deified', harbours in his perspective dangerous propensities. See his *Politics as Religion*.

26. When, in the opening chapters of *Twenty Years at Hull House*, Progressive Era reformer Jane Addams depicts how Christianity and the tradition of domesticity at once stimulated her to adopt a public role and prevented her from engaging in one, she reiterates Stowe's point; Addams fell ill because of this incongruity and only managed to overcome her depression by becoming a social reformer and activist. See Jane Addams, *Twenty Years at Hull House* (New York, 1981 [1910]), particularly ch. 3, 'Boarding-School Ideals'.

27. Jeanne Boydston, Mary Kelley and Anne Margolis, *The Limits of Sisterhood: The Beecher Sisters on Women's Rights and Woman's Sphere* (Chapel Hill, 1988), is one of the books that discuss the sisters' convictions on women's suffrage; see the Introduction and, for Stowe especially, ch. 9, 'Harriet Beecher Stowe: "The Woman Controversy"', 259–65.

28. In the republican ideology George Washington is idolized as the 'true' politician because he was not interested in power and was willing to sacrifice his own interest whenever the public good demanded his presence and contribution in the public domain of politics (for instance when the revolutionary army needed a commander and the newly independent United States a president).

29. Stowe, *Uncle Tom's Cabin*, 376; Stowe's italics.

30. It is tempting to equate Harriet and her sister Catherine in this respect. In her article about the struggle against Indian removal in the 1830s,

Mary Hershberger shows how Catherine's involvement in the women's petition campaign against removal induced her to shy away from this type of political action; Mary Hershberger, 'Mobilizing Women, Anticipating Abolition: The Struggle against Indian Removal in the 1830s', *The Journal of American History* 86 (1999), 15–40.
31. Gregg Crane, *Race, Citizenship, and Law in American Literature* (Cambridge and New York, 2002).
32. The American constitution is often called the godless constitution because it does not mention God.
33. As Crane argues, 'the insistence of Stowe's images on various forms of resemblance as the prerequisite for moral consensus checks her democratic faith in consent'. Crane, *Race, Citizenship, and Law in American Literature*, 70.
34. Pierre Rosanvallon, *Democratic Legitimacy: Impartiality, Reflexivity, Proximity*, trans. Arthur Goldhammer (Princeton, 2011), 190; Rosanvallon's italics.
35. Peter Brooks, *Reading for the Plot: Design and Intention in Narrative* (Oxford, 1984), 216, 234–5.
36. Harriet Beecher Stowe, *A Key to Uncle Tom's Cabin; Presenting the Original Facts and Documents upon Which the Story is Founded, Together with Corroborative Statements Verifying the Truth of the Work* (Boston, Cleveland and London, 1853). The University of Virginia website that has an edition of the work states that 'Although it [the book] claims to be about the sources Stowe consulted while writing the novel [...] she read many of the works cited here only after the novel was published'. Available at http://utc.iath.virginia.edu/uncletom/key/kyhp.html
37. Harriet Beecher Stowe, *Dred; A Tale of the Great Dismal Swamp* (New York, 2009 [1856]).
38. Jonathan Edwards, *A Treatise concerning Religious Affections* (Philadelphia, 1821 [1746]).
39. See particularly her *The Human Condition*.
40. Hannah Arendt, *Love and St Augustine* (Chicago, 1996 [1929]).
41. Lauren Berlant (ed.), *Compassion: The Culture and Politics of an Emotion* (New York and London, 2004).

Part III
Socialism

Religious Aspects of Socialist Imagery, *c*.1890–2000: A Visual Essay

Jolijn Groothuizen and Dennis Bos

In the nineteenth century, the socialist movement developed in reaction to the exploitation and political oppression of the working class. Many different types of socialism emerged, from Christian socialism to revolutionary anarchism. In this visual essay, the emphasis does not lie on the isolated voices that advocated a reconciliation of socialism and religion, but on atheist socialists. They formed the mainstream of the socialist labour movement and remained for a long time hostile to all churches and their doctrines. In the opinion of these socialists, the church and religiously motivated politicians used Christianity to blind the workers, keeping them from freeing themselves from the bourgeoisie. The battle in which socialists and Christian politicians were engaged for the workers' sympathy in election times strengthened this antagonism between socialism and religion even more.

As a result of this rivalry with Christianity, socialists developed a mocking and sometimes even aggressive attitude towards organized religion and religious thought. This became evident in many illustrations by socialists. For the cover of the Sunday paper of the social democratic daily *Het Volk*, the Dutch artist Albert Hahn referred to the oppressing church in his drawing 'De brandkast, beschermd met bijbel en wierookvat' ('The Safe Protected by Bible and Censer', 1902, Fig. 3). The humble Dutch workers are unable to reach the safe of capitalism, as it is shielded by the politicians Herman Schaepman (Roman Catholic leader, left) and Abraham Kuyper (Protestant leader, right), and the threatening sight of devils in the background.

Under revolutionary circumstances, the animosity could lead to socialist violence against the church. Especially in the first two decades after the Russian Revolution of 1917, the confrontation with the church took a turn for the worst. In the Soviet Union, atheism became

Figure 3   Albert Hahn, 'De brandkast, beschermd met bijbel en wierookvat' (The Netherlands, 1902).

state doctrine and Orthodox priests and believers were subjected to harsh persecution. Also in Catholic regions, most notably in Spain, the antagonism between militant socialism and the church sometimes led to violent eruptions. In this famous picture (Fig. 4), taken in 1936 and often used in anti-socialist propaganda publications during the Spanish Civil War of 1936–39, Spanish revolutionaries take aim at a statue of Christ (see also Eric Storm's essay in this volume).

Due to these and numerous other incidents, the idea of an insurmountable opposition between socialism and religion has become dominant in historiography. This conceals the fact that, in their propaganda,

Figure 4   'Fusilaron a Cristo' (Spain, 1936).

socialists also used various elements of the Christian religion in a positive way. As in the case with the anticlerical elements, various images show the political use of religion by socialists. This essay intends to expose some of these remarkable cases in which Christianity was used positively by socialism.[1]

The Hell of Capitalism

In socialist vocabulary, hell and the underworld were not part of the great beyond, but an accurate description of contemporary life under capitalism. The exploitation of labour, the horrors of imperialist war and repression by fascist regimes were consecutively labelled as the infernal consequences of a malfunctioning societal order. Satan himself, bloodsucking vampires and the hounds of hell served to get this meaning across.

In the economically difficult 1930s, the Dutch socialist party SDAP and the trade union NVV tried to help the workers suffering under the crisis by means of a Central Plan Commission. In Plate 1 (see end of essay), a poster dating from 1936, the Central Plan Commission stressed the need for relief measures. As long as politicians refrained from fulfilling this duty, the workers, living in the burning hell of capitalism, found themselves under threat of the hellhound of fascism.

'Let there be light: and there was light' (Genesis 1:3)

Notwithstanding a firm atheist stand and ongoing conflicts with religious institutions, socialists often expressed and presented themselves in forms that referred directly to the Jewish and Christian cultural heritage. A central theme was the sunrise as a visual symbol of the dawning of a new socialist world. According to the social democrats, this world could emerge through universal suffrage. The announcement of a new suffrage law inspired the Dutch artist L.J. Jordaan in 1913 to draw a rising sun with the inscription 'Algemeen kiesrecht' (universal suffrage, Fig. 5). Another possible step closer towards the socialist society was the abolition of privileges. In this 1903 drawing by the famous socialist artist Walter Crane, an angel, wearing a Phrygian cap, leads the workers over the high wall of privilege towards the light (Fig. 6).

The Holy Father

In 1971, the Revolutionary Committee of the Shanghai Drama College published Plate 2 (see end of essay) to celebrate the centennial of the Paris Commune. The advancing revolutionary masses seem to be guided by the holy ghost of Karl Marx, hovering in the skies above them. In the reality of 1871 however, Marx had ignored several invitations to join the communards in Paris, preferring to stay in London and write his famous epitaph for the Commune: *The Civil War in France* (1871).

Patriarchs and Apostles

The new gospel of socialism was initially spread amongst an often unsympathetic audience. The first generations of spokesmen and propagandists therefore had to cope with indifference, ridicule and sometimes violent hostility. Their perseverance and loyalty to the cause earned them the gratitude and respect of their followers, who often honoured them as true apostles. Ferdinand Domela Nieuwenhuis (1846–1919), a Lutheran minister who stepped down from the pulpit and left the

Figure 5 L.J. Jordaan, 'De kiesrechtparagraaf in de troonrede: De zon breekt eindelijk door!' (The Netherlands, 1913).

church in 1877, would become the founding father of socialism in the Netherlands. The draughtsman Willem Papenhuyzen depicted him as 'A rock in the breaking waves of life, reflecting the light of the coming day' (Fig. 7).

Opponents would often ridicule the adoration among socialists for their political leaders, as in this caricature by Wilhelm Schultz (Fig. 8). It shows the (Jewish) German social democrat Paul Singer, who descends from the mountain with the stone tablets containing the Ten Commandments of party leader August Bebel.

Figure 6   Walther Crane, 'Towards the Light' (Great Britain 1903).

Martyrs for the Cause

The worship of slain martyrs formed an important cornerstone of the political culture that developed among revolutionary socialists, communists and anarchists. This cover illustration of a brochure from the German section of the communist International Red Aid (Fig. 9) is taken from an earlier album by the famous Belgian artist Frans Masereel, *The Passion of a Man* (1918). In 25 woodcuts Masereel told the story of a proletarian, born out of wedlock and into poverty, who becomes conscious of his position in class society, rises up against the system and is in the end shot for doing so.

Figure 7 Willem Papenhuyzen, 'Als een rots in de branding van het leven, weerkaatsend het licht van den komende dag' (The Netherlands, undated).

On 11 November 1887, four anarchists, who had been accused of throwing a bomb into a group of police officers, were hanged in Chicago. From that moment on, these men were honoured as the 'Martyrs of Chicago' by socialists all over the world. To honour their fallen comrades, American anarchists sported brass lapel pins such as these (Fig. 10), turning the gallows into a modern variation on the crucifix.

Processions

During the Great Depression, strikers in the Belgium mining district of the Borinage were filmed while parading with a portrait of Karl Marx.

Figure 8 Wilhelm Schulz, 'Die zehn Gebote Bebels' (Germany, 1875–99).

As this still from the documentary *Misère au Borinage* (1933) by Joris
Ivens illustrates (Fig. 11), the parade resembled a Catholic procession.
Comparable parades took place during the Great Proletarian Cultural
Revolution (1966–76) in China. Plate 3 (see end of essay) shows a
propaganda poster displaying Red Guards marching with a portrait of
a young Mao.

'Even though I walk through the valley of the shadow of death...' (Psalm 23:4)

In many respects, the political culture of socialism was a veritable cult
of the dead. Like in Christianity, the dead were mourned and their

Figure 9 Book cover, *Als Opfer sind sie gefallen. Gedenkt der Pariser Kommune!* (Berlin, 1926).

memory was kept alive until the time of redemption. Walther Crane's *Cartoons for the Cause* (1886–96) contains this visualization of a socialist angel of death, grieving for the fallen heroes of class struggle (Fig. 12). After the failed Spartacist Rising of 1919 in Berlin, this picture postcard (Fig. 13) drew a direct analogy between the fate of the leaders of the Rising and that of Christ. Berlin was the Golgotha of 1919, where Karl Liebknecht was crucified and Rosa Luxemburg was tortured to death at his feet.

Inspired by the socialist heroes' graves at Père Lachaise in Paris, at Waldheim Cemetery near Chicago and in Moscow's Red Square,

Figure 10   Brass gallows-shaped lapel pin (United States, 1887).

German communists of the Weimar period erected their own monument to the fallen at the Friedrichsfelde graveyard in Berlin (Fig. 14). Designed by the modernist architect Ludwig Mies van der Rohe, the monument dedicated to Luxemburg, Liebknecht and their fellow Spartacists was up to 1933 regularly used as a site for communist mourning rituals.

A New Jerusalem

Dreams of the 'new Jerusalem' that socialism would bring about varied widely. The modernist interpretation of the Russian artist Vladimir Tatlin, expressed here in his design for a monument dedicated to the Third International (1919), seems a conscious answer to the Bible story of the Tower of Babylon (Fig. 15).

Figure 11   Ivens and Storck, 'A still from the film *Misère au Borinage'* (Belgium, 1933).

More often, however, future socialist society was imagined as the return to a pastoral Arcadia, a world of enduring peace in which justice reigned, all people lived in plenty and 'the lamb will lie down with the lion'. In the period before the First World War, festivities on the first of May offered the occasion for idyllic scenes such as the cover for the German social democratic illustrated weekly *Der Wahre Jacob* in 1893 (Plate. 4; see end of essay). It shows that, despite their aversion to the Christian heritage, socialists accepted the Christian paradise as a mirror image of their own anticipated, classless society.

Religion and religious thought were both mocked and used positively by early socialism. This Janus-faced attitude of socialism towards Christianity is best to be explained within the context of the societal and cultural context in which the early socialists operated. At the end of the nineteenth century, the framework of reference of most Europeans was Christian. Workers knew the Bible well and were brought up with Christian rituals and symbols. This meant that referring to biblical stories and Christian symbols in socialist propaganda could facilitate the acceptance of the socialist message. Therefore, early socialism borrowed religious elements and symbols and used them for their own glorification. Socialist imagery thus offers some of the most striking

Figure 12   Walter Crane, 'In Memory of the Paris Commune' (Great Britain, 1891).

examples of the sacralization of politics. However, as society became more secularized in the second half of the twentieth century, socialists rarely applied Christian references any longer – their frame of reference had disappeared. Just as easily as they had once used religious images, they now applied other imagery in order to reach the workers. The sacralization of politics had therefore not become an end in itself.

Figure 13 Anonymous, 'Golgotha 1919. The murder on Rosa Luxemburg and Karl Liebknecht' (Germany, 1919).

Notes

1. Stefan R. Landsberger and Marien van der Heijden, *Chinese Posters* (Munich, 2009); Vernon L. Lidtke, *The Alternative Culture: Socialist Labor in Imperial Germany* (New York and Oxford, 1985); Hendrik de Man, *Zur Psychologie des Sozialismus* (Jena, 1926); Klaus-Dieter Pohl, *Allegorie und Arbeiter. Bildagitatorische Didaktik und Repräsentation der SPD 1890–1914. Studien zum politischen Umgang mit bildender Kunst in der politisch-satirischen Zeitschrift, 'Der Wahre Jacob' und 'Süddeutscher Postillon' sowie in den Maifestzeitungen* (Osnabrück, 1986).

Figure 14   'Berlin-Friedrichsfelde, Einweihung Gedenkstätte' (Germany, 1926).

Figure 15   Vladimir Tatlin, Monument to the Third International (Soviet Union, 1920).

A Grassroots Sacred Socialist History: Dutch Social Democrats (1894–1920)

Adriaan van Veldhuizen

Socialist philosophers such as Joseph Dietzgen have claimed that socialism and religion are very much alike. In both cases, leaders are treated as prophets, the exegesis of texts is a serious but delicate business, and both the socialist and the Christian ethic reflect on every single part of everyday life. To authors like Dietzgen politics and religion thus appear to be two of a kind. In his *Politics as Religion* historian Emilio Gentile takes this similarity between religion and political organization even further with his claim that since 'the political realm has gained its independence from traditional religion, politics itself has been sacralized'.[1] According to Gentile politics became religion.

Although Gentile claims that 'democracies, autocracies, equality, inequality, nations and humanity' can be sacralized, most of his examples put the state at the centre of the sacralization process.[2] And although he mentions social democracy, his emphasis is on totalitarianism. He is not alone in this; many authors discussing political religion have shared this focus since the 1930s, as discussed in the introduction to this volume. The connection between totalitarianism and the sacralization of politics created a connection between the sacralization of politics and the state.

By using a practical example, this chapter will try to show that the sacralization of politics is not necessarily restricted to the state but can also be found in a democratic political movement and could be initiated by its ordinary members. To make this practical example as concrete as possible, this chapter will focus on only one political organization and on only one particular kind of sacralization. The organization under study is the late nineteenth-century Dutch social democratic party (SDAP). The kind of sacralization that will be discussed is what Gentile has called the emergence of a 'sacred' or 'mythical' history.[3]

115

This 'sacralization of a political past' includes the creation of myths and martyrs involving political predecessors.

In order to discuss this particular kind of sacralization effectively, the two following questions will be asked. First: How did the members of the SDAP sacralize their own history? Second: What circumstances and developments made the party members do this, and who was responsible for it? Was it an initiative from above or did it come from below? But prior to answering these questions, I will provide a short introduction on the origins of the party and the motives of members for joining it in order to show what function the party fulfilled in the lives of its members.

What Did the Party Mean to Its Members?

The founding of the Social Democrat Workers' Party (SDAP) in 1894 was the result of a growing disagreement within the Social Democrat League (SDB). The most important leader of the League, Ferdinand Domela Nieuwenhuis, made a clear distinction between what he called 'economic', 'free' or 'anarchist' socialism, on the one hand, and 'political' or 'parliamentary' socialism, on the other. He initially tried to be a parliamentary socialist. He even became a member of parliament, but when he decided that parliament was nothing but a portmanteau of the French words *parler* (talking) and *mentir* (lying), he quit politics and concentrated solely on anarchist socialism.[4] As a result of this decision the SDB had become a revolutionary though badly organized coalition of many small socialist clubs, associations and societies.

A minority inside the SDB felt uncomfortable with this anarchistic lack of direction and decided to found a new organization. The group was small and internally divided, and their plans were vague and their resources minimal; yet they succeeded in their intentions. On 26 August 1894 the SDAP, the first parliamentary social democratic party in the Netherlands, was founded.

During its first meeting the new party appeared to be quite ambitious and professional, at least compared to the SDB. Nevertheless it was not immediately obvious why anyone would join it. Membership of any socialist party could mean social suicide in many ways. Being a member required time and money, both scarce goods for most workers around 1894. Being a socialist could put family relations and friendships under pressure. And for workers, being a socialist could be the end of one's career. On top of this, the word 'party' was conceptually rather new in the Netherlands and lacked successful extant examples. Success was far from guaranteed, not least because the leaders of the club had not yet proven themselves as politicians.

In addition there was a lot of mutual distrust between the members of the new party. The social differences inside the new party were significant – rich and poor, intellectuals and workers, urban socialists and rural socialists. And finally, most journalists and politicians from outside the party were rather sceptical about the project of the social democrats. Becoming a member was a leap of faith. The seemingly miraculous attraction of the party thus requires explanation. We need to understand what the party meant to its members before we can understand why those members sacralized the history of their organization. In order to discuss the advantages of party membership in an effective way, two developments will be distinguished that made people willing to join the SDAP. One is connected to the past, the other to the future.

The Past: Associations and Traditions

Although the concept of 'party' was new, its structure was not as innovative as it seemed. Many of the first SDAP members had been members of the SDB as well.[5] Most of the other party members were (former) members of other organizations. Some of the branches were former electoral associations, and others had been small local workers' unions, social clubs or even choirs.[6] In most cases the decision to become a branch of the new party was made in consultation with the members of the existing club, but sometimes the organizational metamorphosis took place without the consent of its members.[7]

In every case the party adopted the existing local structures, sometimes over three generations old, which were built up around friendship, kinship and working relations. Many of the local branches had thus been close communities long before the SDAP came into existence. To many members only the name of the organization was new and not the fact that it existed in the first place. Most members of these clubs also lived very close to each other, worked at the same factory or were even family members.[8] This meant that the branches of the SDAP consisted of people who shared political sympathies along with many other characteristics as well. In some cases married couples led a branch, in other cases the branch was led by a father and his son or by a father and his son-in-law.[9]

Despite the novelty of the concept, there was therefore a lot of hidden continuity at the local level. So it might not be surprising that the differences between the various (internally homogeneous) local groups were vast. In the small town of Holwerd almost all members were unskilled farm workers, though in the city of Tilburg most members were railway employees, while in Amsterdam many members were diamond workers.[10] The political style and activities engaged in were just as diverse as the social construction of the branches. Some local branches were very ambitious in the organization of public political meetings, while others focused on providing social engagements for their members. Some branches held their meetings secretly in the small living room of one of their members, while others gathered openly in busy cafés.

So while the name of the party was new, in many small villages and bigger towns its informal structure had already existed in some way or another for a long time. On a local level this was of great importance for the success of the party. In a paradoxical way 'becoming a member of the new party' was thus a tradition within families and social groups even before the party existed. This situation had disadvantages too. Many of the members initially connected to the party primarily on a local level, so to most ordinary members the national bureau of the party was a distant and unknown organization.[11] Since this national bureau had the ambition to be a 'national political machine', it could not afford to remain a motley collection of individuals, gathered in local branches scattered across the country. That the party did not disintegrate had to do with a second advantage that it offered.

The Future: Organization and Ideology

Apart from the opportunity to engage socially with members of an already existing local community, a second element made party membership attractive. On a national level the party offered something the local associations never could. It provided the promise of a better future. The promise was uttered in the same socialist terms as the SDB had done before, but the SDAP claimed to have a new and more successful organization to actually accomplish its goals. This determination was underlined by choosing the concept of 'party' as the new organizational form. During the foundation meeting of the SDAP a fierce debate raged. Some people wanted to form a 'league' or 'association', while others did not want to discuss the name of the new club at all and just wanted to found 'an organization'. Only one ambition was widely shared: the new organization had to be more effective than the SDB had been. It had to be a serious and reliable political organization.[12]

Two of the leading men, Pieter Jelles Troelstra and Jan Fortuyn, came up with the idea to found a 'party'. Although this concept had already appeared in Germany and elsewhere, and in the name of the Christian

Dutch Anti-Revolutionaire Partij, it was a rather ambiguous term at that time.[13] It was mostly used to denote a 'societal group' and was not yet necessarily connected to an organization with a board, statutes and central headquarters like modern parties.[14] Troelstra and Fortuyn nevertheless felt that this concept could be used effectively to distinguish the social democrats from the anarchists; a new kind of organization needed a brand new name.[15]

The founding of the SDAP was accompanied by other developments. In addition to the idea that the party had to be a political organization in parliament, the board of the SDAP tried to strengthen its grip on society in many other ways. In the first years of the party, prominent party members helped publish a newspaper, founded a committee that advocated universal suffrage and became involved in labour unions and several other networks.[16] A relatively large number of party members held different positions inside this larger social democratic environment.

Although not every initiative was immediately successful, there emerged a nationwide network of social democrats that shared experiences and ideas. Not every member of this network was necessarily an active party member. Many people were affiliated with other organizations. Some focused on a local branch, others on a working union or an electoral committee, but they all were members of the same social democratic family. To them the party functioned as an organizational umbrella that connected them to people and groups they otherwise would not have met. At conferences and in newspapers every small step in the right direction – such as a successful local election result or any other increase of socialist influence – was shared with like-minded people. Thus in addition to these social democratic 'best practices', the party network also spread feelings of success and progress.

Despite this organizational fanaticism, the social democratic SDAP members still considered themselves to be revolutionary socialists. In fact, the anarchist SDB and the social democratic SDAP did not differ much in their goals for the future; they only had a different route to that future in mind. The social democratic party was just as attractive for its transcendental properties as the SDB had been. Social democracy gave meaning to peoples' lives in a way that transcended the political. The teleological reasoning of Marxist ideology provided the prospect of a bright future for the workers. The German philosopher Joseph Dietzgen even called the proletariat 'a modern redeemer' since the proletarian revolution would not only better the circumstances of the proletariat but would improve everyone's life.[17] Although this was not a widely shared view among Dutch social democrats, the 'scientific prognosis based on historical evidence' of socialism in general was received very well.

But we should not focus too much on Marxism only. Among ordinary members the conviction that a group of good people could change society was in fact much more important than ideological hair-splitting. This belief in the idea that people could change society was not a product of Marxism; it was rather a prerequisite for Marxism. It was this indestructible faith in justice and the power of people, together with the 'social democratic family feeling' that – in Herman Paul's Wittgensteinian way – resembled religion.

Marxism, however, canalized this faith very well, and some members became ideological zealots. In particular the intellectuals and the *Verspreide leden* (individual members without a local branch) in the SDAP were attracted by the prospect sketched in ideological texts. More often than members affiliated with the local branches, the individual members made their decision to become a party member on ideological grounds.[18] They had become interested in the idea that the SDAP wanted to be a 'serious' social democratic party that continued the well-known socialist struggle by following a parliamentary route.

Of course the local branches embraced the promise of a better future as well. They were not only proud to be a cog in the wheel of an international socialist organization, some branch members also became fierce defenders of its ideology. Although there were differences in understanding what social democracy was or should be, many farmers, workers and schoolteachers wholeheartedly spread the promise of their ideology.

Although it is impossible to ascribe the success of the party to only two factors, it is at least possible to distinguish two trends. First, the party was a new answer to a long-established need for sociability. Many of the ordinary members were already part of structures that became branches of the party. These families, neighbours, colleagues or friends offered stable social contacts. Later on the party also offered new friends, evenings with drinks, traditions and a safe community. Second, the party provided an effective organizational form and gave a new ideological impetus to a need for 'something bigger'. The well-oiled socialist machine was capable of connecting like-minded people on a national level.

These many forms of sociability, organizational advantages, political presence and the ideological promises that the party provided gave many members strong feelings of gratitude and indebtedness towards the party. The whole of the party was far greater than the sum of its parts. Being a member of the party was much more than being part of an organization specialized in political decision-making. Being an SDAP member became a way of life.

Party members often dressed in a recognizable way, had their own way of speaking and shared their own symbols and mannerisms.[19] Even when the party grew larger than a motley collection of local branches, the members kept calling each other brother and sister and gave each other family nicknames like 'aunt', 'uncle' or 'father'.[20] Just like the neighbourhood and the workshop, the party became a place where members met their (new) friends and lovers. These valuable enrichments of life were considered the product of party membership.

This gratitude had great effects on party members' feelings towards the SDAP. In fact it was a crucial factor in the emergence of a sacralized history. Feelings of respect, humility and gratitude were not only uttered at conferences and political meetings, they also can be found in the way party members dealt with their party's past. Since the party meant so much to its members, the genesis of the SDAP was often presented as a story about heroes and martyrs who had to be honoured for their contribution to the present.

To the party members history was not an academic debate but a living collection of personal stories that were repeated over and over again. The most striking consequence of this view of the sacralization of history is the understanding that this sacralization was not a top-down tool, intentionally initiated by a socialist vanguard or state. The members themselves praised their past and predecessors because history was an important part of the party. The meaning of party was bigger than the sum of its parts, so the party's past and its protagonists were cherished.

'Our History' or How We Became Ourselves

The previous section showed *why* party members were inclined to sacralize their party's past, and this section will show *how* they did this. Because the process of sacralization was not only the product of a top-down strategy, it happened in leaps and bounds and had many different manifestations. To describe these different manifestations in a systematic way this section will be divided into four subsections.

First, a brief description will be provided of the rather abstract socialist notion of history: the socialist ideology. This will explain the theoretical context in which the social democrats were operating and emphasize the importance of socialist 'historical thinking' in general. Second, attention will be paid to festschrifts, memoirs and propaganda written and published by party members. Third, the physical celebrations of the party's own history will be discussed. And fourth, contemporary 'professional' historical writing about the party by its members will be reviewed.

Ideology

For social democrats history was much more than the past. It was presented as an ongoing process in which the present and the future are necessarily linked and determined by historical developments. The past, seen by ordinary party members mostly as a collection of worker tragedies, is an overture to the present and, more importantly, to a better future. The past held much suffering, and although it was terrible, it had not been in vain. The impoverishment of the workers had led to revolutions and would lead to a new revolution that would improve their situation. The religious element here is quite obvious: the fallen friends of the past are the co-producers of the future and so they have to be honoured.

This ideological narrative was an important condition for the more concrete celebrations of history that will be discussed in the following paragraphs. So it is important to note that even grassroots members of the Dutch party were aware of the self-imposed historical task of socialism. Their detailed knowledge of Marxism might have been relatively poor, but they were familiar with most of the important themes of the ideology.[21] Though their ideas about socialism may not have been correct according to the books, they had a sense of socialism.

Most members were confronted with ideological debates every now and then. Articles on theoretical topics were published in the newspapers *Het Volk* and *De Nieuwe Tijd*. Although the latter addressed the more intellectual members of the party, it was easily accessible for others too. It could be found on reading tables in socialist buildings and was swapped after socialist meetings. Ideological discussions that were printed in newspapers were comparable to the theoretical discussions during the annual congress and other meetings. And when the SDAP branches organized so-called 'course meetings', local members had the opportunity to listen to prominent guest speakers. These orators held theoretical lectures on 'The necessity of the coming of the revolution' or 'Marx's theory on the value of labour'. And of course, after a theoretical lecture all members attending the meeting were invited to discuss these topics.

While most party members did not read difficult texts on 'dialectical processes' and other vague 'scientific' notions, they had heard about 'the proletariat' and 'the bourgeoisie' and were familiar with the concept of 'historical materialism'. Even though most members gradually grew ambivalent about the proletarian revolution, the 'scientific' importance of the historical roots of social democracy was widely cherished. Although most ideological writings were not translated into the Dutch language, and only a small minority were well informed on Marxism, the majority of the members definitely had a notion of the basic principles of 'their' ideology.

For social democrats this notion was enough to make them realize how important the historical process was. Even the most superficial knowledge of Marxist ideology taught them they were part of a bigger plan in history in which they were directly connected to their predecessors and descendants. History was more than the past; it was a force to be taken into account. This ideological awareness of historicity was a prerequisite for the way the social democrats sacralized their own history.

Festschrifts, Propaganda and Memoirs

The most obvious political celebration of history can be found in festschrifts and memoirs. Nevertheless the first historical narratives appeared as small propaganda booklets. Prominent party members wrote these brochures as an introduction to social democracy for both party members and non-socialists. Titles such as *The Socialists in Parliament* and *Social Democracy and What Is Told about It* were sold in socialist bookstores alongside the *Communist Manifesto* and the party's political programme.[22] A more obvious link to religiosity can be found in W.P.G. Helsdingen's 'peoples' catechism'.[23] This type of publication tried to bridge the gap between ideological hair-splitting, on the one hand, and the practical implementation of parliamentary social democracy, on the other.

These booklets presented the success stories of social democrats who were already members of parliament and at the same time stressed the urgent need for more social democratic MPs. But anyone who reads between the lines will also see signs of a 'social democratic philosophy of history'. In *The Origin, Purpose and Commitment of the SDAP*, for instance, party leader P.J. Troelstra explained how 'social democracy strides from a dark past, towards a bright future'.[24] This 'historical plot' – the product of ideology, on the one hand, and propaganda, on the other – was repeated over and over again.[25]

In another type of publication, history came to the fore in a different, more obvious way. In a *Workers' Yearbook*, published in 1899, every historical moment of import to socialists was recounted. It listed not only the exact dates of the French Revolution and the Paris Commune but also the birthdays of prominent party members.[26] By distributing the yearbook attention was drawn to so-called 'party holidays'. The yearbooks supported ordinary members' awareness of the party's history. The books helped to create a shared past and encouraged both local branches and individual members to celebrate the same festive occasions. By doing so they integrated social democratic history into everyday life. To collectively sacralize the past these kinds of 'historical fact books' were an absolute necessity and, one could argue, synchronized the socialist watches.

The most startling sacralization of history was initiated in 1904. In this year the propaganda booklets were supplemented with a whole new genre: festschrifts. Ten years after its foundation the SDAP published its first festschrift, titled *After Ten Years*.[27] It was a bigger publication than the brochures, and the variety of stories it contained was broader as well. The volume was a celebration of a ten-year-old 'we' with a mission. Party leaders filled most pages with stories they considered important. The festschrift became a canonical text with an endless echo in the history of Dutch social democracy. The festschrift established a solidified corpus of anecdotes and determined who were the party heroes and who were not.[28] The sacralization of the founders of the party was quite obvious since they were called 'the Twelve Apostles'. Through the inclusion of many events – such as fights with the SDB, important meetings and the first election campaigns – many ordinary members were also invited to become part of the sacred social democratic history.

In the years after 1904 more festschrifts appeared. Members of several local branches wrote books that celebrated the foundation of the party in general or their own branch in particular. Not every branch had access to a printing office, so sometimes improvisation was called for. In the small Frisian town of Warga a beautifully decorated minute book was filled with stories of the early days.[29] The book was never published, but members could take a look inside it every now and then. And of course the younger members in particular were invited to do this so as to 'not forget the past'. A few years later the Amsterdam branch acquired the means to print its own festschrift. It became a book very similar to the earlier festschrift of the national party.[30] Smaller branches published less impressive works of remembrance, sometimes only containing a few pages.

Not only branches but also organizations affiliated with the party commemorated their own history, by publishing books, brochures and articles in the same style.[31] In addition to these more or less 'official' publications there is also a relatively large collection of personal memoirs. Many members wrote books, letters, brochures or articles about their first experiences as a social democrat. Because most of these memoirs date from the time that the party was already a stable player in Dutch politics, the stories often had a rather predictable plot.

In books by party leaders like P.J. Troelstra and J. Schaper, for instance, historical facts were presented without violating them, but it is still hard to read them as history books. Most such publications started with the hardships of the pre-political past and concluded with the good times the party had brought. The authors hardly paid any attention to everyday party life or the broader political context. Their books were often composed as a concatenation of personal successes while less spectacular moments and figures were neglected. For instance, party member J.G. van Kuijkhof was only rarely mentioned in any biography. This party secretary is impossible to underestimate, for van Kuijkhof was absolutely indispensable for the work he did; yet in memoirs by his fellow party members he was constantly overlooked.[32] They all focused on the same persons and the same events: 'apostles', fights, big strikes and political victories.

Not only leading party members published their memoirs. Several lesser-known social democrats wrote autobiographies as well. Not all of these publications were printed as books, many only appeared as serial stories in newspapers. Both Hein Mol from Rotterdam and Klaas Geertsma from Arnhem published their memoirs in this way.[33] Another fascinating insight into party life can be found in the memoirs of early member W.H. Meijer, who had numerous small jobs and functions in the party organization and whose inside perspective sheds light on the habits and manners of everyday party life. At the same time his book had a disciplining undertone for younger readers; it said, This is who we are and what we do.[34]

The motley collection of festschrifts, propaganda booklets and memoirs constituted and defined the party's political history. These books made clear who were the heroes and who the villains, what moments had to be celebrated and which to be forgotten. And most importantly, they introduced new members to the historical canon of the party. In this way they had a disciplining effect as well; newcomers were immediately informed about who and what was important and who and what was not.

Despite the disciplining effect, these books were not political tools to suppress the party members or to keep them ignorant. No one was obliged to buy or read them. Nevertheless many of these books – especially the cheaper booklets – were sold. But also the festschrifts must have been published in very large editions.[35] It did not take long before the most important stories of the past became canonical and were repeated over and over again. Probably the best example of this kind of story was the 'Constantia Scuffle' between the members of the two-month-old SDAP and the SDB. In almost every festschrift and memoir this fight is mentioned. Along with less important birthdays, wedding days and funerals, this event became mythical. 'Constantia' – which was the name of the building in which the fight took place – became a metaphor for much more than a single fight, and its history was more than a story from the past. No one considered debunking this story; it had become a mythical event that defined the party's identity.

The Physical Celebration of History

Social democratic history was sacralized not only in books. Party members also re-enacted the party's past in various types of public performances. The Amsterdam branch of the SDAP even had its own 'tableaux group' that re-enacted the stages of the Marxist ideology during party congresses and at several other meetings.[36] This was workers' history par excellence: it was the history of the workers, performed by workers, for workers. The performers thereby made socialist ideology accessible for the relatively large group of nearly illiterate party members.

The *tableaux vivants* invariably had a close link to the well-known ideology of socialism. 'This will be beautiful and propagandistic at the same time', a party member wrote to the party secretary.[37] When 'The Child and the New Era' was portrayed, 'the revolution' and 'the socialist future' would be shown as the closing scenes. This transition from crying to laughter – which of course followed the same plot that was used in ideology and the previously mentioned booklets – made many different appearances in various tableaux. It was not always a historically accurate past that was shown here; the tableaux depicted an artistic interpretation of the social democratic past.

Workers' theatrical groups also brought historical plays to the stage. Performing in these groups was very popular within the SDAP. Many of the branches had their own amateur theatre group. They often put on pieces on the history of social democracy. While the tableaux groups represented the bigger ideological picture, the theatre groups focused on smaller issues. Since many party members wrote their own plays, a relatively high number of the stories were set in the direct environment of the party members.

On the day the decorated minute book was offered to the members in Warga, a neighbouring branch performed a play on the history of their particular branch.[38] And in the small city of Zwolle a piece on the 'Chicago Martyrs' was brought to the stage. Four party members painted their faces grey and pretended to be hanged on stage, from wooden gallows. Now the other party members saw what had happened to socialists in the past.[39] In addition to these rather amateurish plays the party also produced some famous playwrights, like Herman Heijermans, who wrote many plays on the socialist movement.

The same topics were dealt with in socialist songs. Just as in the tableaux and plays, the sacred socialist history was highlighted in musical performances. Hymns like 'De Nieuwe Tijd' ('The New Era') not only celebrated a new historical era, they also emphasized how many friends had lost their lives on their way to the new era.[40] The songs might have been even more impressive than the plays and tableaux as they were sung not only by choirs but also by ordinary party members, particularly during meetings and rallies. For special occasions talented party members also composed theme songs.[41]

Although the remains of the songs and plays are far less tangible than the books described in the previous paragraphs, the artistic mythologizing of the past was probably the most impressive form of the sacralization of party history. This was the case not only because community singing was easily accessible for every member, but also because singing added an extra dimension to the experience of being a party member. If there was a specific moment where the members could actually feel the presence of the heroes of the past, it was during this kind of performance. It was not without reason that these songs were often referred to as 'political psalms'.

Professional Historiography by Party Members

'Professional historiography by party members' might sound like a *contradictio in terminis*, not only because professional history writing at the beginning of the twentieth century was not as advanced as it is nowadays, but also because it would have been difficult for an active member of the SDAP to write a history of his own party that meets modern academic standards. Nevertheless there was a small group of authors who wrote with the intention of objectivity and not from a propagandistic point of view.

Without a doubt the most important author in this genre was Willem Hubert Vliegen (1862–1947). Vliegen was not a trained historian but a typographer from the southern Dutch city of Maastricht. He was a leading member of both the SDB and the SDAP and attended a great number of important meetings and discussions. In the preface to one of his books he stated that he 'would consider it his task to tell about 16 years of sometimes intense and heavy class struggle and its unforgettable moments, as a worker who talks to his younger class members'.[42] Vliegen started to write his first historical work in 1902. Although this book was not meant as a work of propaganda, its appearance was probably motivated by a political development. Around the year 1902 a new generation of members claimed positions in the party. Because of their age most of them had not consciously experienced the party's early years. The break with the SDB was not something that was very important to them. The leaders of the party, on the other hand, derived their status from their role in the split from the SDB.

So the works of Vliegen legitimized the role of the party's leading figures and showed that their leadership was not a coincidence. But at the same time he tried hard not to present too much of an insider's perspective. He tried to be an objective historian. Even people who had become party members only recently were still invited to become part of the story. And that was exactly what happened. Vliegen's *Dageraad der Volksbevrijding* and *Die onze kracht ontwaken deed* became canonical texts for the social democratic movement. They taught workers 'their history' through the stories of their predecessors. The stories Vliegen told were the same as those recounted in the festschrifts, memoirs and propaganda booklets, but they were supplemented with a lot of information on the political process. Because of the broad coverage of Vliegen's books, new members could experience party life from the start all over again.

Apart from making new members feel at home, Vliegen did something else. For years these books were the most important source for research on the SDAP, and even many academic historians who studied the party relied heavily on Vliegen's work. Party members who published their own memoirs often stole and borrowed from Vliegen. Helmig van der Vegt from Zwolle copied many of Vliegen's anecdotes in his memoirs.[43] He did not do that because he thought that no one would find out that it was not his own story. In fact, the stories Vliegen collected became 'collective stories of the party' that were repeated over and over again.[44]

Former Catholic Vliegen, with his extremely detailed and well-informed descriptions, was the Hieronymus of the sacred history of social democracy. With his books he decided what parts, people and processes were important in the party's history. Vliegen's descriptions obviously transcended the political domain. He discussed the personal motivations behind the turn to socialism – often described as 'political conversions' – of the party's leading figures and introduced his readers to the genesis of the social democratic way of life.[45]

Conclusion: A Grassroots History

Social democratic history was a mix of Marx, myths, martyrs and masses that offered 'something to believe in'. For ideological reasons history was important to the party. But the sacralization of history was more than only the celebration of Marxist theory. History functioned as a tie to the party, not only as a top-down strategy in which the party leaders created a shared mythical past, but also in other ways. The sacred history of the SDAP was fabricated in freedom, voluntarily and collectively.

Many party members wrote about their 'conversion' to socialism, read about the 'apostles' and sang the 'socialist psalms' because they liked it; they felt at home in their party. That these party members wrote their own history in religious terms was not without reason. Just as party membership was more than politics only, the party's history was more than a description of the political past. It was the story of a group with a historical task with which these members identified.

This is not a chapter on theoreticians writing on 'politics as religion', nor is it about the party's strategists trying to use religious forms to bind the people to their party. This chapter has dealt with ordinary party members in grassroots politics. Ordinary members took a very active role in this process of sacralization. The histories were written, bought and read voluntarily by members in small local branches. The sacralization of the party's history was democratized, a grassroots sacralization.

Finally, this voluntary choice of a democratic movement that shared some characteristics with totalitarian movements tells us at least two things about political religion in general. First, political religion should not be analysed only from a top-down perspective. Even in totalitarian systems the possibility of voluntary elements should be taken into account. Second, one should look for the religious aspects of political movements not only in big events, theatrical ideologies and mass meetings. Small gestures, manners and forms of address can be indications of the sacralization of politics too.

Notes

1. Gentile, *Politics as Religion*, 3.
2. Ibid., 139.
3. Ibid., 128, 132.
4. F. Domela Nieuwenhuis, *De geschiedenis van het socialisme* (Amsterdam, 1901). Although this book was meant as a historical publication, it is nowadays more valuable as a reflection of Domela's ideas on what socialism is and what it should be.
5. In the Frisian villages of Warga and Wirdum a complete SDB branch was converted into an SDAP branch (J. Frieswijk, *Socialisme in Friesland, 1880–1900* [Amsterdam, 1977], 225). In other places, such as the city of Arnhem, only a group of SDB members formed a new SDAP branch (K. Geertsma, 'De eerste opbouw', *Het Volksblad voor Gelderland* [May–October 1935]).
6. In Dokkum an electoral association became a branch of the party (IISG Amsterdam, Archief SDAP 984, correspondentie eerste afdeling Dokkum). In the small town of Garsthuizen, the local branch was founded by two friends who had previously organized a number of small workers' associations (IISG, Archief SDAP 1043, Letter from G. Th. Beishuizen directed to the party bureau, 9 December 1901).
7. In 1900 a complete singing choir was turned into a local branch of the SDAP (IISG Amsterdam, Archief SDAP 1937, Letter from S. de Boer-van Dijk directed to the party bureau, 21 August 1900).
8. In the branch in the city of Breda at least three pairs of brothers can be found (IISG Amsterdam, Archief SDAP 941a, Letter from Van Oordt directed to the party bureau, 1 July 1905). This situation was far from unique. In most of the administrations of the local branches at least a few brothers can be found. The same goes for the top tier of the party. Party leader Troelstra had both a socialist brother and a socialist sister. The brothers Helsdingen both played important roles in the first years of the party. The siblings Agnes and Jan Bruins both became prominent party members as well. The same happened in the Vos family, which produced a social democratic minister and two social democratic poets.
9. For example, Mr and Mrs Koekebakker in Aardenburg (IISG Amsterdam, Archief SDAP 825, Letter from P. Wage directed to the party bureau, 3 December 1907), or Wilhelm Magnee and his son-in-law August Poppe in Bergen op Zoom (IISG Amsterdam, Archief SDAP 915, Correspondentie afdeling Bergen op Zoom, 1894–95).
10. Holwerd: IISG Amsterdam, Archief SDAP 1155, Ledenlijsten afdeling Holwerd (1896–1921), Streekarchivaat Noordoost Friesland te Dokkum, Boeken burgerlijke stand gemeente Holwerd, uitgave 1900. Tilburg: A.J.M. Wagemakers, *Buitenstaanders in actie, socialisten en neutraal-georganiseerden in confrontatie met de gesloten Tilburgse samenleving 1888–1919* (Tilburg, 1990), 150. Amsterdam: P. van Horssen and D. Rietveld, 'Socialisten in Amsterdam 1878–1898. Een sociaal profiel van de SDB- en SDAP-aanhang', *Tijdschrift voor sociale geschiedenis* 16/4 (1990), 386–406.
11. This situation led to many – often quite humorous – misunderstandings between party members and the national bureau. There were members who thought that the bureau would send them rather random amounts of

money to fund meetings. Others wrote the bureau to 'reserve' prominent party members as guest speakers for small meetings. Usually the secretary answered by patiently explaining the procedures. The first example can be found in J.J. Van der Horst, *Geen ideaalmenschen: De Schiedamse SDAP tot 1917* (Schiedam, 1984), 38. The second example can be found in IISG Amsterdam, Archief SDAP 496, Kopieboek met kopieën van uitgaande brieven van het partijsecretariaat. Alfabetisch register van de geadresseerden 1901–1902, under the name of 'Spaargaren'.

12. 'Sociaal-democratische arbeiderspartij in Nederland', *Provinciale Overijsselsche en Zwolsche courant*, 28 August 1894.

13. From primary sources from around 1894 it appears that the meaning of the word 'party' was undergoing radical shifts at this moment. In both the SDAP and the ARP, the idea that a party is more than a 'societal group' becomes slowly but surely manifest. Nevertheless it was still very normal to consider all socialists (including the SDB members) as members of the same party. The ARP was called a 'party', but in this organization there was also an ongoing debate on the meaning of the concept. This can be seen particularly well in an important meeting in March 1894, when two opposing groups inside the party had different views on the meaning of the concept. See R. Janssens, 'Eenheid en verdeeldheid 1879–1894', in G. Harinck, R. Kuiper and Peter Bak (eds), *De antirevolutionaire partij 1829–1980* (Hilversum, 2001), 92.

14. The ambiguity with respect to this concept can be seen in many letters and books written by party members. Even at the party conference of 1897 the word 'party' was still used for both the SDB and the SDAP (SDAP, 'Verslag congres 1897', *De sociaaldemocraat*, 24 April 1897, Bijlage, 1). In 1907 a party member mentioned that 'the party has existed for thirty years'. In terms of organization this appears to be complete nonsense, but evidently this party member saw earlier organizations as part of the party too. J.W. Gerhard, *Een ernstig woord aan de Leden der SDAP*, a pamphlet, refused by *Het Volk*, 28 February 1907. Moreover, many years later Willem Vliegen described a party as nothing but 'a group in society'. W. Vliegen, 'Verwachtingen', in J.A. Nieuwenhuis, *Een halve eeuw onder socialisten* (Zeist, 1933), 284.

15. 'Sociaal-democratische arbeiderspartij in Nederland', *Provinciale Overijsselsche en Zwolsche courant*, 28 August 1894.

16. Newspaper *Het Volk* was founded in 1901, and the 'Dutch Universal Suffrage Committee' was founded in 1899–1900. A good example of another network that was slowly taken over by the SDAP was the Bond voor Nederlandsche Onderwijzers. This story is described in E.J. van Det, *De Bond van Nederlandse Onderwijzers. Nieuwe uitgave van Zestig Jaren Bondsleven*, ed. S. Karsten and H. van Setten, 2 vols (Amsterdam, 1983).

17. Joseph Dietzgen, *Het evangelie van de sociaaldemocratie. Bewerkt door J. Loopuit* (Amsterdam, 1902), lecture 1.

18. Many of the *Verspreide leden* mentioned their ideological interest in their correspondence. A relatively big group of them can be identified in other correspondence on ideological issues and in the 'letters to the editor' section of the socialist newspaper. IISG Amsterdam, Archief SDAP 1703–1705 (names, addresses and correspondence with the *Verspreide Leden*).

19. In Amsterdam young social democrats tried to look like their hero Frank van der Goes. D. Bos, *Waarachtige Volksvrienden* (Amsterdam, 2001), 314.

20. Prominent party members such as Henri Polak, Jan van Zutphen and Henriette Roland Holst were respectively called cousin, uncle and aunt by the party members.
21. Citing Marx was a very common and popular *argumentam ad verecundiam*.
22. These booklets were printed by party printers like J.A. Fortuyn, H. Masereeuw and later A.B. Soep. They were sold in small social democratic bookstores and during propaganda meetings. They were also spread all over the country by the network of local branches. Some information on this distribution can be found in IISG Amsterdam, Archief SDAP 2827–2836, Kasboeken met gegevens betreffende de afnemers van de brochurenhandel 1899–1906.
23. W.P.G. Helsdingen, *Volkscatechismus* (Amsterdam, 1904).
24. P.J. Troelstra, *SDAP. Haar ontstaan, doel en streven* (Amsterdam, 1899), slotwoord.
25. Another example: W. Vliegen, *Het schuldregister der Regeering* (Amsterdam, 1901).
26. SDAP, *Arbeiders jaarboekje* (Rotterdam, 1899).
27. SDAP, *Na tien jaar. Gedenkschrift bij het tienjarig bestaan der Sociaal Democratische Arbeiders Partij* (Amsterdam, 1904).
28. The festschrift was the final goodbye to the SDB. Even SDB leader Domela Nieuwenhuis recognized that the festschrift closed the discussion between the SDAP and the SDB by placing the SDB in the past. F. Domela Nieuwenhuis, *Van Christen tot Anarchist*, 396 and 538.
29. Tresoar Leeuwarden, 348-6356, 'Notulenboek Afdeling Warga van de SDAP 1908–1917'.
30. P. Hoogland, *Vijf en twintig jaren sociaal-demokratie in de hoofdstad* (Amsterdam, 1928).
31. After its first twelve-and-a-half years the newspaper *Het Volk* devoted a page to its own history, 'Uit onze geschiedenis', *Het Volk; dagblad voor de arbeiderspartij*, 1 October 1912.
32. Troelstra, for instance, mentions van Kuijkhof only a few times in juxtaposition with other party members although he probably spoke to him on a daily basis.
33. For example, K. Geertsma, 'De eerste opbouw', *Het Volksblad voor Gelderland* (May–October 1935). In IISG Amsterdam, Archief SDAP 885, Knipselmap met ongedateerde stukken; H. Mol, *Memoires van een havenarbeider* (Nijmegen, 1980). This is a collection of the articles that Mol wrote as a feuilleton for *Het Dagblad van Rotterdam*.
34. W.H. Meijer, *Terugblik. Herinneringen van een sociaal-democraat* (Amsterdam, 1981).
35. It is one of the classical social democratic books that still can be bought very easily on the Internet and in second-hand bookstores. It is mentioned in descriptions of many personal libraries of socialists as well.
36. In the archives of the annual congresses many programmes of the 'festive evenings' can be found. For many years the tableaux were a recurring element of such evenings. IISG Amsterdam, Archief SDAP 238–258, congresstukken 1895–1912.
37. IISG Amsterdam, archief SDAP 257, Letter from M. Roep to J. Van Kuijkhof, 17 January 1911.

38. Tresoar Leeuwarden, 348-6356, 'Notulenboek Afdeling Warga van de SDAP 1908–1917'.
39. H.J. van der Vegt, 'De klop op de Zwolsche deur V', feuilleton in *Zwolsch Nieuws-en Advertentieblad*, October 1931–September 1932. Collected in IISG Amsterdam, Kleine archieven Nederland, 128.
40. 'De Nieuwe Tijd' was written by O.W. de Nobel.
41. Dirk Troelstra, a brother of the party leader, wrote 'The boodschap op de heide' on the occasion of the opening of a community house in Friesland. The lyrics, however, were not very cheery. Again 'The New Era' is about to begin, but in this song an old grandfather dies on the era's threshold. Nevertheless, the historical inevitability was stressed as well.
42. W.H. Vliegen, *De dageraad der volksbevrijding. Schetsen en tafreelen uit de socialistische beweging in Nederland* (Amsterdam, 1905), 12.
43. Van der Vegt, 'De klop op de Zwolsche deur V'.
44. D.J. Wansink, *Het socialisme op de tweesprong. De geboorte van de SDAP* (Haarlem, 1939).
45. For example, Vliegen, *De dageraad der volksbevrijding*, 167.

Part IV
Nationalism

Nationalism as a Political Religion: The Sacralization of the Irish Nation

Joost Augusteijn

As we have seen in earlier chapters the sacralization of politics is closely associated with the rise of democracy. An important mobilizing factor in democratic politics has always been an appeal to a shared identity, and the strongest basis for such an appeal has no doubt been the concept of the nation. Emilio Gentile has asserted that nationalism became the most universal manifestation of a secular religion in the contemporary world because of its ability to merge with a wide variety of ideologies, institutions and regimes.[1] During the nineteenth century, nationalism acted mostly as a revolutionary force through asserting the sacred nature of the nation and the rights of the sovereign people against traditional powers. In the process, some nationalists elevated their nation to the status of 'most real being', whereby, according to Eric Voegelin, they essentially turned it into a religion.[2]

The symbolic and ceremonial devices of new nineteenth-century states, such as 'the establishment of civic holidays and the spread of national symbols through architecture, town planning, and state monuments', were initially the most influential aspects of this sacralization of the nation.[3] Most new (liberal) regimes were hesitant to stimulate the use of religious models to celebrate the nation, fearing it would perpetuate superstition and prevent the emancipation of the individual. As a result, the sacralization of politics along the lines of nationalist discourse was thus limited in the nineteenth century and remained essentially within the confines of what Gentile has defined as a civil religion, which respects individual freedom, coexists with other ideologies and does not impose obligatory and unconditional support for its commandments.[4]

This can be explained by the fundamental notion contained in all nationalisms that all members of the nation are equal. However, at the same time all nationalisms also exclude those not defined as part of the nation. This became most evident during the First World War when the religious veneration of the nation reached its peak, and internal and external enemies were demonized.[5] In such circumstances the existence, boundaries and features of the nation became indisputable, and it could demand unconditional subordination of the individual and the collectivity to its code of commandments. The demands by governments on citizens in the name of the nation in all states involved in this conflict came close to those associated with a political religion as they represented a desire by the state to permeate every aspect of the individual's personal life and of a society's collective life.[6]

To account for these democratic and totalitarian aspects a distinction has traditionally been made between an inclusive form of political nationalism that allows everyone to join its ranks regardless of background and an exclusivist cultural form that accepts only people with certain characteristics. The question is, however, whether this totalitarian side represents an exception or whether it has simply been contained by nationalism's merger with other ideologies, institutions and regimes. The contention here is that nationalism as an ideology necessarily contains the idea that the collective is more important than the individual by submerging the individual's interests to the nation's will. If so, all cultural as well as political nationalisms have the potential to develop a totalitarian side. There are, after all, limits to nationalism's democratic credentials not only in theory but, as history has shown, often also in reality. It cannot be denied that within National Socialism and Fascism nationalism played a central role even if it was disguised by racist theory or a broader ideology. Fascism has even been described as an extreme form of nationalism and was, according to Gentile, 'perhaps the prototype for the political religions of the twentieth century'.[7]

There is, of course, a substantive difference between fascism and nationalism, but the above makes it interesting to explore the proposition that nationalism itself contains the essence of a political religion. A good object of study to explore this notion is Irish nationalism. In its most recent and violent manifestation during the last decades of the twentieth century, the Irish Republican Army was often accused of actually being a fascist organization, although it described itself as simply nationalist. The accuracy of this charge is not directly relevant here, but it indicates that a nationalist struggle for self-determination can take on extreme features. This chapter will therefore explore the extent to which Irish nationalists sacralized the nation and will try to assess whether their nationalism can be seen as a political religion. It will do this by looking at the various forms and exponents of nationalism in Ireland. The chapter will start off with a look at its most extreme form represented by the thinking of Patrick Pearse (1879–1916), who to many was the ideologue of twentieth-century revolutionary nationalism in Ireland.[8] After that we will analyse the writings of the main exponents of the various forms of Irish nationalism in the long nineteenth century to ascertain how their ideas fitted into the civil–political religion dichotomy and to see whether the concept of political religion can also be of use in the understanding of Irish nationalism itself.

Nationalism in Ireland

Nationalism in Ireland has had many forms, but its origins lay in the Enlightenment ideal of better government. In the turbulent circumstances of the late eighteenth century the organization of United Irishmen based on these ideals evolved from a mainly middle-class reform movement to a revolutionary republican movement which began to emphasize a distinct Irishness. In the nineteenth century two manifestations of what is commonly described as Irish nationalism emerged. One form essentially attempted to obtain autonomy for Ireland through constitutional means, by asking and to some extent forcing Westminster to enact legislation favourable to Ireland. In addition there were organizations which, from time to time, attempted to establish an independent Ireland through the use of force. Although these two forms of political nationalism interacted with each other, cooperated and developed out and into each other, historiography traditionally distinguishes between them as representing constitutional and revolutionary nationalism. Although an interest in the cultural expressions of the Irish nation developed at around the same time as these political forms, they rarely came together. Until the end of the nineteenth century the expressions of cultural nationalism indeed seemed to remain outside the realm of politics. Only in the period leading up to the First World War did it become popularized and politicized, finally culminating in an uprising in 1916 led by activists who for the most part found their roots in the cultural movement. Although revolutionary nationalism became dominant in the wake of this rebellion and forced the independence of southern Ireland, the same divide between constitutional and revolutionary means was maintained, carrying over into 'the troubles' in Northern Ireland from 1969 to 1998.

It is tempting to mirror this constitutional versus revolutionary divide with the distinction between civil and political religion. The constitutional form of Irish nationalism would then be defined as democratic and allowing for competition between various groupings, while the revolutionary form would be seen to force its conception of what constituted the Irish nation on the population. If the thinking behind these two forms can be seen as representing civil and political religion respectively, this would constitute a way to define the difference between them and thereby provide a means to distinguish them from each other and confirming the existence of two forms of political nationalism in Ireland. In the process of assessing the extent to which the various forms can be seen as political religions it may also be possible to see to what extent the dichotomy sketched in Irish historiography may be illuminated by the use of the concepts as defined by Gentile.

Pearse's Rise to Prominence

After a century of constitutional and occasional revolutionary demands by Irish nationalists the political relationship between Ireland and the rest of the United Kingdom had developed into a stalemate around 1900. The failure of physical force had become apparent after the last uprising in 1867 which had shown the inability of the Irish to stage a successful take-over of power. The growing military dominance of the modern state over a civilian population had already manifested itself violently in the Paris Commune of 1871. The great majority of the Irish had subsequently come to support the constitutional demands of the Irish Home Rule Party, which was striving for the introduction of an Irish parliament dealing with domestic affairs within the United Kingdom. Although the Liberal Party under Gladstone came to support this demand in 1886 and attempted to introduce it, this was impossible due to the opposition of the House of Lords which was dominated by Conservatives who feared that home rule for Ireland would spell the end of the British Empire.[9]

This state of affairs lasted roughly from the 1870s to the First World War. Considering the strong support for the demand for autonomy among the Irish – since the franchise extension of 1886 more than 80 per cent of Irish MPs were elected each time under this ticket – it is not too surprising that more extreme forms of nationalism resurfaced in this period. Partly in reaction to the emergence of a strong Home Rule Party, a greater interest in what made Ireland different developed among large sections of the population in the late nineteenth and early twentieth centuries. The resulting interest in cultural nationalism was initially more or less apolitical. However, at the end of the first decade of the

Plate 1   Poster for the Centrale Plan-Commissie, Dutch Social Democratic Party, NVV (trade union), 'Fascisme' (The Netherlands, 1936).

巴黎公社就是工人阶级夺取政权。——列宁

巴黎公社万岁
纪念巴黎公社一百周年

Plate 2 Revolutionary Committee of the Shanghai Drama College, 'Bali gongshe wansui!' ('Long Live the Paris Commune!') (China, 1971).

Plate 3 Revolutionary Committee Political Propaganda Group, 'Qianli yeying lian hongxin' ('To go on a thousand "li" march to temper a red heart') (China, 1971).

Plate 4   H.G. Jentzsch, 'Germany' (*Der Wahre Jacob*, Germany, 1893).

twentieth century a more radical form of nationalism developed among the members of the cultural organizations and of the remnants of the physical-force movements of the nineteenth century.[10]

When the veto power of the House of Lords came under attack in 1910 as a result of its refusal to accept the budget of the then Liberal government, the introduction of home rule became a distinct possibility. This generated a strong reaction among the large minority of mostly Protestant unionists in Ireland, who were particularly strong in the northeast of Ireland. After the veto power was indeed curtailed in 1912 they threatened armed resistance and received almost unconditional support for this from the Conservative Party. These actions confirmed the already existing suspicions among many Irish nationalists that when it came down to it the English would never grant them any form of autonomy. Consequently, they began to arm themselves as well in an attempt to safeguard the introduction of home rule. A relatively small section of those who were central in setting up the paramilitary force saw a potential opportunity to attempt another uprising. Despite the threat of armed resistance by unionists, a home rule bill was nevertheless passed in September 1914. However, due to the outbreak of the First World War and the fear that home rule would generate a conflict in Ireland, the government added two caveats: home rule would not be implemented until after the war and then a solution would have to be found for the resistance of unionists.[11]

This postponement confirmed the fears of radical nationalists, who turned to an old Irish adage: 'England's difficulty is Ireland's opportunity'. As soon as the war broke out they decided to initiate a rebellion. A central figure in the nationalist paramilitary organization was Patrick Pearse, who had come to prominence in the language organization, the Gaelic League, around 1900 and had become the figurehead of the radical movement. As editor of the Gaelic League's newspaper and frequent public speaker he was one of the few radicals with a public profile, which was an important consideration for the underground revolutionaries to bring him on board. Pearse was also one of the few radicals who had clear ideas about Irish nationality and the rationale behind a rebellion, which he expressed frequently. All these elements gave him a central role in the rebellion which started on Easter Monday 1916 and of which he became the officially appointed leader. Afterwards Pearse thus became the central figure in nationalists' conception of nationality.[12]

The 1916 Rising failed after six days of fighting, and Pearse and 14 other rebels were subsequently executed. It nevertheless contributed strongly to a resurgence of the fortunes of physical-force nationalism. Following a reorganization of the rebels into the Irish Republican Army and the founding of a political wing in Sinn Féin, a successful guerrilla campaign developed after 1919 which eventually led to the foundation in the south of Ireland of a dominion of the British Empire in 1921. The partition of Ireland and the subordinate status of the south this entailed caused a substantial section of the IRA to continue their struggle. Following an unsuccessful civil war with their compatriots, who had accepted the new position of Ireland, in 1922–23, the organization conducted violent campaigns in 1939–44, 1956–62 and 1969–95. To legitimize their struggle they always based themselves on the ideas of Patrick Pearse. Up to the 1970s this also applied to the new rulers of the southern state who also located their roots in the IRA of the 1917–21 period. Only the association with the violence unleashed by the Provisional IRA in Northern Ireland after 1969 made his ideas, particularly regarding the militarization of society, suspect in their eyes.[13] The fight by the Provisional IRA was much harder to defend as an exercise in the expression of the democratic rights of the Irish people due to the presence of a majority of unionists in the North who opposed a united Ireland. Although democracy, the IRA argued, could be truly expressed only within an all-Ireland context, the accusation of fascism was easily hurled at them.

Pearse's Thinking

Pearse's ideas thus stand at the heart of Irish nationalism in most of its guises during the larger part of the twentieth century. They were particularly instrumental in legitimizing the IRA campaigns and there-fore form the main source for an analysis of the more extreme forms of twentieth-century Irish nationalism. To assess whether nationalism by itself can function as a political religion with totalitarian demands on its followers, his thinking therefore forms the crucial starting point. The main document that defined the claim to independence for most Irishmen is the Proclamation of the Republic, essentially written by Pearse a few days before the 1916 Rising with some minor contributions from a number of the other signatories. Written in the name of the self-styled Provisional Government of the Irish Republic and addressed to the people of Ireland, it provides a concise definition of what made Ireland a nation and how the nation related to its citizens:

> IRISHMEN AND IRISHWOMEN: In the name of God and of the dead generations from which she receives her old tradition of nationhood,

Ireland, through us, summons her children to her flag and strikes for her freedom. [...]

We declare the right of the people of Ireland to the ownership of Ireland, and to the unfettered control of Irish destinies, to be sovereign and indefeasible. The long usurpation of that right by a foreign people and government has not extinguished the right, nor can it ever be extinguished except by the destruction of the Irish people. In every generation the Irish people have asserted their right to national freedom and sovereignty; six times during the last three hundred years they have asserted it in arms. Standing on that fundamental right and again asserting it in arms in the face of the world, we hereby proclaim the Irish Republic as a Sovereign Independent State, and we pledge our lives and the lives of our comrades-in-arms to the cause of its freedom, of its welfare, and of its exaltation among the nations.

The Irish Republic is entitled to, and hereby claims, the allegiance of every Irishman and Irishwoman. The Republic guarantees religious and civil liberty, equal rights and equal opportunities to all its citizens, and declares its resolve to pursue the happiness and prosperity of the whole nation and all of its parts, cherishing all of the children of the nation equally and oblivious of the differences carefully fostered by an alien government, which have divided a minority from the majority in the past.

Until our arms have brought the opportune moment for the establishment of a permanent National Government, representative of the whole people of Ireland and elected by the suffrages of all her men and women, the Provisional Government, hereby constituted, will administer the civil and military affairs of the Republic in trust for the people.

We place the cause of the Irish Republic under the protection of the Most High God. Whose blessing we invoke upon our arms, and we pray that no one who serves that cause will dishonour it by cowardice, in humanity, or rapine. In this supreme hour the Irish nation must, by its valour and discipline and by the readiness of its children to sacrifice themselves for the common good, prove itself worthy of the august destiny to which it is called.[14]

In calling upon God and the deeds of the dead generations and referring to Ireland's exaltation among the nations and its august destiny Pearse clearly attempts to confer an aura of sanctity upon the Irish Nation. At first sight, the requirements for members of the nation in this document place it well within the confines of the definition of a civil religion provided by Gentile.[15] By directly referring to the establishment of a national government elected by the suffrage of all men and women it appears to guarantee a plurality of ideas, free competition in the exercise of power, and the ability of the governed to dismiss their governments through peaceful and constitutional methods. By guaranteeing religious and civil liberty, equal rights and opportunities to all its citizens it also seems to reject any identification with a particular ideology or religion and acknowledges the separation of church and state.

As the Proclamation clearly espouses these liberal objectives one could argue that indeed Irish nationalism even in this extreme form constitutes a civil religion. However, a close reading of the text also brings out a number of features that demand a much closer association between citizens and the Irish nation closely mirroring the character-istics of a political religion.[16] The Irish Republic is here constituted as a living entity that is entitled to and claims the allegiance of every Irishman and Irishwoman regardless of their aspirations, even asserting the willingness of the nation's children to sacrifice their lives for the nation. It effectively imposes loyalty by calling upon its children to rally to its flag and pledge their lives to the cause of the Republic's freedom and sees its exaltation among the nations and the august destiny to which it is called as its mission. The references to the nation's past and mythical willingness to assert the people's right to national freedom and sovereignty in arms create a certain political liturgy for the adora-tion of the Irish nation. Even in its more social democratic objective 'to pursue the happiness and prosperity of the whole nation' it subsumes individual interests to those of the whole. Although prevented from putting their ideas into practice, this programme does seem to indicate that the Irish nation as the 1916 rebels imagined it could be particularly prescriptive. The fact that Pearse gained Christ-like status after 1916 also indicates a tendency to create a cult around him as the embodiment of the nation.[17]

On the basis of the Proclamation of the republic we thus have to conclude that a nation engaged in a struggle for liberation can show at least some overt elements of a political religion. To see to what extent this constitutes the essence of this form of nationalism we need to take a further look at Pearse's thinking, using Gentile's definition of a politi-cal religion as our starting point. According to this definition, a political religion has a number of interrelated constitutive elements. It needs to be exclusive and fundamentalist and therefore intolerant of other political ideologies and movements, it denies the autonomy of the individual in relation to the collectivity, sanctifies the use of violence as a legitimate weapon in the fight against the nation's enemies and as an instrument of regeneration, and in relation to traditional religious institutions, it either adopts a hostile attitude or attempts to establish a symbiotic relationship.

It is not difficult to find elements in Pearse's writing which give Irish nationalism an exclusivist character. First, he defines freedom as 'a divine religion' which 'bears the marks of unity, of sanctity, of catholicity, and of apostolic succession'.[18] For him the nation was one and holy, embraced all the men and women of the nation, and it or the aspiration for it was passed down from generation to generation. Pearse thus placed the nation in an exclusive untouchable position. Furthermore, he makes clear throughout his writings that the Gaelic language and tradition were superior to all others, in particular to English civilization:

> Newspapers, politicians, literary societies are all but forms of one gigantic heresy, that like a poison has eaten its way into the vitals of Irish nationality, that has paralysed the nation's energy and intellect. That heresy is the idea that there can be an Ireland, that there can be an Irish literature, an Irish social life whilst the language of Ireland is English.[19]

He also clearly saw the nation as a separate entity with a life of its own and called on the Irish to be part of it and live as part of it. In the pamphlet *The Spiritual Nation*, published in 1916, he set out that a nation is not just a group of people but has a spirit of its own, which can be compared to the soul of a person and which lives within the language in its broadest sense, consisting not only of the sounds and idiom but also of its literature and folklore. This national spirit can reveal itself entirely, he argued, only in a free nation, in its institutions, the arts and the inner life and actions of the nation. This subordination of the individual under the collectivity remained part of republican thinking. Pearse's successor as leader of the republican movement, Eamon de Valera, put it most succinctly in 1922 when a treaty with England was under discussion: 'The people have no right to do wrong.'[20]

The people are also called upon to sacrifice their own life for the nation. 'A man's life for a nation's happiness! What a magnificent exchange that would be!'[21] Pearse took this a step further by comparing it to the sacrifice of Jesus Christ: 'One man can free a people as one Man redeemed the world. I will take no pike, I will go into the battle with bare hands. I will stand up before the Gall[22] as Christ hung naked before men on the tree!'[23] Although he interpreted much of this personally – 'the deed that I see / And the death I shall die'[24] – implicitly he argued a good Irishman should follow his example. The use of force was sanctified on many occasions in his writings, most famously on 1 August 1915 in his oration over the grave of Jeremiah O'Donovan Rossa, a leading nineteenth-century revolutionary:

> Rulers and Defenders of Realms had need to be wary if they would guard against such processes. Life springs from death; and from the graves of patriot men and women spring living nations. The Defenders of this Realm have worked well in secret and in the open. They think that they have pacified Ireland. They think that they have purchased half of us and intimidated the other half. They think that they have foreseen everything, think that they have provided against everything; but the fools, the fools, the fools! – they have left us our Fenian dead, and while Ireland holds these graves, Ireland unfree shall never be at peace.[25]

Sacrificing oneself for the nation became something positive, as he made clear in an oft-quoted comment on the battlefields of the First World War:

> It is good for the world that such things should be done. The old heart of the earth needed to be warmed with the red wine of the battle-fields. Such august homage was never before offered to God as this, the homage of millions of lives given gladly for love of country.[26]

The regenerative powers of sacrifice were put most clearly by Pearse's contemporary, the popular Irish writer Canon Sheehan, in 1914: 'As the blood of martyrs was the seed of saints, so the blood of the patriot is the seed from which alone can spring fresh life, into a nation that is drifting into the putrescence of decay.'[27] Pearse made similar statements after the rising had failed: 'We seem to have lost. We have not lost. To refuse to fight would have been to lose; to fight is to win. We have kept faith with the past, and handed on a tradition to the future.'[28]

His attitude towards established religious institutions was somewhat ambiguous but still within the two possible approaches given by the definition of a political religion: either a hostile attitude or an attempt to establish a symbiotic relationship. In most cases he is seen as deferential to the church when he is trying to mobilize its support, but when it refused to follow his thinking he is unusually willing to stand up against it: 'The hand of God is with us, – yea, even though, for the moment, the hands of the Bishops may be raised against us.'[29] If he cannot work together with them in a mutually beneficial way, he shows his hostility to the institution but never to the fundamental belief underlying the faith of most Irishmen, as we can see when he called upon his men to start the rebellion that was certainly not supported by the church: 'the day of the Lord is here, and you and I have lived to see it. And we are young. And God has given us strength and courage and counsel. May He give us victory.'[30]

In his writing we thus recognize the four characteristics of a political religion. The nation to Pearse and others like him is also a secular collective entity that provides meaning and an ultimate purpose to social existence and prescribes the principles for distinguishing between good and evil:

> Pax Britannica, is peace with sin, peace with dishonour, the devil's peace. Christ's peace will not come to Ireland until she had taken Christ's sword. The Irish should now not shy away from the shedding of blood and welcome war when it comes as she would welcome the Angel of God. It was always the few who fought for the good thing and the many for the evil thing, but with God's help the few would ultimately win. That they had not always won in the past was because they had been guilty of some secret faltering, some infidelity to their best selves, some shrinking back in the face of a tremendous duty.[31]

Ultimately people should be willing to lay down their lives for the nation. Together the Irish fulfil a messianic role in bringing freedom to what is constituted as holy Ireland: 'the people itself will perhaps be its own Messiah. The people labouring, scourged, crowned with thorns, agonising and dying, to rise again immortal and impassable.'[32]

By calling upon a sacred history, particularly laid down in the mythical assertion that all Irish generations have asserted their right to independence through arms, a certain political liturgy is created for the adoration of the sacralized collective entity. In a sense Pearse himself became the person who embodied the nation. He had already put himself in the position of the saviour of the Irish as Christ had been the saviour of humanity. In a poem he composed shortly before his execution, written from the point of view of his mother, he again reiterated that: 'Receive my first-born into thy arms, / Who also hath gone out to die for men.'[33] This was picked up by people shortly after his death. Pearse became the ideal in every sense:

> in [the] person and life of P.H. Pearse, the novelist will find the most fertile field for his pen. [...] The soldier will find in him the most disinterested patriotism [...] the statesmen may well learn from him what goes to make for real democracy and true contentment [...] the countrymen will see in him Irish thought, culture and nationality developed to their highest.[34]

By 1932 he was even considered to be worthy of sainthood: 'He possessed all the qualities which go to the making of a saint to a degree that it is hardly within my province to analyse.'[35]

Although Pearse's ideas may not offer a point-by-point match with the characteristics of a political religion, it is clear that the position he gave to the nation and the demands it could make on its citizens went far beyond what would constitute a civil religion. We see how nationalism can take on the form of a political religion. To ascertain whether this is an essential part of Irish nationalism or associated only with Patrick Pearse and revolutionary nationalism, we will now look a little more closely at a number of icons of Irish nationalist thought in the nineteenth century, ranging from the main examples of what were seen as constitutional nationalists, such as Daniel O'Connell and Charles Parnell, to some icons of the revolutionary movements, such as Wolfe Tone, Thomas Davis and the Fenians, who were also among Pearse's heroes.

Irish Nationalism in Perspective

The first expressions of what is commonly referred to as nationalist thinking in Ireland were formulated in the late eighteenth century by the United Irishmen. They were initially a reform movement based on the ideas underlying the French Revolution that strove for the abolition of inequalities based on religion and also demanded a share of political power for the middle classes. Although initially successful, their demands became suspect when war broke out in 1793 between Great Britain and revolutionary France, which was associated with Catholicism and anti-aristocratic ideas. The end to further reform caused a radicalization of a portion of the United Irishmen, who began to strive for an independent Ireland in which their ideals could be implemented. As Wolfe Tone, the leader of this movement and seen by

Pearse as one of the fathers of Irish freedom, indicated, their demands were purely aimed at gaining better rights and did not refer to some sort of ethnic nation in a Herderian sense:

> To subvert the tyranny of our execrable government, to break the connection with England, (the never-failing source of all our political evils,) and to assert the independence of my country – these were my objects. To unite the whole people of Ireland; to abolish the memory of past dissensions; and to substitute the common name of Irishman in place of the denominations of Protestant, Catholic and Dissenter – these were my means.[36]

Apart from the forcible nature of their attempt to establish an independent Ireland, the ideology did not show any clear elements of a political religion. Following their failed uprising of 1798 the movement became defunct, and apart from a short, violent episode in 1803 more peaceful means to change Irish society were tried subsequently.

Arguably the most influential Irish leader following the demise of the United Irishmen was Daniel O'Connell (1775–1847), who came to prominence in the 1820s when he popularized the middle-class reform movement demanding full emancipation for Catholics. After achieving this goal through a combination of parliamentary politics and mass mobilization, he changed his objective to the creation of an independent Irish Parliament within the United Kingdom. O'Connell had achieved mythical status in Ireland by 1829 when the Emancipation Act was passed and he was widely described as 'The Liberator'. As had been the case in the struggle for emancipation, the campaign for an autonomous parliament generated mass support in Ireland, but this time O'Connell was unable to gain support for it in parliament. His unwillingness to use the potential revolutionary forces contained in the Irish masses caused the movement to disappear after O'Connell's death in 1847.

A study of O'Connell's writings reveals that he never really described the nation as a cultural entity. Like the United Irishmen he saw his main objective as 'the restoration to old Ireland of her independence', stating in later life that he lived 'to see Ireland free and independent'.[37] Although one of his most trusted colleagues, P.V. Fitzpatrick, spoke of nationalizing Ireland as a paramount objective and 'the progress of Ireland to the position of a nation', this goal did not mean much more than political independence.[38] The closest O'Connell came to defining a difference between Britain and Ireland was in a letter to Paul Culllen, later the Cardinal of Ireland:

> For we are, thank Heaven, a separate nation still and have preserved through ages of persecution – English persecution, political as well religious – our separate existence and so much of our royal and national station as consists in a national hierarchy complete in all its parts from our most dignified and venerated archbishops down to the humblest acolyte who serves at the foot of our altars – of the Catholic altars of the most high God. British!!! I am not British. You are not British.[39]

Apart from such references to Catholicism as an identifiable characteristic of the Irish, what exactly constituted the Irish nation was not defined, certainly not in linguistic or ethnic terms.[40] Although O'Connell saw Protestants as Irish, he did expect Protestantism to disappear after Ireland's independence: 'the great mass of the Protestant community would with little delay melt into the overwhelming majority of the Irish nation. Protestantism would not survive the Repeal ten years. Nothing but persecution would keep it alive and the Irish Catholics are too wise and too good to persecute.'[41] In a letter to the Liberal MP Charles Buller he stated that churches would be treated equally,[42] but to Catholic churchmen and fellow politicians he indicated that an independent Ireland would be Catholic: 'So rich, so prosperous a country with a legislature devoted to Religion, to Catholic truth in doctrine, discipline and submission to authority, with an undeviating attachment to the authority of the Holy See'.[43] Essentially an independent Ireland would thus be a Catholic nation. O'Connell justified this outcome by the connection he made between Anglicanism and repression: 'We have never yet been a people. A faction has ruled and a prostate population yielded an unwilling and coerced obedience.'[44]

O'Connell used the term nation in effect to describe statehood. There are no indications he gave the term any other meaning. He used strong language to describe the negative impact of the link with Britain: 'the domination of England is the sole and blighting curse of this country. It is the incubus that sits on our energies, stops the pulsation of the nation's heart and leaves to Ireland not gay vitality but the horrid convulsions of a troubled dream', but added that his objective was simply to improve the condition of the Irish people.[45] It is not entirely clear whether his primary objective was the improvement of the lot of the people or the freedom of Ireland. It seems most likely that freedom was simply seen as the best way to achieve the desired improvement in conditions in Ireland.

This duality in objectives was later objected to by Pearse. Following the successful campaign for Catholic emancipation which made Catholics equal citizens within the United Kingdom, O'Connell began to campaign for repeal of the legislation which had merged the Irish Parliament with that of Great Britain. However, when this did not yield any results in Parliament, he entered into a political arrangement with the liberal Whig Party to obtain further improvements for the Irish people. The liberals saw this as the way to get the Irish to accept the union between Ireland and Great Britain. Although O'Connell argued that 'Every popular concession, as I know, advances the cause of Repeal',[46] it seems likely that if reforms were successful, the support for repeal of the union would dwindle. Making Ireland an independent nation therefore seemed in the end the secondary ambition. O'Connell acknowledged this in Parliament in 1836: 'Ireland was not a province, but a pitiful colony [...] Do justice to Ireland and England had nothing to apprehend from the further agitation of repeal, nothing to apprehend from Ireland, but everything to hope. Henceforth separation was at an end'.[47] Although this may have been a tactical statement to some extent, he also took immense pride in the Irish military contribution to the empire and wanted Ireland to remain in the empire.[48]

O'Connell's refusal to go beyond a demand for reform in the absence of the possibility of gaining autonomy through Parliament included his rejection of the use of illegitimate means.[49] He put it most succinctly when he said, 'Nothing is politically right which is morally wrong.' He explicitly rejected the use of violence:

> The principle of my political life [...] is, that all ameliorations and improvements in political institutions can be obtained by persevering in a perfectly peaceable and legal course, and cannot be obtained by forcible means, or if they could be got by forcible means, such means create more evils than they cure, and leave the country worse than they found it.[50]

He felt that whatever was gained by violence would not last: 'The altar of liberty totters when it is cemented only with blood'.[51] He was nevertheless a strong believer in the power of agitation to force the English to make concessions. 'Whatever little we have gained, we have gained by agitation, while we have uniformly lost by moderation.' The early leaders of what is commonly seen as the Irish nationalist movement were thus essentially out for political improvements – not for independence on the basis of ethnic distinctions. The claims of the nation were limited to support for autonomy and did not go into the realms of what could be seen as a political religion.

The first to connect politics with the romantic notion of the nation introduced by Johann Herder was Thomas Davis (1814–45), a young, half-Welsh Protestant and another of Pearse's fathers of Irish freedom. To some extent his background might explain Davis's liberal attitude towards who belonged to the Irish nation. Striving for the unity of Catholics and Protestants, he asserted that anyone who wanted to be Irish could be so. Ireland was made up of different tribes from different places who had merged into something that became Ireland. The Saxons and Normans, however, had subjugated Ireland and refused to participate in an Irish nation as others had done before them.[52] He clearly did not believe that internal divisions in Ireland would hinder the demand for independence:

> He who fancies some intrinsic objection to our nationality to lie in the coexistence of two languages, three or four great sects, and a dozen different languages, creeds, and races in Ireland, will learn that in Hungary, Switzerland, Belgium and America, different languages, creeds, and races flourish kindly side by side, and he will seek in English intrigues the real well of the bitter woes of Ireland.[53]

It was by joining together that Irish Catholics and Protestants would ultimately win over England and 'would make this country comparatively a paradise'.[54]

It is clear that Davis did not define Ireland as an ethnic nation. In that sense he mirrored his predecessors who focused on political independence and equated the nation with the state. His criticism of English rule was also based on the suffering it caused, referring to the presence of a state church, high taxation and the absence of employment opportunities, which made Ireland economically poor. 'We must believe and act to the lessons taught by reason and history, that England is our interested and implacable enemy – a tyrant to her dependants – a calumniator of her neighbours, and both the despot and defamer of Ireland for nearly seven centuries.'[55] The treatment of Ireland by Britain would eternally mark their relationship:

> Ireland is changing the loose tradition of her wrongs into history and ballad; and though justice, repentance, or retribution may make her

cease to need vengeance, she will immortally remember her bondage, her struggles, her glories, and her disasters. Till her suffering ceases that remembrance will rouse her passions and nerve her arm. May she not forgive till she is no longer oppressed and when she forgives, may she never forget![56]

However, he made clear that a redress of grievances by Britain would not be enough: 'we would spurn your gifts, if the condition were that Ireland should remain a province. [...] we tell you, in the name of Ireland, that Ireland shall be a Nation!'[57]

In Davis's mind freedom would bring benefits to Ireland nationally and internationally: 'A People known and regarded abroad will be more dignified, more consistent, and more proud in all its acts. [...] A nation with a high and notorious character to sustain will be more stately and firm than if it lived in obscurity'.[58] Part of this new-found pride was to be based on at least an awareness of Irish cultural identity. 'The Irish Press is beginning to teach the People to know themselves and their history; to know other nations, and to feel the rights and duties of citizens.'[59] Davis was the first leader to put an emphasis on language as the distinguishing feature of the Irish nation: 'A people without a language of its own, is only half a nation. A nation should guard its language more than its territories – 'tis a surer barrier, and more important frontier, than fortress or river.'[60]

With this he started to develop his sense of nationalism in the direction of a political religion. The nation in his eyes became an entity in itself, separate from the individuals that constituted the nation: 'On nations fixed in right in truth, / God would bestow eternal youth.'[61] He also started to celebrate a willingness to die for Ireland: 'No saint or king has tomb so proud / As he whose flag becomes his shroud.'[62] Thus the essence of nationalism changed from a demand for better government freely chosen by the people to a personification of a nation worth dying for. Indeed some members of the loose organization of which Davis was a part, the Young Irelanders, attempted an uprising in 1848, including Pearse's third and fourth fathers of Irish freedom. Fintan Lalor's main contribution to nationalist thinking were his assertions that the public right of the nation stood above the private right of the individual and that the nation should control the conditions for life, including the nation's soil and its resources. John Mitchel is best known and respected by Pearse for his unconditional hatred of England. Although in the circumstances of the Great Famine the rebellion failed miserably, it inspired a new generation of revolutionaries among the Fenians.

The Fenians originated among the many Irish who had been forced to emigrate by the dire economic conditions of the 1840s and beyond. The initiative in 1858 was taken by some of the banished members of the Young Irelanders in the USA who subsequently brought the organization to Ireland. Leading Fenians like John O'Leary later stated they were inspired at a young age by Thomas Davis and the newspaper he had helped to found. 'In leading article, and poem we read, from week to week, the story of Ireland's sufferings under English rule; and now and then we heard of other countries groaning under alien domination, and of their efforts, successful and unsuccessful, to shake it off.'[63]

The Fenians again focused on independence and did not seem to take on board the ethnic elements of Irish nationality which Davis had begun to develop. Their inspiration and motivation lay purely in the repression by the English. As O'Leary put it, 'If the English had not come to Ireland, and if they had not stayed there and done all the evil so many of them now allow they have been doing all along, then there would have been no Fenianism.'[64] They referred in particular to the Famine and the lack of success of the tenants' rights movement which sought more rights for Irish farmers. In this they followed the ideas of Young Irelanders like Terence Bellew MacManus, who famously stated at his trial in 1849,

in no part which I have taken was I actuated by enmity towards Englishmen individually, whatever I may have felt of the injustice of English rule in this island; I therefore say, that it is not because I loved England less, but because I loved Ireland more, that I now stand before you.[65]

He was subsequently transported to Australia from where he escaped before settling in the USA. After his death in 1861 his body was brought to Dublin where the Fenians organized a huge funeral. In the oration they emphasized MacManus's willingness to fight, and apart from mentioning that it was better for the soul to be buried in Irish soil, no references were made to the Irish nation.[66] In a sense O'Leary even made light of the ethnic differences between Ireland and England: 'Nearly all our misdoings – i.e., doings the English disliked – used to be set down to some sort of innate wickedness of our nature, variously traceable to race, religion, climate or the Lord knows what.'[67]

The Fenians staged an unsuccessful rising in 1867 which also led to their demise. Although the organization continued to exist as an oath-bound secret brotherhood, Irish nationalism again turned to constitutional means in the last great political movement before the 1916 Rising brought revolutionary nationalists of the IRA to the fore. Unofficially termed the 'uncrowned king of Ireland', Charles Stewart Parnell (1846–91) became the towering figure of this movement that popularized the demand for home rule among the masses in Ireland.

As a Protestant landlord Parnell was an unlikely candidate for this position. His brand of nationalism was again not fundamentally different from that of his predecessors. In a House of Commons debate over the introduction of a Coercion Bill in Ireland in 1881 he connected the amount of repression in Ireland with the spirit of nationality just as the Fenians had done: 'The more you tyrannize – the more you trifle with the Irish people – the stronger will burn the spirit of nationality, the more they will free themselves from the yoke which renders such things possible.'[68] Elsewhere he claimed that the position of Irish tenants lay at the heart of the problematic relationship between Ireland and Britain: 'the great and all absorbing topic in Ireland, agricultural country as she is, depending upon the soil for her very existence, is the land question [...] the land question is at the root of all other questions'.[69] The essential fight, Parnell argued, was 'for the rights of the people to make their own laws on the soil of Ireland',[70] and the feeling that the Irish did not benefit from the fruits of the union with Britain:

> there were many people – in fact, the majority of the people of Ireland – who now thought that the time had come when this practice should cease, and that they should have the opportunity of living in their own country, and of obtaining prosperity from the natural riches and resources of the country – an opportunity which the laws of England had denied them for so long a period.[71]

Nationality here thus again constituted the desire for political independence.

Parnell did allude to a nationality which went beyond simple political independence. When radical nationalists attacked him for degrading their 'country into the position of a province', he claimed that there was 'no reason why Ireland under Home Rule will not be a nation in every sense and for every purpose that it is right that she should be a nation'.[72] This, of course, begged the question what the nation then was in his eyes, but he never answered that. To justify his demand for political independence he argued that it was an impossible task for one nation to govern another, as was happening in Ireland.[73] Even prominent liberal politicians of that period like Gladstone and, to some extent, Chamberlain accepted that Ireland was a separate nation but, of course, rejected the necessity for independence.[74] Some have asserted that to Parnell home rule was only a temporary staging post and that he fundamentally desired Irish independence. Although not universally accepted, this position seems to be inherent in his statements, most famously in a speech he gave in Cork in 1885 and which he repeated many times after. It was later inscribed onto the monument dedicated to him in Dublin's O'Connell Street:

> We can not, under the British Constitution, ask for more than the restitution of Grattan's Parliament [i.e. home rule]. But no man has the right to fix the boundary to the march of a nation; no man has the right to say to his country: 'Thus far shalt thou go and no further', and we have never attempted to fix the *ne plus ultra* to the progress of Ireland's nationhood, and we never shall.

For the moment he was content to settle for home rule, but in the future anything seemed possible:

> while we struggle today for that which may seem possible for us with our combination that we shall not do anything to hinder or prevent better men who may come after us from gaining better things than those for which we now contend.[75]

Although Parnell might ultimately have desired complete independence, like O'Connell he did not believe the use of force was an option. He nevertheless did not oppose the Fenians on principle:

> I have the greatest respect for men who announce themselves publicly to be Fenians – who believe in the separation of England from Ireland by physical force, and who do not look to Constitutional agitation. [...] But though I have this respect for those men, I have never been able to see that a physical force policy was practicable or possible to adopt, either in Ireland or out of it.[76]

This was part of the reason why Pearse admired Parnell and not O'Connell. Parnell also reiterated O'Connell's assertion that England had never given Ireland anything except when it had been pressed to do so, by war or by Irish agitation or even rebellion:

> There was an old maxim that England's difficulty was Ireland's opportunity, and it had been verified in times past. They had never been

able to get the attention of England to their claims unless public opinion was acted upon by some pressing danger.[77]

His party thus stood on 'a platform with one plank only and that one the plank of national independence'. When that was granted the myriad of other nationalist grievances would be dealt with, and Ireland would voluntarily help England in times of difficulty.[78]

Conclusion

This cursory glance at the ideas of Irish political leaders has revealed that if the nation was sacralized at all in nineteenth-century Ireland, it never obtained the features of a political religion. Practically all movements and leaders strove for simple independence and did not place any stronger demands on the people than a willingness to support that effort. Only the Young Irelander Thomas Davis went somewhat further in constituting a nation which had a life of its own, but apart from references to linguistic differences he explicitly rejected the existence of an ethnic nation. Others occasionally alluded to the nation in a sense broader than a desire for political independence but never came to define this entity. If it is argued, therefore, that the Irish did develop a form of nationalism as a religion in the nineteenth century, this always remained a civil and never became a political religion. It could even better be argued that what emerged in Ireland in this period did not go beyond patriotism.

The merger of cultural-identity formation and this patriotism or political nationalism around 1900 brought in a new element. Although the thinking of Patrick Pearse, as the most coherent representative of this development, was strongly rooted in a civil religion, his ideas contained all the ingredients constituting a political religion. The way he defined nationalism and its relationship with the people clearly showed that nationalism itself can constitute a political religion. In that sense it did not need the emergence of fascism or other totalitarian ideologies. It could well be argued that the popularization of cultural nationalism in late nineteenth-century Ireland laid the foundation for this development to emerge there.

What are the implications of using the distinction between constitutional and revolutionary nationalism to typify the various political movements in nineteenth-century Ireland? In light of the study of the ideas of the main leaders of the various movements, the distinction loses a lot of its power. Essentially the objectives and justification were not different, nor was their analysis of the attitude of the British government. All essentially equated the nation with statehood and did not provide any content regarding what constituted the Irish nation. The only fundamental difference seems to have lain in their attitude towards the use of force. The real distinction which should be identified within Irish nationalism thus lay between these expressions of nationalism and the movement which first came to the fore in 1916. The merger between cultural and political nationalism which had taken shape in the years leading up to this constituted a truly new form of nationalism that was a form of political religion.

We must therefore conclude on the basis of the Irish example that nationalism itself does not necessarily constitute a political religion. Passionate political nationalists who sacralize the nation do not place totalitarian demands on their adherents. It seems to be the emergence of cultural nationalism that subsumes this early political nationalism and brings in an objectified nation with its own identity and its own demands on the people. The contention made at the start of this chapter that all nationalisms subjugate individual freedom to the nation's will is therefore shown to be false.[79]

Notes

1. Gentile, *Politics as Religion*, 1, 30.
2. Eric Voegelin, 'The Political Religions' (1938), in idem, *The Collected Works of Eric Voegelin*, ed. Manfred Henningsen, vol. 5 (Columbia, MO and London, 2000), 32.
3. Gentile, *Politics as Religion*, 30.
4. Ibid., xv, 139–40.
5. Ibid., 32. See also the chapter by Patrick Dassen in this volume.
6. Ibid., xv, 139–40.
7. Ibid., 36
8. His thinking was also described as fascist. Hedley McCay, *Pádraic Pearse: A New Biography* (Cork, 1966), 13, 27, 31, 49.
9. D. George Boyce, *Nineteenth-Century Ireland: The Search for Stability* (Dublin, 1990), ch. 6.
10. Ibid., ch. 8.
11. A.T.Q. Stewart, *The Ulster Crisis: Resistance to Home Rule 1912–14* (London, 1997), passim.
12. Joost Augusteijn, *Patrick Pearse: The Making of a Revolutionary* (Houndmills, 2010), passim.
13. Ibid., ch. 6.
14. Dorothy Macardle, *The Irish Republic* (London, 1968), 157.
15. Gentile, *Politics as Religion*, 140.
16. Ibid., 140.
17. Augusteijn, *Patrick Pearse*, ch. 6.
18. Pádraic H. Pearse, *Ghosts* (Dundalk, 1916).

19. Letter dated 13 May 1899, in Seamus Ó Buachalla (ed.), *The Letters of P.H. Pearse* (Gerrards Cross, Bucks, 1980), 9.
20. Diarmuid Ferriter, *Judging Dev: A Reassessment of the Life and Legacy of Eamon De Valera* (Dublin, 2007).
21. Quoted by Jerome F. Cronin in *Irish Independent*, 27 March 1957.
22. Term to describe the English.
23. 'The Singer' (1915), in idem, *Collected Works of Padraic H. Pearse. Plays, Stories, Poems* (Dublin et al., s.l.), 1–5.
24. 'Renunciation', ibid.
25. Macardle, *The Irish Republic*, 128. See also www.youtube.com/watch?v= OHPEWF5Jlrc (retrieved July 2012).
26. *The Spark*, December 1915.
27. Canon Sheehan, *The Graves at Kilmorna*, quoted in Charles Townshend, *Easter 1916: The Irish Rebellion* (London, 2005), 114.
28. Ó Buachalla (ed.), *Letters*, 378–80.
29. *An Claidheamh Soluis*, 26 June 1909.
30. Padraic Pearse, *The Sovereign People* (Dublin, 1916).
31. Ibid.
32. 'The Coming Revolution', *An Claidheamh Soluis*, 8 November 1913.
33. Letter dated 3 May 1916, Ó Buachalla (ed.), *Letters*, 381–2.
34. M.J. Hannan, *Irish Leaders of 1916 – Who Are They?* (Butte, MT, 1920), 1.
35. Louis N. Le Roux, *La vie de Patrice Pearse* (Rennes, 1932). Translated into English by Desmond Ryan (Dublin, 1932), x.
36. *An Argument on Behalf of the Catholics of Ireland by a Northern Whig* (September, 1791), taken from William Theobald Wolfe Tone (ed.), *Memoirs of Theobald Wolfe Tone* (London, 1827), 64.
37. Donal McCartney, *The World of Daniel O'Connell* (Dublin and Cork, 1980), 94.
38. Maurice R. O'Connell (ed.), *The Correspondence of Daniel O'Connell*, vol. IV (Dublin, 1977), 430–3. See also, ibid., vol. VII (Dublin, s.l.), 125, 351–4.
39. Ibid., vol. VII, 156–7.
40. Ibid., vol. VII, 157, 159. See also the chapter by Maartje Janse in this volume.
41. Ibid., vol. VII, 158. See also ibid., vol. IV, 442; McCartney, *The World*, 95.
42. O'Connell (ed.), *The Correspondence*, vol. VIII, 235.
43. Ibid., vol. VII, 202.
44. Ibid., vol. IV, 465.
45. Ibid., vol. IV, 387.
46. Ibid., vol. VII, 353.
47. McCartney, *The World*, 94–5. See also O'Connell (ed.), *The Correspondence*, vol. VIII, 235.
48. McCartney, *The World*, 94, 96.
49. O'Connell (ed.), *The Correspondence*, vol. VIII, 141, 142.
50. *The Nation*, 18 November 1843.
51. Quoted by F. O'Ferrall, *Daniel O'Connell* (Dublin, 1981), 12.
52. 'Celts and Saxons', in *Thomas Davis, Selections from His Prose and Poetry* (London, Leipzig, 1914), 354–8.
53. 'Foreign Policy and Foreign Information', in *Thomas Davis*, 269.
54. 'Conciliation', in *Thomas Davis*, 277. See also 'Orange and Green Will Carry the Day', 291–3.

55. 'Foreign Policy and Foreign Information', in *Thomas Davis*, 270. See also, 'No Redress – No Inquiry', 257–8, and 'Orange and Green', 291–3.
56. 'No Redress – No Inquiry', in *Thomas Davis*, 257–8.
57. Ibid.
58. 'Foreign Policy and Foreign Information', in *Thomas Davis*, 267.
59. 'No Redress – No Inquiry', in *Thomas Davis*, 257–8.
60. 'Our National Language', *Thomas Davis*, 172.
61. 'Nationality', *Thomas Davis*, 334.
62. Ibid. See also the poems: 'The Green above the Red', 'The Vow of Tipperary', 'Tipperary' and 'The West's Asleep', in *Thomas Davis*, 345–50.
63. John O'Leary, *Recollections of Fenians and Fenianism* (Dublin et al., 1968), 3–4.
64. O'Leary, *Recollections*, 78–9. See also 4–13.
65. www.irishfreedom.net/Fenian%20graves/TBMcManus/TBMcManus.htm (retrieved July 2012).
66. O'Leary, *Recollections*, 165–7.
67. O'Leary, *Recollections*, 77.
68. *HC (House of Commons), Deb(Debate), 04 March 1881 vol. 259 cc335–66* (all references from House of Commons Debates retrieved June 2011, http://hansard.millbanksystems.com). See also, *HC Deb 13 June 1882 vol. 270 cc988–1110.*
69. Speech of 11 October 1885, in Alan O'Day, *Parnell and the First Home Rule Episode, 1884–87* (Dublin, 1986), 108.
70. Robert Kee, *The Laurel and the Ivy: The Story of Charles Stewart Parnell and Irish Nationalism* (London, 1993), 249.
71. *HC Deb 17 June 1880 vol. 253 cc210–64.*
72. Kee, *The Laurel*, 126.
73. *HC Deb 23 February 1883 vol. 276 cc716–812.*
74. For Gladstone see *HC Deb 08 April 1886 vol. 304 cc1036–141*; for Chamberlain, O'Day, *Parnell*, 4.
75. O'Day, *Parnell*, 12.
76. *HC Deb 04 March 1881 vol. 259 cc335–66.*
77. *HC Deb 18 January 1878 vol. 237 cc159–223.*
78. Speech 24 August 1885, in O'Day, *Parnell*, 83; *HC Deb 26 April 1875 vol. 223 cc1640–83*; *HC Deb 18 January 1878 vol. 237 cc159–223.*
79. The author wishes to thank the Netherlands Institute for Advanced Study in the Humanities and Social Sciences for providing the opportunity to work on this essay.

The German Nation as a Secular Religion in the First World War? About the Problem of Unity in Modern German History

Patrick Dassen

> The *Volk* has risen up as the only thing which has value and which will last. Over all individual fates stands that which we feel as the highest reality: the experience of belonging together.[1]
>
> – Eduard Schwartz, October 1914

Introduction

'War! It was purification and a relief which we felt, and an incredible hope'. Thus wrote the German writer and later Nobel Prize-winner Thomas Mann about the First World War in the autumn of 1914 in his essay 'Thoughts in Wartime'.[2] According to Mann, the war was the best thing that could happen to Germany because the 'old', civilized world, 'crawling with vermin', was at its end. Four years later, in his *Reflections of an Unpolitical Man*, Thomas Mann still wrote that the war had brought about revolutionary optimism: it reinforced the belief in 'the human being', in an 'earthly empire of God and of love, an empire of freedom, equality, fraternity'.[3]

There can hardly be any doubt about the enthusiasm of German intellectuals and artists when the First World War broke out.[4] The German-Jewish writer (and later pacifist) Ernst Toller, for example, wrote, referring to the first month of the war, 'We constantly live in a chauvinist glow. The words "Germany", "fatherland" and "war" are magically attractive to us'.[5] Even the usually sober sociologist Max Weber wrote in a letter of 28 August 1914, *'this war is great and wonderful'*.[6]

For a long time historians have assumed that almost every German was enthusiastic about the outbreak of the war. However, as the American historian Jeffrey Verhey and others have shown, this is only partially true. The 'spirit of 1914' was largely limited to students and a small section of the better-off, educated middle classes in the big cities. By contrast, the workers in the cities (57 per cent of the population) were rather resistant to the war enthusiasm. Instead of cries of jubilation an atmosphere of fear and despair was prevalent in working-class areas. And the farmers in the countryside were equally unfavourably disposed towards the war. They were plagued by a lot of concrete worries, like bringing in the harvest and the absence of wage earners and requisitioned horses.[7]

Nevertheless, no matter how small the group of the educated middle class, the *Bildungsbürgertum*, actually was (approximately not even one per cent of the population),[8] it was this educated elite which largely dominated public discourse during the war. These were the schoolteachers who gave their chauvinistic lessons; the journalists who defended Germany's war in the newspapers and the weekly magazines; the majority of the politicians who tried to get or retain the support of their electorate; the professors at the universities who gave their biased lectures; the clergymen and priests in the Christian churches who preached about the battle as a religious war and the Germans as God's heroes; the artists who produced their nationalistic paintings and the writers who wrote their exalting and patriotic pamphlets and poems – all claiming that the Germans had to defend their culture (*Kultur*) and that the war was a *defensive* war, a response to the aggression of Russia and its Western allies. Because the 'hearts and minds' in the First World War, which from 1916 became more and more a 'total' war, *did* matter, this elite is important.

This chapter, consciously one-sided, focuses on this intellectual and cultural elite in Germany. It addresses the question to what extent the German nation, as a secular entity, was sacralized during the First World War and how attitudes changed over the course of the war. The starting point is that 'religion' has several functions and that 'politics' – in this case, the German nation during the First World War – can adopt some of those functions. As the Swiss historian Philippe Burrin, among others, has made clear, politics and religion share many common features.[9] For its believers, religion gives meaning to life and death, answers to ineradicable metaphysical questions and direction to human action. It can mobilize 'hearts and minds', makes a clear distinction between 'good' and 'evil', provides comfort, security and 'identity', and creates unity and a feeling of solidarity and community. In this chapter I will focus on this last aspect, the feeling of 'belonging together', which initially was clearly the dominant feeling among the 'believers' in the German nation under the conditions of war, instability and crisis. In this way I link up with Emilio Gentile's description of a 'religion of politics' as 'a sacralized secular entity inspiring faith, devotion, and togetherness among believers'.[10] My argument also connects with the approach of Emile Durkheim (in 1912) to regard religion mainly as societal 'cement'. This functionalist approach asserts, in the words of Gentile, that religion is able

> to elevate people beyond themselves and have them live a superior life in the collectivity to which they belong. Religion is the condition in which the individual [...] transcends himself or herself through deep involvement in the collectivity to which he or she belongs as a result of shared beliefs. [...] The divine is the society itself, and society venerates itself.[11]

The concepts of 'community' and 'collectivity' will play a crucial role in the first, and largest, part of the chapter, which is mainly devoted to 'the Spirit of 1914', that is, the war enthusiasm of German intellectuals in particular. In this context special attention will be paid to the specific idea of a German *Volksgemeinschaft* (literally 'people's community'). The second part of the chapter will address the disillusion with the war. Soon after the armed conflict began, the war turned out to be a divisive element in Germany: nationalism not only integrated but also polarized the German people. I will try to explain why the German nation experienced difficulties in functioning as a secular religion and in integrating its people during the First World War. In the conclusion I will also try to make clear how and why the Nazis tried to construct a line of continuity between the experiences of 1933 and 1914, using the concept of *Volksgemeinschaft*.

The 'Spirit of 1914' and the German *Volksgemeinschaft*

What is particularly remarkable at the outbreak of the war is the explicitly *religious* language in which it was described. For many intellectuals the German nation at war seemed to give meaning to life. For them the nation seemed to embody a kind of identity, unity, sanctity, sacrifice and solidarity. Germany was flooded with a wave of countless pamphlets, articles, poems and books in which intellectuals wrote about the German 'mission' (*Sendung*) or 'crusade'. 'We have to follow this crusade in the service of the *Weltgeist* through till the end', professor of political economy Johann Plenge wrote. 'God wants it. For the salvation of us

and the world'.[12] Another economist, Werner Sombart, wrote in his
famous war book *Traders and Heroes* (1915) about the Germans as the
'chosen people'.[13] For some the First World War was an experience of
salvation, the meaning and goal of history; others described the war in
religious terms like rebirth, redemption or revelation. Hearing the first
gunshots, the Jewish philosopher Martin Buber wrote that he did not
know 'what' it was, 'just that it was annihilation [...], and – purification
of the mind. [...] for a while I lived overwhelmed and *relieved*'.[14]

How is this war enthusiasm in the German intellectual world to be
explained? What is striking in almost all primary sources is the feeling
of extreme happiness about the *national unity* the war brought about.
Many intellectuals had the feeling that the ranks were finally closing and
that Germany seemed to be united as *one* people. To the intellectuals
the war meant the union of the poles of 'spirit' (*Geist*) and 'power'
(*Macht*), which had thus far been separated. The mission to propagate
German *Kultur* was impossible without political-military power, but,
conversely, military power was also dependent on cultural and ideological
motivations. As the historian Friedrich Meinecke wrote in August 1914,
'The days of alienation between culture [*Kultur*] and politics, which
was so noticeable in us during the last decades, are over'.[15] And the
theologian Ernst Troeltsch stated in his 'Ideas of 1914' that 'The new
idealism [...] has recognized the military, political, technical and social
effort as its material, which is just as dead without spirit as the spirit
is empty without material.'[16] That's why many wrote enthusiastically
about the unity which had emerged since August 1914. 'One notices',
Friedrich Meinecke wrote in a letter of 1 September 1914, 'that our
people in no time have coalesced into one single personality'.[17] And
the philosopher Max Scheler wrote in his widely read *Genius des Krieges
und der deutsche Krieg* (1915), 'We were no longer what we had been for
such a long time: alone! The broken lifeline [*Lebenskontakt*] between the
levels: individual – people – nation – world – God was closed in one
moment'.[18] For many intellectuals the German nation turned out to
be an excellent social cement, which created a feeling of mutual solidarity and common destiny and ethics. The new national *Gemeinschaft*
(community) offered a sense of security and a common aim. Dedication
to the nation gave meaning to life to the extent that during the war
the devotion or sacrifice of one's own life was regarded as rewarding.
Max Weber wrote in 1915 about the *meaning* which war could give to
human existence. Interestingly in light of our theme of the 'sacralization of politics', he stated that in times of war the terrain of politics can
become a direct competitor to religious ethics. War, according to Weber,

can release a pathos and a feeling of community, which bring with them an unconditional spirit of sacrifice and submission. War breaks through the natural relations and sparks off a massive feeling of love for all those who are threatened. Through war death becomes a meaningful event because one 'can know to *believe*: that he dies "for" something'.[19] And in a lecture of August 1916 Weber said that at home one dies 'of' something, on the battlefield 'for' something.[20]

Weber's colleague and friend, the sociologist Georg Simmel (1858–1918), pointed out that in times of turmoil and harrowing experiences – such as war – the distinction between the individual and the collective seems to disappear. Simmel wrote in 1914 that the individual is swallowed up into the whole and feels responsible for it. Thus life takes on a higher meaning because all thoughts and feelings are connected to a 'supra-individual totality'.[21] The war met the individual's need to get totally absorbed into the whole. Marianne Weber, Max Weber's wife, even pathetically wrote in February 1915, 'We have become a people, and those standing here are my brothers [...]. Hot love rises in me [...] I want to destroy myself in this community'.[22] Similarly, the historian Otto von Gierke wrote in August 1914, 'For a time I seemed to lose my individual personality. A higher patriotic individuality had taken full possession of the consciousness of all its members. I had seen the "spirit of the people" [*Volksgeist*]'.[23] Such descriptions refer to, in Gentile's words, the 'inexpressible spiritual experience that cannot be understood rationally and occurs in the presence of the *numinous*'.[24] These 'mystical' experiences, however, were rather rare in Germany during the war and were mostly restricted to the first months and to the intellectual elite.

The Internal Division of Society and the Problem of Modernity on the Eve of the War

The joy over national unity in the summer of 1914 must be seen against the background of the deep political, social and religious divisions within the Second German Empire. Bismarck may have united Germany in 1871, but he did not unite the Germans themselves. The gulf between the middle class and the workers remained huge. The working class, the 'red danger', was regarded as a revolutionary and internationally oriented group that was seen as a direct threat to the political and social system. This gap was widened when Bismarck proclaimed the discriminatory Socialist Laws (1878–90), which would be a heavy burden on the political and social relations of the next decades. When, despite strong opposition, the Social Democratic Party (SPD) became the largest political party in the national parliament in 1912, they would remain 'political outsiders'. In addition to this political division there was a deep religious contrast between the Protestants and the Catholics, very much enhanced by the *Kulturkampf* (1871–78), the fight by Bismarck and the modern secular state, supported by liberals, against the Catholic Church, which was depicted as 'backward' and as an 'enemy within'. Church property was confiscated and clergy were arrested. The Catholic lawyer and publicist Julius Bachem even compared the state's actions to the persecution of the early Christians in the Roman Empire.[25] Roman Catholics, one-third of the population, did not hold key positions in German society (the army, bureaucracy etc.). They didn't identify very much with the Second German Empire, which they saw as a largely *Protestant* empire, and so they did not erect statues honouring Bismarck or the Emperor. Thus, the German Empire was to a considerable extent a society divided into different religious, social and cultural 'segments'. When the war broke out in 1914, the Catholics and Social Democrats were nevertheless loyal to the German state. The rejoicing over the – presumed – end of the internal political and religious division of Germany was intense: now everybody seemed to struggle for the same, common goal.

Another factor accounting for the war enthusiasm was the feeling that the war would offer a solution to the so-called 'problem of modernity'.[26] Cultural writings around 1900 frequently lamented that modern German culture was not bound together by a single connecting principle. Many members of the *Bildungsbürgertum* complained that modern, industrial society lacked *common* ethics and beliefs and a spiritual bond. That's why they were searching for the 'cement' that could bind together the individuals in such a fragmented society. It is in this context that one should see the great interest in religion around 1900, as religion was regarded as an important factor of integration and a source of common values and standards. Georg Simmel, for example, stated in his work *Die Religion* (1906) that religion had an important function not only for the individual but also for society itself, as a kind of social cement. He was convinced that society could not exist without religion; the belief in a 'whole' (*Gesamtheit*), according to Simmel, was 'one of the strongest ties, which holds society together'. The human desire for integration emerged where there was a lack of unity – that is, in social life. In this way God could provide 'the unity of existence'.[27] It is no coincidence that Simmel's view on religion resembles that of his French contemporary Emile Durkheim (1858–1917). Both described the fundamental lack of coherence in the complex, industrializing societies of around 1900: modernity creates feelings of disintegration, uncertainty and the loss of identity.

Again, in the work of Max Weber, the trenchant observer of the Wilhelmine Empire, this problem of modernity plays a crucial role. His diagnosis of modernity focused on the 'disenchantment' of the world, which means that there are no public, generally acknowledged values anymore: values compete with each other; there is no hierarchy, just 'struggle' (*Kampf*). At the same time he witnessed the countless attempts of his contemporaries to *re-enchant* the world: life should again get coherence, colour and a new content. Through the disappearance of a coherent Christian worldview the need for *new religions* arose, especially in times of crisis. Art and science, but also socialism, were to develop as substitute religions (*Ersatzreligionen*), which were expected to bring salvation. Therefore, in his famous speech 'Science as Vocation' (1917) Weber stated that the 'ancient gods' had risen from their graves again and had resumed their eternal struggle.[28]

Significantly, Weber, himself an impassioned nationalist, considered the German *nation* the most important substitute religion of his time. Many expected the war to bring a feeling of relief and to stir up unknown energies. As a nationalistic leader stated in 1913, 'Let us regard war as holy, like the purifying force of fate, for it will awaken in our people all that is great and ready for selfless sacrifice, while it cleanses our soul of the mire of petty egotistical concerns'.[29] This quote not only contains religious language, like 'cleansing the soul' and 'selfless sacrifice', but also refers to the end of 'egotistical concerns': now everyone would become part of a *mental*, supra-individual entity, namely the nation. In many cases one witnesses the expectation that an end would come to the predominance of a 'materialist' culture. Condemnation of banal materialism had been dominant in the cultural criticism in Germany since around 1900.[30]

It is hard to imagine writings that expressed this cultural criticism and the hope of war as redemption from pessimism more clearly than the works of economist Werner Sombart (1863–1941). In his post-1900 writings, which were very well received by a great part of the *Bildungsbürgertum*, Sombart criticized modern culture and the material-ism of the masses, modern capitalism and technology, the estrangement of 'modern man' from nature and so forth – in short, the usual song of German cultural criticism around 1900. In the beginning of 1915 Sombart's very influential *Traders and Heroes* was published, which brought together several of the above-mentioned themes, including the cultural pessimism before the war, the hope for a renewal of German culture by a new *Volksgemeinschaft* and a clearly religious language, invoking sacrifice, salvation and rebirth. Chapter 11 was even called 'Redemption from Evil' ('Erlösung von dem Übel'). Sombart's book was permeated with the idea that, because of the war, every German was aware again of the existence of the community of the Germans (*Volksgemeinschaft*), 'the supra-individual, a whole, a life outside us: the people, the fatherland, the state'.[31]

The New *Volksgemeinschaft*

Thus, to intellectuals the war meant above all that Germany would form a united national community. The so-called *Burgfrieden*, a truce between all political parties at the beginning of the war, played an important role in this regard. Internal differences were to be resolved in order to create a closed front in the face of 'a world of enemies'. On 4 August 1914 Kaiser Wilhelm II addressed the members of the Reichstag, the German parliament, with the famous words, 'I no longer recognize parties, I know only Germans.'[32] These words would become the most memorable quotation of the whole war. In the late afternoon that same day all political parties, including the SPD, approved the war credits to finance the war; an 'Enabling Law' was also passed, by which the Reichstag almost eliminated itself. It had been anything but self-evident that the social democrats would be loyal to the German state rather than to their internationalist Marxist orientation. Only one week earlier the leadership of the SPD had mobilized well over 100,000 demonstrators in greater Berlin against the war.[33] One important reason for the social democratic approval of the war credits and Enabling Law was their conviction that Germany was fighting a defensive war against the aggression of the Russian reactionary autocracy, those 'half barbarian hordes';[34] other reasons were the hope of political reforms and the end of their isolation. The relief of the government and large parts of the population at the SPD's expression of solidarity with the nation was nonetheless great. The approval seemed to put an end to the SPD's role of opposition to the state. Many were convinced that a new era in German history had begun. In the first month of the war the enthusiasm captured many, especially from the elite. The so-called 'August experience' refers to the many war volunteers, the countless war sermons, people dancing on market squares and the many thousands of war poems that were composed.[35] In this respect, though, Germany was no exception: war euphoria was also to be observed in the big cities of Great Britain, France and Russia.

In the first months of the war anything that could spread discord was forbidden; for example, all anti-social democratic, anti-Catholic and anti-Semitic organizations were banned.[36] Workers were able to organize themselves through the recognition of trade unions as legitimate organizations. Soon after the outbreak of the war soldiers and students were allowed to read social democratic literature in military barracks and schools. As Alfred Riedl, a pacifist author, joyfully recorded in his diary on 20 August 1914, '*Vorwärts* can be sold in Prussian train stations! That is the most unbelievable event of this era, which will overturn all that exists.' And the liberal journalist Hellmut von Gerlach wrote in December 1914 that in Germany 'there no longer existed first- and second-class citizens'.[37] Also at the war front there were signs that national integration was succeeding. As Alfred Zweig, a Jew, wrote in a December 1914 letter, 'in the field there are no Catholics, no Protestants, no Jews, no Centrists, no Social Democrats [...] but only Germans, as our *Kaiser* has already proclaimed'.[38]

An infinite number of examples can demonstrate that during the first months of the war many were carried away by the feeling of unity and solidarity. For the argument of this volume it is important explicitly to note that this sentiment was not only imposed from above by the government by means of propaganda: the feeling of unity was, initially, authentic and also came 'from below'. But, as argued before, the enthusiasm about the 'spirit of 1914' was largely limited to the intellectual and cultural elite, including professors, authors, artists and journalists (though there was a significant distinction between their *public* statements and the less ecstatic, sometimes even terrified *private* manifestations in diaries and letters).[39] Small though this group was, they were very active and had a huge audience, especially at the beginning of the war. The many lectures they gave were very well attended. For example, in Munich no fewer than 3000 to 3500 people came to these talks.[40] Possibly the most popular professor in Germany, Rudolf Eucken, professor of philosophy and Nobel Prize-winner for Literature in 1908, gave 36 lectures in the first year of the war. In Nuremberg he spoke to several thousand on two successive nights till after midnight.[41]

In numerous articles, lectures and pamphlets the intellectuals described the feeling of unity, fraternity and equality as a newly created *Volksgemeinschaft*.[42] Again, it is revealing that the language about the new national unity and feeling of togetherness was very religiously coloured. The Berlin Germanic scholar Gustav Roethe, for example, publicly talked about the 'miracle' of unity; through German mobilization 'salvation' had come. Anyone who had experienced the days between 1 and 4 August 'could not lose the holy gain again. The wonderful experience, it binds together, [...] and it will purify and chasten us'.[43]

The Berlin professor of philosophy, Alois Riehl, stated in 1914, 'Never was a people so united as in those early, unforgettable August days [...]. Each of us felt we lived for the whole and that the whole lived in all of us [...]. The whole population was possessed of the truth and reality of a religious power'.[44] The sacralization of politics can hardly be more clearly expressed.

The new *Volksgemeinschaft* that had come into being was conceived as the end of – and as a reaction to – the deep social, political and religious division associated with the industrial class society of the German Empire before the war. The essence of the *Volksgemeinschaft* is the organic unity of the people and the subordination of the individual to the community. The concept, used since the 1860s by anti-Semites and Zionists alike, was picked up around 1900 by the German Youth Movement, and after that increasingly used by liberal imperialists and *völkisch* militarists.[45] But the right wing of the SPD also used the concept of the *Volksgemeinschaft*, namely as the integration of the SPD into the nation. The social democrat Konrad Haenisch, for instance, still found in 1916 that the social democratic approval of the war credits symbolized the party's loyalty to 'the *Volksgemeinschaft* in misery and death'.[46]

Interestingly, the idea – or better, the myth – of the *Volksgemeinschaft* played an important role not only on the home front but also on the front lines, for example during the notorious Battle of Langemarck on 10 November 1914, where about 2000 youthful, inexperienced German war volunteers did not stand a chance against the machine guns of the enemy. The many students and schoolboys, mainly of bourgeois origin, were just other ranks. They did not experience this as a kind of degradation but as a result of the August awakening. Here for the first time a connection seemed to be brought about beyond class boundaries in the sense of an empathically underlined *Volksgemeinschaft*. Langemarck would be symbolic not only of youthfulness and self-sacrifice, but also of the levelling of social differences and the fraternization of the social classes in a united community (*Solidargemeinschaft*).[47]

An extremely popular book during the First World War idealized this good-fellowship at the front (*Frontkameradschaft*), which was connected to the Youth Movement's philosophy of life. The war volunteer Walter Flex (1887–1917) paints in his autobiographic war story *The Wanderer between Both Worlds: An Experience of the War* (1917) (*Der Wanderer zwischen beiden Welten. Ein Kriegserlebnis*) the friendship between the fallen Ernst Wurche, member of the *Wandervogelbewegung*, and the narrator. Ernst Wurche is the idealized picture of the 'new man', a protagonist of a new idealism and spirit of sacrifice enhanced by the war, who is at home in 'both worlds', heaven and earth, life and death. The indisputable message of Flex's writings is that the individual should make himself subordinate to the organic *Volksgemeinschaft* and should be absorbed by the community and, ultimately, by death. Walter Flex himself died a 'hero's death' in 1917 on the eastern front. *Der Wanderer*, a clear example of aestheticization of the war, was a bestseller, perhaps even the most successful book by a German author during the First World War, and would become one of the most popular books in twentieth-century Germany.[48]

The subordination of the individual to the community is, along with fraternization among social classes, the second core element of the concept of the *Volksgemeinschaft*. This subordination can be directly connected to Wilhelmine cultural criticism. Many German intellectuals welcomed the values of self-sacrifice, fraternity, sharing and courage – as opposed to the values of the modern capitalist society, such as selfishness, materialism and individualism. This opposition has a long tradition in German history and can be connected to the idea of an allegedly deep – often very stereotypical – contrast between German *Kultur* and Western *Zivilization*, which had been influential since the end of the eighteenth century and culminated in the First World War and in works like Oswald Spengler's *The Decline of the West* (*Der Untergang des Abendlandes*, 1918/1922).[49] German *Kultur* stood for inner values and idealism, whereas the 'superficial' *Zivilization* of the French and, especially since the First World War, the British, stood for outer appearances and materialism. An important part of the contrast was between the German *Gemeinschaft* (community) and the Western *Gesellschaft* (modern society), which represented atomized individuals. The problem was, of course, that pre-war modern Germany itself was more and more imbued with Western, capitalist values. But the war seemed to solve this problem, as the sociologist Emil Lederer concisely addressed in 1915: 'during the days of mobilization the society [*Gesellschaft*] which had existed transformed itself into a community [*Gemeinschaft*]'.[50] It is no coincidence that many German intellectuals described the First World War as a *Kulturkrieg*, conflating and inflating several stereotypes of the contrast.

The antithesis between *Kultur* and *Zivilization* also included a very important political contrast, namely between the 'ideas of 1914' and the 'ideas of 1789'. The German 'ideas of 1914' entailed a harmonious, organic *Volksgemeinschaft*, including all classes, and were directed against the Western idea of a democratic society.[51] That Germany 'must consider itself fortunate' that it avoided the 'civil revolution' of 1789 is one of the messages of Thomas Mann's essay 'Thoughts in Wartime' of 1914.[52] The 'ideas of 1914' were celebrated not only as the antithesis of French and Western democratic and liberal ideas but also as an expression of a real German revolution, comparable to the French Revolution 125 years before, through which a new era of history would begin. As Johann Plenge, not without self-confidence, stated about the mission of German *Kultur* in the world, 'in us lies the twentieth century. No matter how the war ends, we are the ideal people. Our ideas will be the goals of humanity'.[53] Plenge, an economist and sociologist who coined the term the 'ideas of 1914', wanted an anti-capitalist, anti-liberal *Volksgemeinschaft* of a 'national socialism' without conflicts. The fusion of these two powerful currents – nationalism and socialism – would overcome the antagonisms of modern class society. As the German historian Hans-Ulrich Wehler makes clear, these ideas of a 'German socialism' were to be a 'breeding ground' for the Nazis.[54]

Part of the 'ideas of 1914' was also a specific German conception of 'freedom' (*deutsche Freiheit*), which needed to be defended against the unbounded liberalism and 'vulgar' democracy of the Western world. At stake was again the victory of German *Kultur* over Western *Zivilization*. German 'freedom' meant the supra-individual bond and voluntary adaptation from inner conviction and self-restraint to the whole of the nation. The subordination of the individual to the collective was essential because in a true *Volksgemeinschaft*, which was seen as an organic unity, the interest of the people as a whole, rather than individual interests, reigned. This specific idea of German 'freedom' was represented by the theologian and historian Ernst Troeltsch, who was one of the most popular professors in the German Empire and gave many lectures throughout the war. In his lecture presented in the autumn of 1915, 'The German Idea of Freedom', Troeltsch described German freedom as 'the free, conscious, dutiful submission [*Hingabe*] to [...] the whole'. German freedom, as opposed to French or Anglo-Saxon ideas of freedom, was more about duties than about rights. German freedom was 'not equality' but 'service of the individual' to the whole, part of the German 'mystery of the state' (*Staatsmystik*).[55] This idea of the primacy of the whole and the subservient role of the individual, here merely expressed by a moderate liberal intellectual and later *Vernunftrepublikaner*, was deepened by the war and would become very influential in modern German (and European) history. It contained the germs of modern collectivism and of the 'political religions' of the totalitarian states of the Interbellum period.[56]

The Reality of the War:
Polarization and Exclusion by Nationalism

As we have seen, the former 'inner enemies' were largely integrated into the German Empire at the beginning of the war: the government, for example, tried to prevent discrimination against social democrats, and in return the social democrats approved the war credits and trade unions forbade all strikes. Like the Catholics and the Jews, the socialists did not want to be seen as traitors to the Fatherland at the 'moment of truth'. As Hugo Haase, the leader of the SPD in parliament, stated in the Reichstag on 4 August, 'In the hour of danger we do not let our own fatherland down'.[57]

This internal peace, however, was not to last for very long. Soon after the armed conflict began and the war showed its real face, internal tensions resurfaced. After four years of war, Germany would actually be more divided and strife-torn than ever before and became involved in revolutionary disturbances. The contrast between August 1914 and November 1918 could not be bigger. During the war the problem of German disunity was brought to light very clearly. In the course of the war the still much-proclaimed 'spirit of 1914' would become more a myth than a reality. The celebrated and idealized *Volksgemeinschaft* of a united German people soon proved to *exclude* certain groups, like social democrats and Jews, as 'inner enemies'.[58]

Thus, German nationalism not only integrated but also divided the German people.[59] Why? There are several reasons. The first one has to do with the process of radicalization during the war, which led to tensions between militaristic nationalists who formulated increasingly extreme war aims and the wish for peace and social reform by the largest part of the population. In the course of the war the right-nationalistic camp in society and army became increasingly influential regarding politics and warfare – at the expense of civil politics – particularly after August 1916, when Paul von Hindenburg and Erich Ludendorff took over the army leadership from Erich von Falkenhayn. There is no doubt that in reality Ludendorff (1865–1937) was the real leader of this Third Supreme Army Command and was largely responsible for many important military *and* political decisions after August 1916, including the unrestricted submarine warfare (January 1917); the dismissal of the moderate Chancellor Bethmann Hollweg in the summer of 1917; the harsh conditions of the Peace of Brest–Litovsk (March 1918), which served as a basis for plans for further expansion into the east; the great, unsuccessful, Spring Offensive of 1918; and the attempt to transfer responsibility for the lost war onto the moderate political parties. Under his radical leadership Germany became a near-dictatorship for two years and attempted to wage a total war (though not very successfully).[60] Ludendorff tried to mobilize all material and human resources, based on the idea 'that during the war the power of every individual belongs to the state', as he wrote in his war memoirs.[61] Considering the rife dissension within Germany it is important to note that Ludendorff pursued a rigorous policy towards the 'inner enemies', like the social democrats. In the opinion of the later theorist of *Der totale Krieg* (1935), maintaining a united home front was crucial to winning a total war. Therefore every possible inner opponent should be eliminated. Ludendorff's importance for the development of Germany during the war and the early Weimar Republic (where he was involved in the Kapp–Lüttwitz coup of 1920 and in Hitler's coup of 1923) can hardly be overestimated.[62]

Although a key figure, Ludendorff of course was not the only person responsible for the extreme war aims. From the beginning of the war Germany had been divided between 'annexionists' and 'moderates'. The first group consisted of rich industrialists from the Rhineland, the radical nationalist Pan German League (*Alldeutscher Verband*), a large section of the academics and intellectuals, National Liberals and Conservatives and the majority of the Catholic *Zentrumpartei*. On the opposite side were the 'moderates', consisting of the majority of the social democrats and the left-liberal *Fortschrittspartei*.[63] The annexionists asserted themselves through a wave of memoranda. From the beginning of the war, Heinrich Class, the radical leader of the Pan German League, had let it be known that Germany should focus on a policy of expansion, including the 'germanisation' or even 'ethnic cleansing' of the subdued population.[64] In May 1915 six big economic pressure groups of industrialists and agrarians presented an important memorandum with a very ambitious programme of annexations, including of Russia and the Baltic states.[65] A clear manifestation of the radicalization of the political and military climate of Germany during the war was the founding of the German Fatherland Party (Deutsche Vaterlandspartei) in September 1917, warmly welcomed by Ludendorff's Third Supreme Army Command.[66] The Fatherland Party was a right-radical mass organization, which, on the one hand, favoured increasingly extreme war aims and opposed a peace policy and, on the other hand, wanted to obstruct domestic political reforms, like the demand for equal suffrage in Prussia.[67] Monopolizing the concept of 'Fatherland' at the expense of the social democrats and the Catholics, the attitude of the *Vaterlandspartei* meant a clean break with the *Burgfrieden*.

The two camps of radicals and moderates drifted further apart during the war, with the radicals losing popular support. As the mayor of Nuremberg, Otto Gessler, wrote in the summer of 1917, 'The people have had enough, nothing matters to them anymore. They lack an understanding what a lost war will bring [...]. Those who support strong war aims are at present the most hated people in the world'.[68]

So, instead of bringing unity the First World War only increased the tensions within Germany: not just between the radicals and moderates but also between the rich and the poor, the war front and the home front, men and women, town and countryside, consumers and producers, the establishment and the outsiders, and also within the left-wing political camp itself.[69]

A second reason for the polarization of German society during the war was the gap between the rich and the poor. Undoubtedly, the workers in Germany bore the heaviest burden and suffered most, both on the war front and the home front.[70] 'Ordinary men' were increasingly suffering from hunger and cold. It is estimated that nearly 500,000 people died on the home front from the consequences of undernourishment.[71] Yet a small elite group hardly suffered at all and continued to live in luxury: 'the trains to the sea side resorts at the Baltic Sea were full', a so-called mood-report noted.[72] Unsurprisingly, the producers of weapons and munitions, like Krupp and Stinnes, took advantage of the war on an enormous scale. The big industrial enterprises were supported and given preferential treatment by the German state.

Against this background of increasing exhaustion and protracted hardships among the lower social classes combined with extreme war profits, powerless state authorities and an arrogant military elite deaf to the real needs of the population, resistance against the German Empire grew. For example, on 28 May 1915 1500 women demonstrated in front of the Reichstag in Berlin chanting the slogans, 'We want peace and our men back! We want bread for our children!'[73] And a pastor who had been enthusiastic in 1914 cynically wrote in his diary on 16 October 1915 that 'the famed German unity consists of one class enriching itself at the expense of the other'.[74] From the spring of 1916 the number of protests, food riots and strikes rose (evidence, by the way, that Germany was at that time still far from being a dictatorial state).[75] The rejection of the war and the growing anger towards the state were expressed in many letters and diaries. In the army itself the class distinctions, expressed in the privileges for arrogant officers, for example, were very apparent and diametrically opposed to the melodrama of the national 'community of the trenches' (*Schützengrabengemeinschaft*).[76] The initial feelings of national unity and loyalty were increasingly undermined, and the existing political order in Germany, unlike in France and England, increasingly lost its legitimacy.[77] As a result the German nation was no longer able to function as a secular religion, elevating and integrating the people, as it had in August 1914. As the German historian Benjamin Ziemann put it, 'The national language [...] lost even more than the religious language its persuasiveness in the course of the war'.[78]

Conversely, socialism became more attractive, including, from 1916, among soldiers as well.[79] It is no coincidence that a revolution broke out at the end of the war. The yearning for peace and the many domestic problems and tensions, including hunger and the long-standing demand for political and social reforms, culminated in a dramatic outburst in November 1918. As Walther Rathenau wrote in a letter on 8 November 1918, 'What has happened, I've seen coming for four long years, but every warning was in vain.'[80] This is not the place to deal with this revolution extensively.[81] For the sake of the argument of this chapter it is sufficient to note that the revolution produced severe internal disruption on two fronts. First, as a consequence of the revolution Germany got a government under socialist leadership, which encountered much resistance among the old conservative elite, including industrialists, army officers, high bureaucrats and the like. The birth of the Weimar Republic, in the midst of revolution and defeat, could hardly be more unfortunately timed, and its many opponents took advantage of the situation. Second, during the revolution the split within the socialist camp itself was tragically exposed. In April 1917 the USPD (Unabhängige Sozialistische Partei Deutschlands), the Independent Socialist Party of Germany, was founded. This heterogeneous party, with Karl Liebknecht and Rosa Luxemburg in its ranks, wanted an immediate end to the war, whereas the 'mother-party', the (M)SPD, pursued a negotiated peace but remained loyal to the German civilian and military authorities. Friedrich Ebert, since November 1918 the moderate social democratic leader of the Council of People's Commissars and a fierce opponent of a radical Bolshevik revolution, wanted to avoid chaos and introduce full parliamentary democracy. He was severely damaged by the dissension within the socialist camp. Tensions dramatically exploded in January 1919, when an insurrection of 'Spartacists', the radical left-wing minority within the USPD, was ruthlessly suppressed by pro-government troops and the contra-revolutionary Free Corps, under responsibility of the SPD (Gustav Noske), which was extremely suspicious of any 'Bolshevik threat'; Karl Liebknecht and Rosa Luxemburg were brutally murdered. Significantly, the SPD-led government appealed to the myth of the dangerous 'internal enemy'.[82] The accusation of 'betrayal' of the revolutionary cause and the rift within the socialist camp would place heavy burdens on the Weimar Republic, which was attacked from left- and right-extremists from the beginning.

Finally, in an atmosphere of polarization and radicalization images of inner enemies can emerge, often leading to the exclusion of groups deemed not to belong to the 'true nation' or who are under suspicion of disloyalty to the nation and representing a harmful element. This pattern can be amply demonstrated by the increasing stigmatization and exclusion of a small but important minority, namely the Jews. Of course this is a burning question, particularly given their terrible fate in the Third Reich. At the very beginning of the war most Jews were enthu- siastic: out of the 550,000 Jewish inhabitants in Germany (*c*.1 per cent of the population), 10,000 Jews presented themselves as volunteers; about 100,000 Jews served as soldiers. Most Jews clearly wanted to prove themselves as 'genuine Germans', sometimes even 'overfulfilling' their duties. During the first months anti-Semitic utterances were forbidden by the state, and, uniquely for Germany, about 2000 Jews were even appointed officers.[83] However, very soon old, latent anti-Semitic feel- ings and stereotypes resurfaced. Jews were depicted as war-profiteers and were accused of speculation and usury. But even more serious was the accusation that the Jews were refusing to fight. In October 1916 the Prussian Ministry of War conducted the infamous Jewish census (*Judenzählung*) to investigate whether 'enough' Jews were dying for the 'fatherland'. This clearly discriminatory census marked a serious rift in the relationship between Jews and 'Germans', probably even a turning point in Jewish self-perception.[84] Diaries and letters show that many Jews who had had the illusion of being integrated into German society were extremely disappointed. During the last two years of the war Jews were increasingly portrayed as the 'internal enemies' of the German people. The propaganda of the Pan German League, led by Heinrich Class, intensified the witch-hunt against the Jews. At the end of the war the leaders of the Pan German League realized that the 'Jewish Question' was the most successful means to get support from the masses.[85] In April 1918 there was a blockade of the border against Eastern Jews, and in that same year, for the first time during the war, there arose fear of pogroms. The Jews were becoming what they had been so often before: scapegoats for all disasters. Both the military defeat and the revolution of November 1918 were portrayed as Jewish conspiracies. In this context, the impact of the post-war myth of the 'stab in the back', the legend that the German army was defeated not by the enemy on the battlefield but by the treacherous civilians on the home front, especially Jews (and socialists and others), can hardly be overestimated.[86] Up until the collapse of the Third Reich in 1945, Hitler and his accomplices would obsessively refer again and again to the treacherous 'November criminals', who needed to be eliminated to prevent Germany from suffering another defeat. In *Mein Kampf* (1925–26) Hitler had written that had 12,000 to 15,000 Jews been killed by 'poison gas' in the First World War, this might have saved the lives of one million 'decent' Germans.[87]

Conclusion

'But where is the mood of August 1914?', Karl Hampe, a German medievalist and professor in Heidelberg, wrote in his diary on 8 July 1916.[88] The hope of the German, educated middle class for a transformation of relationships among Germans at the beginning of the war, the hope for a real *Volksgemeinschaft* without class boundaries in which all Germans belonged together, had not been realized. Quite the contrary. Germany came out of the war more divided than ever before, the result of a process during the war itself, which has often been obscured by the preoccupation with the war's outcome, the defeat and the revolution of 1918. Despite all the propaganda over the 'spirit of 1914', the internal developments in Germany throughout the war were marked by increasing polarization and the exclusion of several groups. Thus, in the course of the war a clear pattern emerged. In the beginning the *Volksgemeinschaft* had 'democratic' features because everybody seemed to be included and seen as equal; in that sense the *Volksgemeinschaft* can be related to a 'civil religion'. But during the course of the war the *Volksgemeinschaft* took on an increasingly exclusive, fundamentalist and intolerant nature, and in that sense became more and more a 'political religion', as defined by Emilio Gentile.[89]

Consequently, the German 'nation' no longer functioned as a unifying, integrating force, as it had in August 1914. That was a reality that even the German intellectuals could not deny. The German nation was not able to function as a sacralized entity and to elevate the people (*Volk*) as a whole any longer because the German nation and people were, more than ever, totally fragmented. It is no coincidence that military chaplains stopped speaking about war aims and nationalism in their sermons.[90] The propaganda from above, designed to improve the morale of the population, failed because most people understood that perseverance (*Durchhalten*) was not in their interest. The war had created quite the opposite of 'shared beliefs' and a feeling of 'belonging together'. Most people just wanted an end to the war (and the hunger, cold and so forth) and were not willing to sacrifice their lives to the German nation any longer. They did not regard that nation as a kind of supra-individual and sacred abstract entity, bigger than themselves and worth dying for, but rather as a group of concrete state or military authorities who were mainly seen as corrupt, incompetent, greedy and unresponsive to the people's real needs. In sum, the German nation as a secular religion had almost totally failed to integrate the German people. 'The' German nation was not able to mobilize the 'hearts and minds' of the population any longer; its religious aura and belief in transcendent moral purposes had disappeared.

And yet, after the war, it is remarkable that the idea of a German *Volksgemeinschaft* still – or again – held uncommon appeal, as Jeffrey Verhey and Stefan Bruendel have made clear.[91] This persistence testifies to the power of myths in history, particularly in times of crisis. Interestingly, in the 1920s the hope of a new *Volksgemeinschaft* can be found throughout all political spectra: anarchists, Catholics, Jews, Protestants, social democrats, liberal democrats, conservatives and national socialists.[92] But, as in the First World War, the meaning of the concept varied from inclusion to exclusion. The liberal Theodor Heuss, for example, who later became the first president of the German Federal Republic, hoped in 1919 that the Weimar Republic would 'open the door to a new feeling of community'.[93] To the Reichs President, the social democrat Friedrich Ebert, the *Volksgemeinschaft* was a symbol of inner unity and national solidarity, beyond class egotisms;[94] and liberals like Hugo Preuss hoped to build a new *Volksgemeinschaft* with a new constitution and democratic structures.[95] By contrast, the conservatives took the view that the equality of a modern, democratic civil society *atomized* the people – at the expense of the good of the whole. This contrast of an allegedly atomized democratic society versus a unified *Volksgemeinschaft*, which had its roots in a long tradition, was to become in the 1920s and 1930s an influential view on which the radical nationalists built and added an ethnic principle. They placed all their hope in the 'people', now understood as a *völkisch*, ethnic community, using radical principles of exclusion. After the disappearance of the old form of government, the huge political, social and economic crises of the first years of the Weimar Republic, the loss of German territories and colonies and so on, only the German 'people' could guarantee continuity and homogeneity, the nationalists argued. In order to preserve the people from disintegration, all the 'unsound' elements, such as the Jews, should be excluded.

The *Volksgemeinschaft* also played an important role in the ideology of the national socialists and was presented as a community of unity, solidarity and fellowship, transcending class distinctions. The new Nazi-*Volksgemeinschaft* represented modern collectivism, making the individual totally subordinate to the community. In his 'Appeal to the Nation' of 15 July 1932, Hitler, significantly, referred to the victory of a religious community and the defeat of the divided class society: 'A religious community of people has come into being, which will slowly defeat the prejudices of the insanity of classes [*Klassenwahnsinn*] and arrogance of social position [*Klassendünkel*]'. Since 1919 Hitler's predecessors had not been able to achieve unity: 'they played people off against one another, the city against the countryside [...], the manual worker against the white-collar worker, the people of Bayern against the Prussians, the Catholics against the Protestants, and so forth and the other way round'.[96] So, Nazi propaganda created the illusion of a new unity of the German people, which, after so many years of the social and political chaos of the Weimar Republic, was now striving for a single righteous cause, a 'national awakening'.[97] The reference to the *Volksgemeinschaft* by Joseph Goebbels, the prospective Nazi Minister of Propaganda, on 30 January 1933 is revealing. On this day of Hitler's assumption of power Goebbels commented on the radio while witnessing a huge torchlight procession from the balcony of the Berlin Reichskanzlei, 'We are all immensely happy! [...] For me it is moving to see how in this city [...] really the whole people rises, how the people are marching below, workers and civilians and farmers and students and soldiers – *one* big Volksgemeinschaft'.[98]

Interestingly, the Nazis tried to construct a line of continuity between 1933 and August 1914 by referring to the renewal of the unity of the people.[99] In that context the 'Day of Potsdam', 21 March 1933, was important because at this ceremonial opening of parliament the unity of the old Prussia and the new Germany was very consciously constructed. In his official speech the Prussian minister Otto Dibelius underlined 'that this event meant a "rebirth of the spirit of 1914"', and now 'we all want to be once again what God has created us to be, we all want to be Germans'.[100] This enthusiasm over a new unity of the German people was the essence of the similarity between the 'spirit' of 1914 and 1933 and was, like a religion, able to mobilize the hearts and minds of many people again. As Claudia Koonz has argued, to most Germans the 'positive' message of the new solidarity of the German people was a more compelling reason to support the NSDAP than was the motivation of anti-Semitism.[101]

Thus, the Nazis seized upon a fundamental problem of modern German history, namely the lack of internal unity, which they promised to solve definitively. This issue of 'fragmentation' becomes very clear, for example, in a speech of Joseph Goebbels, 'The new tasks of German culture', on 15 November 1933:

> The purpose of the revolution which we have carried out is the forging of the German nation into a single people. This has been the longing of all good Germans for two thousand years. Attempts have been made through legal processes countless times; each of these attempts failed. Only the fervent explosion of the national passions of our people made it possible. [...] What was not possible, and often not even wanted, from above, we have achieved from below. The German people, once the most fragmented in the world, atomized into its component parts and hence condemned to impotence as a world power, [...] rose up in a unique demonstration of its sense of national strength.[102]

The success of the Nazis can partly be explained by their attempt to fill this gap with their new (political) religion. They tried to forge a *Volksgemeinschaft* by creating the illusion of belonging together through organizations like 'Kraft durch Freude' ('Strength through Joy') and 'Winterhilfswerk' ('Winter Aid').[103] Interestingly, the support and obedience of most people in the Third Reich are to be explained less by the terror, fear and violence characteristic of totalitarian regimes in the Interbellum period than by mainly 'neutral' religious categories, such as the promise of unity, salvation and redemption, the new bond of the 'belief' after so much confusion, the leader who is looked upon as a Messiah and the important role of rituals and celebrations as unifying forces. But a crucial difference with 'August 1914' is that the *Volksgemeinschaft* of the Third Reich was explicitly defined in racial terms and that the exclusion of the 'inner enemies', such as the Jews (and the communists and so forth), was far more radical than in the First World War: violence was seen as a legitimate weapon in the battle against such enemies. The political religion of the totalitarian Nazi regime with its ideal of a racially pure society and a racial empire ultimately ended in a ruthless war of massive destruction (*Vernichtungskrieg*) and in a genocide of the Jewish people.

Notes

1. Quoted in Jeffrey Verhey, *The Spirit of 1914: Militarism, Myth and Mobilization in Germany* (Cambridge, 2000), 5. The quote of the conservative minister

Eduard Schwartz is from his speech 'Der Krieg als nationales Erlebnis' (October 1914).

2. Thomas Mann, 'Gedanken im Kriege', in idem, *Essays. Bd. 2: Politik*, ed. Hermann Kurzke (Frankfurt am Main, 1977), 23–37 (27). Mann won the Nobel Prize for Literature in 1929.
3. Thomas Mann, *Betrachtungen eines Unpolitischen* (Munich, 1988 [1918]), 509.
4. There are only a few exceptions, like Thomas Mann's brother, Heinrich Mann. For the reactions of the German artists, see Joes Segal, *Krieg als Erlösung. Die deutschen Kunstdebatten 1910–1918* (Munich, 1997). For the intellectuals, see Wolfgang J. Mommsen (ed.), *Kultur und Krieg. Die Rolle der Intellektuellen, Künstler und Schriftsteller im Ersten Weltkrieg* (Munich, 1996); Kurt Flasch, *Die geistige Mobilmachung. Die deutschen Intellektuellen und der Erste Weltkrieg. Ein Versuch* (Berlin, 2000); Alan Kramer, *Dynamic of Destruction: Culture and Mass Killing in the First World War* (Oxford, 2007), esp. 159–210. A very nice collection of primary sources is Peter Walther (ed.), *Endzeit Europa. Ein kollektives Tagebuch deutschsprachiger Schriftsteller, Künstler und Gelehrter im Ersten Weltkrieg* (Göttingen, 2008).
5. Ernst Toller, *Een jeugd in Duitsland* (Amsterdam, 1981), 46 (transl. of *Eine Jugend in Deutschland* [1933]).
6. Quoted in Marianne Weber, *Max Weber. Ein Lebensbild* (Munich, Zürich, 1989 [1926]), 530 ('*dieser Krieg ist gross und wunderbar*').
7. See Verhey's well-documented study, *Spirit*, esp. 1–114 (chs 1–3). See for more local studies which take the edge off the war enthusiasm of August 1914, Verhey, *Spirit*, 6–7.
8. Hans-Ulrich Wehler mentions the figure of 540,000–680,000 *Bildungsbürger* before 1914, only *c*.0.8 per cent of the population. See Wehler, *Deutsche Gesellschaftsgeschichte. Bd. 3. Von der 'Deutschen Doppelrevolution' bis zum Beginn des Ersten Weltkrieges 1849–1914* (Munich, 1995), 732.
9. Philippe Burrin, 'Political Religion: The Relevance of a Concept', *History and Memory* 9 (1997), 321–49 (328); cf. 334. For the 'family resemblance' between religion and politics see also the chapter by Herman Paul in this volume.
10. Gentile, *Politics as Religion*, 138.
11. Ibid., 8. The functionalist interpretation of religious phenomena is one of the four interpretations that Gentile presents; see 4–16.
12. Quoted in Hans-Ulrich Wehler, *Deutsche Gesellschaftsgeschichte. Bd. 4. Vom Beginn des Ersten Weltkrieges bis zur Gründung der beiden deutschen Staaten 1914–1949* (Munich, 2003), 19. 'Weltgeist' means something like 'world spirit'.
13. Werner Sombart, *Händler und Helden. Patriotische Besinnungen* (Munich and Leipzig, 1915), 142.
14. Martin Buber, 'Pescara', *Zeit-Echo* 1 (1914–15), nr 3, 38.
15. Friedrich Meinecke, 'Politik und Kultur', in idem, *Politische Schriften und Reden*, ed. Georg Kotowski (Darmstadt, 1958), 76–82 (81).
16. Ernst Troeltsch, 'Die Ideen von 1914 [1916]', in idem, *Deutscher Geist und Westeuropa. Gesammelte kulturphilosophische Aufsätze und Reden*, ed. Hans Baron (Tübingen, 1925), 31–58 (40–1).
17. Friedrich Meinecke, *Ausgewählter Briefwechsel*, ed. Ludwig Dehio and Peter Classen (Stuttgart, 1962), 45 (letter to Alfred Dove).

18. Max Scheler, *Genius des Krieges und der deutsche Krieg* (Leipzig, 1915), 2.

19. Max Weber, 'Zwischenbetrachtung', in idem, *Gesammelte Aufsätze zur Religionssoziologie I*, ed. Marianne Weber, 9th edn (Tübingen, 1988), 536–73 (548).

20. Max Weber, 'An der Schwelle des dritten Kriegsjahres', in *Max Weber Gesamtausgabe [MWG]*, I/15, *Zur Politik im Weltkrieg. Schriften und Reden 1914–1918*, ed. Wolfgang J. Mommsen in cooperation with Gangolf Hübinger (Tübingen, 1984), 656–89 (658).

21. Georg Simmel, *Deutschlands innere Wandlung* (Strassburg, 1914), 3.

22. Marianne Weber (anonymous), 'Erlebnisse der Seele', in *Die Frau* 22/5 (1915), 258. Quoted in Günther Roth, 'Marianne Weber und ihr Kreis', in Marianne Weber, *Lebensbild*, ix–lxxii (xxxiii).

23. Quoted in Verhey, *Spirit*, 67.

24. Gentile, *Politics as Religion*, 10.

25. David Blackbourn, *History of Germany 1780–1918: The Long Nineteenth Century*, 2nd edn (Malden, MA et al., 2003), 197.

26. Cf. my dissertation, Patrick Dassen, 'De onttovering van de wereld. Max Weber en het probleem van de moderniteit in Duitsland 1890–1920' (Amsterdam, 1999), esp. 244–7.

27. Georg Simmel, *Die Religion*, 2nd edn (Frankfurt am Main, 1912 [1906]), 48, 86.

28. Max Weber, 'Wissenschaft als Beruf', in idem, *Gesammelte Aufsätze zur Wissenschaftslehre*, ed. Johannes Winckelmann, 7th edn (Tübingen, 1988), 582–613 (605).

29. Quoted in Roger Chickering, *Imperial Germany and the Great War, 1914–1918*, 2nd edn (Cambridge, 2004), 8–9.

30. See Dassen, *Onttovering*, 107–36, esp. 110.

31. Sombart, *Händler*, 118.

32. Quoted in Verhey, *Spirit*, 136 ('Ich kenne keine Parteien mehr, ich kenne nur Deutsche'). Within a few days postcards went on sale with the picture of the Kaiser and his words.

33. Gunther Mai, *Das Ende des Kaiserreichs. Politik und Kriegführung im Ersten Weltkrieg*, 2nd edn (Munich, 1993), 13, 18–19; cf. Verhey, *Spirit*, 52–7. Verhey writes that over 750,000 people throughout Germany participated in the anti-war demonstrations (55).

34. Matthew Stibbe, *Germany 1914–1933: Politics, Society and Culture* (Harlow et al., 2010), 15; Roger Chickering, *The Great War and Urban Life in Germany: Freiburg, 1914–1918* (Cambridge, 2007), 66; cf. Wehler, *Gesellschaftsgeschichte*. *Bd. 4*, 41, 43 (quote). Wehler also points out the 'fear of a brutal repetition of the Socialist Laws' (42).

35. Cf. Mommsen, 'Das Deutsche Reich im Ersten Weltkrieg', in idem, *Der Erste Weltkrieg. Anfang vom Ende des bürgerlichen Zeitalters* (Bonn, 2004), 37–60 (39): 'The national euphoria of "August 1914" was no myth'. Verhey mentions the reliable figure of *c.*185,000 volunteers in August 1914, fewer than normally presumed (*Spirit*, 97).

36. Verhey, *Spirit*, 143–4.

37. Both quotes in ibid., 148.

38. Quoted in David Engel, 'Patriotism as a Shield: The Liberal Jewish Defence against Antisemitism in Germany during the First World War', *Leo Baeck Institute Year Book* 31 (1986), 147–71 (152).

39. See, for example, the diaries and letters collected in Peter Walther, *Endzeit*. This volume shows much more fear and anxiety than generally assumed. See, for instance, Gerhart Hauptmann in his diary on 1 August 1914: 'I had difficulty not to break into sobs regarding the dreadful foreboding annihilation [*Völkermord*]' (27). (Hauptmann's attitude towards the war was ambivalent, but he would contribute to the mental mobilization with poems like 'Komm, wir wollen sterben gehen' ['Come, We Want to Die'].) On 4 August 1914 Stefan Zweig wrote in his diary as a result of the recent developments, 'It is the most terrible day of my whole life' (34).
40. Verhey, *Spirit*, 116.
41. For Rudolf Eucken see Flasch, *Die geistige Mobilmachung*, esp. 15–35.
42. As Jeffrey Verhey states, 'The most important value gained in 1914 was community'. Verhey, *Spirit*, 130.
43. Quoted in Steffen Bruendel, 'Die Geburt der "Volksgemeinschaft" aus dem "Geist von 1914". Entstehung und Wandel eines "sozialistischen" Gesellschaftsentwurfs', in *Zeitgeschichte-online, Thema: Fronterlebnis und Nachkriegsordnung. Wirkung und Wahrnehmung des Ersten Weltkriegs* (May 2004), online at www.zeitgeschichte-online/md=EWK-Bruendel (retrieved February 2012), 5.
44. Quoted in Verhey, *Spirit*, 130.
45. Bruendel, 'Die Geburt', 8. For the concept of *Volksgemeinschaft* see also the excellent study by Peter Walkenhorst, *Nation – Volk – Rasse. Radikaler Nationalismus im Deutschen Kaiserreich 1890–1914* (Göttingen, 2007), esp. 86–98, 128–31, 147–50.
46. Quoted in Bruendel, 'Die Geburt', 9 ('in Not und Tod').
47. Gerd Krumeich, 'Langemarck', in Etienne Francois and Hagen Schulze (eds), *Deutsche Erinnerungsorte Bd. III* (Munich, 2001), 292–309, esp. 296–7.
48. For Walter Flex, see Lars Koch, 'Der Erste Weltkrieg als Medium der Gegenmoderne – Zu den Werken von Walter Flex und Ernst Jünger' (diss. Groningen, 2004), esp. 61–204, about the new *Volksgemeinschaft*, 115–24.
49. For the background and history of this contrast, see Arnold Labrie, '"*Kultur*" and "*Zivilization*" in Germany during the Nineteenth Century', *Yearbook of European Studies* 7 (1994), 95–120.
50. Quoted in Verhey, *Spirit*, 5; cf. 127 and 231.
51. See e.g. W.J. Mommsen, 'Der Geist von 1914: Das Programm eines politischen "Sonderwegs" der Deutschen', in idem, *Der autoritäre Nationalstaat. Gesellschaft und Kultur im deutschen Kaiserreich* (Frankfurt am Main, 1990), 407–21, esp. 412ff.
52. Mann, 'Gedanken im Kriege', esp. 30.
53. Quoted in Verhey, *Spirit*, 132.
54. Wehler, *Gesellschaftsgeschichte, Bd 4*, 20.
55. E. Troeltsch, 'Die deutsche Idee von der Freiheit', in idem, *Deutscher Geist*, 80–107 (94) (Troeltsch writes about the untranslatable *Organstellung*). See also, more generally, W.J. Mommsen, 'Die "deutsche Idee der Freiheit"', in idem, *Bürgerliche Kultur und politische Ordnung. Künstler, Schriftsteller und Intellektuelle in der deutschen Geschichte 1830–1933*, 2nd edn (Frankfurt am Main, 2002), 133–57.
56. Cf. Gentile, *Politics as Religion*, 140: a political religion 'denies the autonomy of the individual in relation to the collectivity'. Cf. xv.

57. Haase's statement can be found in Eduard David, *Die Sozialdemokratie im Weltkrieg* (Berlin, 1915), 9–10 (10).
58. See for this exclusion Bruendel, 'Die Geburt', esp. 11–13.
59. See Patrick Dassen, 'Radicalisering, polarisatie en totale oorlog. De Eerste Wereldoorlog als splijtzwam voor Duitsland', in Patrick Dassen and Petra Groen (eds), *Van de barricaden naar de loopgraven. Oorlog en samenleving in Europa 1789–1918* (Amsterdam, 2008), 237–84.
60. The total mobilization of the economy was no success: the Hindenburg plan (autumn 1916), for example, didn't increase war production and instead deepened the instability of the economy, and also the 'total control' of the population – the mobilization of the hearts and minds by propaganda – was not very effective.
61. Erich Ludendorff, *Meine Kriegserinnerungen 1914–1918* (Berlin, 1919), 259. Ludendorff wrote this in the context of the conscription for men between 16 and 60 years old.
62. See for his role during the war, the recent, reliable study by Manfred Nebelin, *Ludendorff. Diktator im Ersten Weltkrieg* (Munich, 2010), whose title is its central message.
63. Thomas Nipperdey, *Deutsche Geschichte 1866–1918. Bd 2. Machtstaat vor der Demokratie* (Munich, 1992), 804.
64. See for the plans for 'ethnic cleansing', Alan Kramer, 'Etnische Säuberungen vom Ersten Weltkrieg zum Nationalsozialismus', in Gerd Krumeich (ed.), *Nationalsozialismus und Erster Weltkrieg* (Essen, 2010), 323–45, esp. 326–30, and W.J. Mommsen 'Der "polnische Grenzstreifen". Anfänge der "völkischen Flurbereinigung" und der Umsiedlungspolitik', in idem, *Der Erste Weltkrieg*, 118–36.
65. For the flood of memoranda see Heinz Hagenlücke, *Deutsche Vaterlandspartei. Die nationale Rechte am Ende des Kaiserreichs* (Düsseldorf, 1997), esp. 49–72; Wehler, *Gesellschaftsgeschichte. Bd. 4*, 28–32; Nipperdey, *Deutsche Geschichte 1866–1918. Bd. 2*, 806–7; Mommsen, 'Das Deutsche Reich', 41–2.
66. See Ludendorff, *Kriegserinnerungen*, 369.
67. For the Fatherland Party see Hagenlücke, *Deutsche Vaterlandspartei*. Hagenlücke regards the Vaterlandspartei as the culmination of the agrarian-industrialist-conservative 'Sammlungspolitik'.
68. Quoted in Verhey, *Spirit*, 155. Compare what one farmer's son wrote in April 1918: 'The biggest traitors of the Fatherland are the members of the Fatherland Party. The leaders of these rascals belong in prison'. Quoted in Stibbe, *Germany 1914–1933*, 48.
69. For a good overview see Chickering, *Imperial Germany*, esp. 94–165 (chs 4–5); Stibbe, *Germany 1914–1933*, esp. 38–66.
70. Stibbe, *Germany 1914–1933*, 46, 48; Wehler, *Gesellschaftsgeschichte. Bd. 4*, 81–6, 224; Mommsen, 'Das Deutsche Reich', 49–50.
71. Jay Winter, 'Surviving the War: Life Expectation, Illness and Mortality Rates in Paris, London and Berlin, 1914–1919', in idem and J.-L. Robert (eds), *Capital Cities at War: Paris, London, Berlin 1914–1919* (Cambridge, 1997), 487–523 (517 n. 34). The demographic historian Winter writes about 478,500 'excess civilian war-related deaths in Germany'.
72. Quoted in Wehler, *Gesellschaftsgeschichte Bd. 4*, 73 ('Stimmungsbericht').
73. Quoted in Stibbe, *Germany 1914–1933*, 40.

74. Quoted in Verhey, *Spirit*, 148.
75. The first wave of food riots was in October 1915, and the first strike of national significance was on 28 June 1916, supported by 55,000 workers in Berlin, as a result of the imprisonment of Karl Liebknecht, the radical socialist and one of the leaders of the Spartakusgruppe.
76. See for the features of a class society in the German army, Wehler, *Gesellschaftsgeschichte. Bd. 4*, 186–7; Chickering, *Imperial Germany*, 97–8.
77. See, for example, Belinda Davis, *Home Fires Burning: Food, Politics, and Everyday Life in World War I Berlin* (Chapel Hill and London, 2000), 237; Mommsen, 'Das Deutsche Reich', 51; Stibbe, *Germany 1914–1933*, 42.
78. Benjamin Ziemann, 'Soldaten', in Gerhard Hirschfeld, Gerd Krumeich, Irina Renz (eds), *Enzyklopädie Erster Weltkrieg* (Paderborn, 2009), 155–68 (165).
79. Ziemann, 'Soldaten', 165ff. Karl Kautsky (though not unbiased) stated in 1916, 'Today Liebknecht is the most popular man in the trenches' (quoted in Wehler, *Gesellschaftsgeschichte. Bd. 4*, 111).
80. Walther Rathenau, *Briefe. Teilband 2: 1914–1922*, ed. Alexander Jaser, Clemens Picht and Ernst Schulin (Düsseldorf, 2006), 2019 (letter to Poul Bjerre) (part V.2 of the *Walther Rathenau-Gesamtausgabe*).
81. See for the Revolution of 1918/19, the classic study by Heinrich August Winkler, *Die Sozialdemokratie und die Revolution von 1918/19. Ein Rückblick nach sechzig Jahren* (Bonn, 1979); see also Wehler, *Gesellschaftsgeschichte. Bd. 4*, 174–97.
82. Kramer, *Dynamic*, 310.
83. For these figures, see Massimo Ferrari Zumbini, *Die Wurzeln des Bösen. Gründerjahre des Antisemitismus. Von der Bismarckzeit zu Hitler* (Frankfurt am Main, 2003), 613.
84. For the Jewish census, see Werner T. Angress, 'The German Army's "Judenzählung" of 1916. Genesis – Consequences – Significance', *Leo Baeck Institute Year Book* 23 (1978), 117–37; Wehler, *Gesellschaftsgeschichte. Bd 4*, 128–34, 495ff.; see for a general overview, Christhard Hoffmann, 'Between Integration and Rejection: The Jewish Community in Germany, 1914–1918', in John Horne (ed.), *State, Society and Mobilization in Europe during the First World War* (Cambridge, 1997), 89–104.
85. Cf. Hagenlücke, *Deutsche Vaterlandspartei*, 410.
86. See for the stereotypes of the enemy and conspiracy theories during the war and the Weimar Republic, Boris Barth, *Dolchstosslegenden und politische Desintegration. Das Trauma der deutschen Niederlage im Ersten Weltkrieg 1914–1933* (Düsseldorf, 2003).
87. Adolf Hitler, *Mein Kampf* (Munich, 1936), 772.
88. Karl Hampe, *Kriegstagebuch 1914–1919*, ed. Folker Reichert and Eike Wolgast (Munich, 2004), 414. Hampe noted this as a result of an 'illicit rise in prices'.
89. Gentile, *Politics as Religion*, 140. See also the Introduction of this volume.
90. Stibbe, *Germany 1914–1933*, 46.
91. Verhey, *Spirit*, 213–19, 236; Bruendel, 'Die Geburt', 13–26.
92. Verhey, *Spirit*, 213.
93. Ibid., 214.
94. Bruendel, 'Die Geburt', 15–16.
95. Ibid., 16; Verhey, *Spirit*, 214–15.

96. Adolf Hitler, 'Appell an die Nation', online at www.dhm.de/medien/lemo/ audios/hitler (retrieved 3 March 2012).
97. Cf. Stanley Stowers, who writes about 'a powerful nostalgia for a mythical unity of meaning, purpose and values in many Germans. National Socialism promised such a holistic communitarian future'. Stanley Stowers, 'The Concepts of "Religion", "Political Religion" and the Study of Nazism', *Journal of Contemporary History* 42/1 (2007), 9–24 (21).
98. Quoted in W.J. Mommsen, '1933: Die Flucht in den Führerstaat', in Carola Stern and Heinrich August Winkler (eds), *Wendepunkte deutscher Geschichte 1848–1990* (Frankfurt am Main, 1994), 127–58 (155–6).
99. Cf. Verhey, *Spirit*, 4, 116, 224, 238; Bruendel, 'Die Geburt', 23.
100. Quoted in Bruendel, 'Die Geburt', 23, and Verhey, *Spirit*, 224. Interestingly, Dibelius chose the same text the Generalsuperintendent Dryander had chosen on 4 August 1914, namely Romans 8:31: 'If God is for us, who can be against us'.
101. This is the central contention of Claudia Koonz's book, *The Nazi Conscience* (Cambridge, MA, 2003). Cf. also Ian Kershaw, *Hitler 1889–1936: Hubris* (London, 1998), 332: Kershaw states that 581 life stories, collected in 1934, make it clear that the idea of social solidarity was the most important reason to become a member of Hitler's NSDAP (*c.*33 per cent). To only *c.*12 per cent was anti-Semitism the most important ideological factor. Cf. Wehler, who writes about 'an immensely attractive utopia of the "egalitarian Leistungs-Volksgemeinschaft"', *Gesellschaftsgeschichte, Bd. 4*, 988; cf. 548.
102. Quoted in Roger Griffin (ed.), *Fascism* (Oxford, 1995), 134–5.
103. See for the *Volksgemeinschaft* in the Third Reich, David Welch, *The Third Reich: Politics and Propaganda*, 2nd edn (London and New York, 2002), esp. 62–80. See also Richard Evans, *The Third Reich in Power 1933–1939* (New York, 2005), ch. 5, 'Building the People's Community', 414–503. Evans aptly points to the gap between the ideal of solidarity and reality but has to confess that ultimately the rhetoric of the *Volksgemeinschaft* convinced probably most Germans on the political level: everybody seemed to be in agreement under Hitler's leadership.

History or Civil Religion? The Uses of Lincoln's 'Last Best Hope of Earth'

Adam Fairclough

Lincoln as the Patron Saint of American Civil Religion

Like Shakespeare and the translators who gave us the King James Bible, Abraham Lincoln (1809–65) has enriched the English language with phrases that are instantly recognizable and endlessly quotable. 'Government of the people, by the people, and for the people' is one of the most concise and memorable definitions of democratic government that we have. Similarly, the words from Lincoln's second inaugural address, 'With malice toward none, with charity for all, let us bind up the nation's wounds', beautifully express the wisdom of a victorious power extending the hand of reconciliation to a vanquished foe. A third Lincoln phrase has also entered the vernacular. At the conclusion of his second annual message to Congress, in December 1862, Lincoln ended his proposal for voluntary, gradual, compensated emancipation with the words, 'In giving freedom to the slave we assure freedom to the free. We may nobly save or meanly lose the last best hope of earth'.[1]

This chapter locates Lincoln's 'last best hope of earth' formulation within a long tradition of 'American exceptionalism'. The phrase expressed a belief that the United States was not only uniquely fitted to teach liberty and democracy to other peoples but also had a providential mission to do so. Indeed, Lincoln's words are so frequently quoted in connection with the superiority of American institutions that they function as a kind of précis of American civil religion. The chapter goes on to argue that belief in American exceptionalism is so potent in the United States that Lincoln's phrase has led many historians to exaggerate – indeed, fundamentally to misconceive – America's role in the development of democracy. It also questions the assumption that America's civil religion has rested upon a broad national consensus on values by drawing attention to its coercive and intolerant aspects. For example, white southerners have historically endorsed racial inequality and demonstrated a weak commitment to democratic freedoms, indicating that civil religion may be more contentious than that term suggests. The chapter concludes by suggesting that civil religion, as defined by a strong belief in American exceptionalism, is now largely associated with a particular kind of conservatism.

Lincoln and American Civil Religion

What did Lincoln mean by 'last best hope of earth'? He was trying to define liberty as the core principle of the United States, and to associate that principle with the abolition of slavery. In the main body of the message he had pleaded for a constitutional amendment providing for gradual, compensated emancipation, to be accompanied by the deportation of freed slaves and their resettlement in some foreign territory. Although a reluctant abolitionist – his hand forced by the exigencies of war – he came to regard emancipation as completely consistent with the principle of equality that, in his eyes, undergirded the United States. In extending American liberty to blacks, Lincoln differed from all previous presidents. Indeed, some have gone so far as to claim that Lincoln redefined the very meaning of America by making liberty racially inclusive and placing a fresh emphasis upon equality.[2]

The phrase 'last best hope of earth' also conveyed a larger message about the role of the United States in world history. Britain had abolished slavery in 1833, France in 1848, yet Lincoln believed that the United States, not Britain or France – both of which claimed to exemplify liberty – represented the 'last best hope of earth'. And although he viewed the abolition of slavery as politically desirable and morally right, his primary concern was that the Union crush the attempted secession by 11 states that claimed to constitute a new nation, the Confederate States of America. Secession had violated the fundamental principle of democracy, Lincoln believed. Only a Union victory could assure the future of the United States and its republican, democratic system of government that was, in Lincoln's eyes, uniquely wise and uniquely successful. A Union defeat would be a catastrophic setback for the republican, democratic principle.

If Lincoln's role as the 'Great Emancipator' set him apart from his predecessors, his conception of the United States as the 'last, best hope of earth' was as old as the republic itself. By 1776, writes Bernard Bailyn, 'Americans had come to think of themselves as in a special category, uniquely placed by history to capitalize on, to complete and fulfil, the promise of man's existence'. According to this national optic, peoples suffering under monarchical and aristocratic rule would be inspired by America's success as a great republic. Indeed, the United States had a providential mission to show the rest of the world the path of liberty and freedom. Like the ancient Hebrews, Americans had entered a covenant with God; unlike the ancient Hebrews but like the first Christians, they had a duty to spread the good news. Underpinning this faith lay a theology of, to use Mark Noll's phrase, 'Christian republicanism', a blend of evangelical Protestantism, republican principles, and 'commonsense moral reasoning'. The assertion that the United States had developed the freest, most successful form of government ever seen ('best') was boilerplate political rhetoric in the new republic. So was the notion that the United States provided the rest of the world with an example of liberty for others to emulate.[3]

George Washington set the tone in presidential rhetoric. In his first inaugural address (1789) he proclaimed that 'The sacred fire of liberty and the destiny of the republican model of government are [...] staked on the experiment entrusted to the hands of the American people'. This assertion became a staple of presidential inaugural addresses, and the inauguration ceremony itself a central element of what has come to be known as American civil religion. Twelve years later, Thomas Jefferson, taking office after the first peaceful transfer of power from one political party to another, described the United States as 'the world's best hope'.

Presidential assertions of this kind reflected a widespread belief in the early republic that the rest of the world closely watched the United States and that at some point, noting America's stability and success, it would emulate America's form of government. 'The eyes of all nations are fixed upon our republic', claimed Jackson in 1833. 'The event of the existing [Nullification] crisis will be decisive in the opinion of mankind of the practicability of our form of government.' Twelve years later, James K. Polk described the American polity as the 'most admirable and wisest system of well-regulated self-government among men ever devised by human minds'.[4] Even as the slavery question divided America and destroyed national institutions, James Buchanan expressed his 'humble confidence' that 'the most perfect form of government ever devised by man will not [...] perish until it shall have been peacefully instrumental by its example of civil and religious liberty throughout the world'.

Words like 'crisis' and 'perish' revealed that the boastful self-confidence of 'best' contended with anxiety that the United States, as a federal republic of enormous extent, might fall prey to party or sectional divisions and fall apart. By 1850 America had demonstrated its power to withstand foreign enemies, but its ability to preserve domestic cohesion was very much in question. Hence the spread of republicanism as a form of government depended upon the survival of the United States. From Washington to Lincoln, presidents and other political leaders warned about the divisive consequences of partisanship, excessive presidential power, sectionalism, agitation of the slavery issue and disunion.

Here, then, is the significance of the word 'last'. Should the United States disintegrate, Lincoln believed, the world's progress toward liberty and equality would falter and even spin into reverse. The outcome of the Civil War would determine 'not only the civil and religious liberties of our own dear land, but in a large degree the civil and religious liberties of mankind in many countries and through many ages'. In the classic formulation of the Gettysburg Address, only a Union victory could ensure that republican and democratic government – 'government of the people, by the people, and for the people' – did not 'perish from the earth'.

Historian of religion Mark Noll has suggested that the Civil War caused Lincoln to doubt the existence of a special bond 'between God and his American chosen people'. But Lincoln's humility regarding God's inscrutable ways never undermined his belief in America's providential mission. As Gentile writes, Lincoln

> perceived history as the implantation of God's will, and firmly believed that God had chosen the American people to carry out his work in history [...]. He had a mystical concept of the Union, which he identifies with liberty and democracy, and he interpreted the Civil War as a punishment for the disunity of the American people, who had broken their sacred pact with the Omnipotent.

Hence, while viewing the war through his own moral optic, Lincoln affirmed a belief that was already an important element of American nationalism. As Jean Baker puts it, faith in the 'virtuousness uniqueness' of the United States 'framed the political culture of his time'.[5]

The enduring popularity of the phrase 'last best hope of earth' reflects the fact that it reinforces a patriotic narrative of national destiny. God had selected Americans to be, in the words of Reinhold Niebuhr, 'the tutors of mankind in its pilgrimage to perfection'. Along with 'American Dream' and 'City on a Hill', the phrase 'last best hope of earth' has helped to define America's core ideology. That set of beliefs has been variously labelled the 'American Dream' (James T. Adams, 1931), the 'American Creed' (Gunnar Myrdal, 1944), 'Messianic consciousness' (Reinhold Niebuhr, 1952), the 'American idea of mission' (Edward M. Burns, 1957) and 'American civil religion' (Robert N. Bellah, 1967).

Lincoln himself has been described as the 'preeminent prophet of American civil religion', the veneration of whom constitutes 'the spiritual center of American history'. Although the Washington Monument is, literally, the most visible public monument in the nation's capital – regulation forbids any building to stand taller – the Lincoln Memorial is by far the most impressive. Dedicated in 1922, it bears an unmistakable resemblance to the Parthenon. It has the look and feel of a shrine; it is a place of pilgrimage.[6]

The outward expressions of America's civil religion – what might be called its *liturgy* – resemble those of many other nations. Independence Day, the Pledge of Allegiance, the national anthem, flag rituals and the president's annual address to Congress, all have their foreign equivalents. It is, rather, in the realm of its *theology* that America's civil religion seems most distinctive. As Swedish economist Gunnar Myrdal argued in his classic work *An American Dilemma: The Negro Problem and Modern Democracy* (1944), the United States 'has the most explicitly expressed system of general ideals' when compared with 'every other country in Western civilization':

> These ideals of the essential dignity of the individual human being, of the fundamental equality of all men, and of certain inalienable rights to freedom, justice, and a fair opportunity represent to the American people the essential meaning of the nation's early struggle for independence [...] [T]hese tenets were written into the Declaration of Independence, the Preamble of the Constitution, [and] the Bill of Rights.

Foreign observers recognized the all-pervading influence of American civil religion early on, even if they did not use that particular phrase. In 1835 Alexis de Tocqueville noted the 'garrulous patriotism' (which he found intensely irritating) of the average American. 'For the past fifty years', he wrote, 'no pains have been spared to convince the inhabitants of the United States that they constitute the only religious, enlightened, and free people'. Indeed, such was their 'overweening opinion of their superiority' that Americans 'are not very remote from believing themselves to belong to a distinct race of mankind'.[7]

When Lincoln referred to the Union as the 'last best hope of earth', therefore, he was expressing a commonplace confidence in the moral and political superiority of American institutions. The civil religion to which Lincoln subscribed helped Americans believe that their history and destiny were exceptional. However, as S.N. Eisenstadt argues, it was not so much the history that was exceptional as the *belief* in that exceptionalism. 'The collective identity [...] that developed in American civilization was based on a political ideology transformed from a religious experience but maintaining its religious identity, a hitherto unique occurrence in the history of mankind'.[8]

Reinhold Niebuhr and Edward Burns, both writing in the early years of the Cold War, identified some of the factors that have nurtured American exceptionalism. Geography made it easy to sustain the notion of an innocent nation in a wicked world. Distance afforded cheap security, allowing the young nation to heed George Washington's admonition to avoid 'entangling alliances', thereby sustaining the illusion of a virtuous America uncontaminated by a corrupt Europe. Celebration of the Revolution promoted the conviction that the United States represented, to quote Niebuhr, 'a new beginning for mankind'. Veneration of the Founding Fathers allowed Americans to congratulate themselves for 'having invented the most perfect system of government on earth [... and] upon having originated constitutionalism'. The conceit that North America was an 'empty' land inhabited by small numbers of nomadic savages and Mexican 'greasers' (Lincoln's term), and the carving out of new states from territory acquired through conquest – states with strong rights of self-government – made the continental expansion of the United States appear different from European imperialism. Mass immigration, symbolized by the Statue of Liberty, reinforced America's self-image as a nation both divinely favoured and morally superior. Above all, America's astonishing economic, political and military success afforded comparatively little challenge to that self-image. To be sure, the nation endured grave crises – the Civil War, the Great Depression – but it emerged from each one stronger than before.[9]

The Development of American Civil Religion over Time

American civil religion was not handed down on tablets of stone: its symbols and language have been developed by individuals, organizations and Congress. The Cold War, for example, made the Christian element in America's civil religion more explicit. The Pledge of Allegiance, written in 1892 by Francis Bellamy, a Christian socialist, had contained no reference to God. In 1954, however, 12 years after it had made the Pledge part of the official 'flag code', Congress added the words 'under God'. The same year saw Congress add the words 'In God We Trust' – which replaced 'E Pluribus Unum' as the national motto – to the currency. Having featured on some coins, but not others, since 1864, it now appeared on coins and bills of every denomination. All of this accentuated America's abhorrence of 'atheistic communism'.

Changes in the civil religion have not been devoid of controversy. In 1983, for example, when Congress voted to make the third Monday in January a holiday for federal workers in honour of Martin Luther King, Jr, a number of states refused to follow suit. Even in 2000, by which time all 50 states had acknowledged King Day, some of them diluted that recognition by deliberately downgrading King. Virginia, for example, called the holiday 'Lee-Jackson-King Day', yoking the black civil rights leader to two white defenders of slavery, Confederate generals Robert E. Lee and Thomas J. 'Stonewall' Jackson. Over time, nevertheless, a mythologized Martin Luther King, Jr has been admitted to that select group of national heroes that peoples the pantheon of civil religion. The Martin Luther King, Jr. National Memorial originated in a private initiative, but received backing from Congress in 1996 and was unveiled by President Obama in 2011. The monument's site – on federal parkland near memorials to Thomas Jefferson and Franklin D. Roosevelt – underlines the fact that King stands in the company of demi-gods.

The most obvious example of conflict over civil religion has been the South, where whites in the former Confederacy openly celebrated the 'Lost Cause' and, well into the twentieth century, declined to observe the Fourth of July. To this day, displays of the Confederate battle-flag, especially on public property, produce bitter controversies that sometimes wind up in court. More to the point, white southerners' nostalgia for the 'Lost Cause' has often indicated a rejection of the liberal values of the 'American Creed'. Indeed, Charles Reagan Wilson has argued that in the late nineteenth and early twentieth centuries, the 'Lost Cause' constituted its own, rival, civil religion. Nevertheless, as the Civil War veterans died and young southerners demonstrated their loyalty to the nation in the Spanish–American War and the First World War, the North deemed the Lost Cause and American civil religion to be compatible. In 1905 Congress voted to allow Confederate battle-flags that had been captured during the war to be returned to the southern states. Nine years later President Woodrow Wilson, a native southerner, dedicated a monument to the Confederate dead in Arlington National Cemetery.

Today, many military bases are named after Confederate generals who were, in fact, traitors: Fort Lee, Fort Hill, Fort Hood, Camp Beauregard. Robert E. Lee is often presented as a *national* hero, despite the fact that Congress never granted him a full pardon before he died in 1870.[10]

That both the Lost Cause and the civil rights movement became part of civil religion underlines the point: 'Americanism' is not a given. It is often a battleground. For example, reconciling Confederate memory with American patriotism rested upon a definition of the political nation, accepted by both parties as well as the Supreme Court, that excluded blacks. Black leaders then embarked upon a decades-long struggle to utilize civil religion in the cause of racial equality. The Lincoln Memorial became the symbolic focus of their efforts. In 1939, Marian Anderson, a world-class classical singer who happened to be black, was refused permission to perform in Washington's Constitution Hall because that venue's owner, the Daughters of the American Revolution, operated a 'whites only' policy. Thereupon the National Association for the Advancement of Colored People – the nation's leading civil rights organization which had allies in the Roosevelt administration and a friend in Eleanor Roosevelt – gained permission from the federal government to relocate the concert to the Lincoln Memorial, where Anderson sang to 75,000 people. After the Second World War, Martin Luther King, Jr repeatedly yoked the Lincoln Memorial to the civil rights cause, speaking before mass demonstrations there in 1957 and 1959 and, most memorably, the 1963 March on Washington.[11]

Conservatives, for their part, have equated civil religion, and patriotism generally, with the politically charged concept of 'Americanism'. As defined by congressional and state investigating committees, 'Americanism' was incompatible with Communism, Marxism, or social democracy. From the 'Red Scare' of 1919–20 to the 'McCarthyism' of the late 1940s and 1950s, 'Americanism' operated as a coercive force against the left. It decimated the American Socialist Party between 1917 and 1920, and by the mid-1950s it had virtually destroyed the Communist Party. The charge of 'un-Americanism' also weakened the labour unions and intimidated many liberals. Southern segregationists exploited it to portray advocates of racial equality as 'un-American'. In some States, children in public schools were force-fed highly tendentious courses on 'Americanism'. A Senate committee, chaired by James Eastland of Mississippi, interrogated civil rights activists and even seized their records.[12]

One effect of the association between 'un-Americanism' and 'foreign' ideologies was to force liberals to continuously accentuate their patriotism, creating, in effect, a liberal interpretation of civil religion. No one was more skilful in this respect than Martin Luther King, Jr. Identifying the cause of racial equality with Christianity, the Declaration of Independence, the Constitution and Abraham Lincoln, he covered his own radicalism with a cloak of patriotism. He ended his most famous speech, 'I Have a Dream', with lines from the song 'My country 'tis of thee'.[13] Even the American Communist Party, during its heyday in the 1930s, tailored its image to fit civil religion. It named its political schools after Thomas Jefferson. Communists who fought for the Spanish Republic were soldiers of the Abraham Lincoln Brigade.[14]

The Enduring Power of Civil Religion

Reinhold Niebuhr and Edward M. Burns, writing at a time when America's confrontation with the Soviet Union made it the undisputed leader of the 'Free World', warned against the exaggerated self-righteousness associated with civil religion. 'Every nation has its own form of spiritual pride', noted Niebuhr in *The Irony of American History* (1952). 'Examples of American self-appreciation could be matched by similar sentiments in other nations'. At various times in history, wrote Edward M. Burns in *The American Idea of Mission* (1955), the Chinese, the Greeks, the Romans, the Muslim Arabs and Turks, the Dutch, the French and the British – among others – had 'conceived of themselves as superior and as endowed with a mission to dominate other peoples or to lead the rest of the world into paths of light'. For each of these civilizations, however, illusions of omnipotence and superiority eventually crumbled as defeat or decay humbled them.[15]

The Second World War, however, had unleashed forces that seemed only to confirm the notion that the United States represented the 'last best hope of earth'. In 1941 Henry R. Luce, publisher of *Time* and *Life*, issued a clarion call for America to reject isolationism and embrace the challenge of world leadership. The United States had become 'the most powerful and the most vital nation in the world', and its democratic idealism, 'once regarded as the dubious eccentricity of a colonial nation', was now 'the faith of a large majority of the world'. President Harry S. Truman articulated the same vision of a freedom-loving America guiding the destiny of the world. The United States, he stated in 1952, had 'finally stepped into the leadership which Almighty God intended us to assume a generation ago'. Speaking in 1965, President Lyndon B. Johnson invoked the familiar Old Testament trope: 'The American covenant called on us to help show the way for the liberation of man'. Nine years later Ronald Reagan, then governor of California, urged Americans to embrace 'The leadership of the free world [that] was thrust upon us two centuries ago in that little hall of Philadelphia'. Upon becoming president in 1981 he vowed that America would 'again be [...] a beacon of hope for those who do not now have freedom'. William J. Clinton began his first inaugural address by observing that the United States was 'the world's oldest democracy'. He expressed his joy at seeing American ideas embraced 'across the world'. George W. Bush described the 'democratic faith' of the United States as 'a trust we bear and pass along'.[16]

Although American civil religion is alive and well, despite the withering critiques of Niebuhr, Burns and others, we cannot assume that all Americans, or even a majority of them, subscribe to its theology. Indeed, like an actual religion, outward observance often accompanies lack of inner conviction. Just as many Christians who weekly recite the Nicene Creed feel no need to take it literally, many Americans engage in a 'soft' version of civil religion, partaking of such simple rituals of patriotism as singing the national anthem at sports events and – especially after September 11 – displaying the national flag. These Americans often reject the 'hard' version of civil religion that equates America with a providential destiny.

In recent years, American conservatives – now mainly Republicans – have latched onto Lincoln's 'last best hope of earth' phrase to buttress their case for the moral and political primacy of the United States. They equate American exceptionalism with the idea that the United States, possessing a near-perfect economic and political system, has nothing to learn from Europe and the outside world. Making 'last best hope of earth' a kind of litmus test of patriotism, conservatives insist on the absolute superiority of American values and institutions. William J. Bennett, Secretary of Education in the Reagan administration, called his three-volume history of the United States, *America: The Last Best Hope*. Former Republican congressman and television pundit Joe Scarborough published a book with the self-explanatory title, *The Last Best Hope: Restoring Conservatism and America's Promise*.[17]

When Barack Obama failed to affirm with sufficient conviction that the United States is still the 'last best hope of earth', Republicans depicted him as unpatriotic, un-American and anti-American. Obama's worldview, states former Arkansas governor Mike Huckabee, is 'dramatically different' from that of any other president: 'To deny American exceptionalism is [...] to deny the heart and soul of this nation'. Republican presidential hopefuls (for the 2012 election) Sarah Palin,

Newt Gingrich, Mitt Romney and Rick Santorum have all reiterated the point, insisting that the United States is exceptional because it is superior. 'America is the single greatest nation in all of human history', boasted Senator Marco Rubio, another Republican with presidential ambitions. A vote for the Democratic party, he went on, would be a vote for America becoming 'just like everyone else'. A Republican vote would help ensure that America would 'continue to be exceptional'. According to Republican political adviser Craig Shirley – also known for his popular histories – Obama fails to understand the United States. He 'was asked if he believed in American exceptionalism', complains Shirley, 'and he equated American exceptionalism with Greek exceptionalism, which most people would view as nonsense'. The United States 'is a unique country', Shirley explains. 'It's unique because [...] never in the history of the world has there been a country as selfless as America, as willing to do more and ask for less from the rest of the world'.[18]

Opinion polls confirm that belief in American exceptionalism, in the sense of American superiority, is especially strong among conservative voters. According to a 2010 Rasmussen Report, half of all Americans 'believe that the United States is the last best hope', including a large majority of conservatives but only 29 per cent of liberals. Likewise, while half the population thinks that 'the United States has had special protection from God', evangelical Christians were twice as likely to hold this belief as mainline Protestants and Catholics.[19]

Historians and Civil Religion

During the twentieth century the historical profession produced a rich body of work that disputed civil religion and rejected the idea of American exceptionalism. A mixed group of liberals, 'progressives', Marxists and products of the 1960s New Left questioned the notion that the history of the United States can be analysed in terms of a shared national commitment to fundamental ideals and principles. In reality, they noted, the United States has sanctioned slavery, genocide and the exploitation of workers, while on the world stage it has behaved in a not dissimilar fashion to imperialist powers like Britain and France. In 1907, for example, J. Allen Smith interpreted the Constitution as an anti-democratic document that worked mainly to the benefit of the wealthy and the powerful. In 1912 Charles A. Beard depicted the Founding Fathers as a propertied elite that was guided as much by economic self-interest as by civic virtue. During the 1930s writer and journalist Matthew Josephson popularized Marxian critiques of American history with *The Robber Barons* (1934), *The Politicos* (1938) and *The President Makers* (1940). Southern-born C. Vann Woodward, in a career spanning the 1930s to the 1990s, depicted the South as a region scarred by racism, poverty and anti-democratic values. But rather than seeing the South as an anomaly, he contended that the North's historic commitment to equality and democracy was honoured as much in the breach as in the observance. An admirer of Reinhold Niebuhr's *Irony of American History*, Woodward treated American exceptionalism as a national myth. The disastrous intervention in Vietnam encouraged the writing of 'revisionist' histories of American foreign policy that disputed the ideas that the USA has been an innocent in a guilty world, and that its actions have invariably been guided by democratic idealism.[20]

So pervasive is American civil religion, however, that it has been, and still is, reflected in the work of many historians. In his 1950 presidential address to the American Historical Association, Conyers Read argued that 'total war, be it hot or cold, enlists everyone and calls upon everyone to do his part', the historian included. For Read, historical scholarship and civil religion were not in conflict. 'We recognize certain fundamental values as beyond dispute [...]. As historians we must carry back into our scrutiny of the past the same faith in the validity of our democratic institutions which, let us say, the astronomer has in the validity of the Copernican theory'. Four years later G. D. Lillibridge wrote that 'the American destiny' was to lead the world to freedom and happiness. School and college textbooks reflected this theme, and the Americans who read them imbibed, to quote Godfrey Hodgson, 'assumptions about the exceptional historical destiny of the United States as uncontested as the air they breathed'.

By the 1970s, however, civil religion had lost much of its force as a promoter of ideological cohesion. The civil rights movement, the Vietnam War, the counter-culture, second-wave feminism and Watergate not only accentuated America's social and political divisions but also questioned the very idea that the nation rested upon moral foundations. Influenced by these developments, and following the identity politics of the era, an increasing number of historians focused their research on historically excluded Americans such as blacks, women, Native Americans and homosexuals. This scholarly trend – which is still evident today – made the idea of a nation committed to core values increasingly difficult to sustain.

After 1980 a conservative reaction set in. In his successful presidential campaign Ronald Reagan skilfully appealed to civil religion, asserting the moral superiority of the United States in its struggle to vanquish the 'evil empire' of the Soviet Union. The disintegration of that empire, and of the Soviet Union itself, evoked a wave of Cold War triumphalism. A number of prominent historians urged their colleagues to elaborate a more celebratory account of the American past. In 1996, worried that critiques of civil religion had gone too far, Diane Ravitch and Arthur Schlesinger, Jr, a conservative and a liberal respectively, pleaded for historians to place 'the nation's democratic ideals at the center of its history'. Eric Foner, a prominent historian of the Civil War era, did just that, placing the expansion of freedom at the heart of a grand narrative. Freedom, Foner argues, has been 'fundamental to Americans' sense of themselves': this idea 'anchors the American sense of exceptional national identity'. After the Civil War, he writes, the Republican Party's effort to guarantee civil and political equality for the ex-slaves reflected the depth of America's democratic idealism. The grant of suffrage to blacks showed that Americans were attempting 'to live up to the noble professions of their political creed – something few societies have ever done'.[21]

Analysing how various historians have treated Lincoln's 'last best hope of earth' reveals the frequent confusion of history and civil religion. Distinguishing between them, however, is not helped by the fact that some historians use Lincoln's words rather like novelists plunder Shakespeare and the Bible for catchy titles. Thus *The Last Best Hope of Earth: Abraham Lincoln and the Promise of America* (1993), by Mark E. Neely, Jr, says remarkably little about the idea of the United States as the spearhead of liberty and equality, despite quoting the phrase several times in the text. Similarly, Sean Wilentz uses the phrase 'world's best hope' – Jefferson's phrase, the inspiration for Lincoln's – to end his prize-winning *Rise of American Democracy*, but without pondering its international implications or, indeed, its relevance for the development of the United States after 1861, the end point of his study. Still, the implication is that the United States *has* functioned as the 'last best hope of earth'.[22]

Other scholars have explicitly interpreted Lincoln's words as a description of historical reality. 'While Lincoln eloquently maintained that the issue of the Civil War involved more than the fate of democracy on American soil', wrote G.D. Lillibridge in 1954, 'English democrats three thousand miles from the battleground underwrote his words in a calculated risk in which they publicly gambled their struggle for liberty in England upon the victory of [the] defeat of freedom in America'. The eminent political scientist William H. Riker made an even bolder claim. The success of the Union cause, he wrote in 1965, 'determined the repute of democracy everywhere. The present ascendancy of democratic theory is in no small part a consequence of the fact that American democracy survived the Civil War'. Forty years later, James McPherson, one of the foremost authorities on the Civil War – and unquestionably the most widely read – made the same argument. 'For liberals, reformers, radicals, and revolutionaries of all stripes', the United States was the model democracy, and the victory of the Union decisively strengthened their hand. 'The Civil War shaped the destiny not only of America', McPherson believes, 'but also, as Lincoln put it, of "the whole family of man"'.[23]

Among Lincoln scholars, Allen G. Guelzo is perhaps the more assiduous promoter of the 'last best hope of earth' view of the United States. Twice the recipient of the Lincoln Prize, Guelzo argues that although it might seem 'inexcusably boastful' for Americans to claim that their democracy was 'a template for all other nations to follow', this indeed has been, and still is, the case. The survival and growth of democracy, Guelzo asserts, owed everything to the Union victory in 1865. That victory not only vindicated democracy as a political system but also 'invested democracy with a transcendent story [and] made its progress providential'. The survival of democracy in the United States meant that 'eight decades later' the United States 'constituted nearly all that stood between civilization and the universal midnight of Nazism'. According to Allen Guelzo, moreover, only Americans have developed a true understanding of democracy. Other nations might acquire 'aspects of democracy', he reasons, but even in the most advanced European democracies 'old habits of noblesse oblige, of social guarantees, of [...] deference to the wiser and better' persist as 'relics of the feudal past'.[24]

The United States as the Model for Modern Democracy

Historians who portray the United States as the exemplar of democracy stress the fact that the United States was the *first* large nation to adopt universal suffrage for white men. Although France prescribed universal suffrage in the Constitution of 1793, this experiment quickly failed. The French Revolution of 1848 ushered in another period of universal suffrage, but it was also short-lived. This was in stark contrast to the United States, where by 1825, according to historian Gordon Wood, 'every state but Rhode Island, Virginia, and Louisiana had achieved universal white manhood suffrage'. Equally important, the new democratic politics persisted. In other words, the United States attained universal manhood suffrage two decades before Switzerland, and six decades before even a bare majority of men in Great Britain had gained the right to vote. The United States also pioneered modern political parties and electioneering techniques. In the nineteenth and early twentieth centuries, writes John Keane, these innovations 'set the United States apart from the rest of the world' and 'set the agenda for all representative democracies'.[25] To Wood, pre-eminent historian of the American Revolution, the emergence of an egalitarian and democratic United States was a remarkable achievement and one worth celebrating. The emergence of American democracy, he argues, was less a development rooted in British constitutionalism or Enlightenment thought than a radical break with the past. Similarly, Sean Wilentz, while acknowledging that 'the radicalism of the seventeenth century belongs to the genealogy of American democracy', stresses the innovative character and singular achievement of America's universal suffrage.[26]

There are plenty of sceptics, however, who dispute the notion of the United States as the first democracy and global trendsetter. In the first place, they point out, American democracy rested upon a tradition of representative government in Britain that included, in the words of John Keane, 'such basic practices as office holding, parliaments, [and] liberty of the press'. A longer time-frame, agrees Michael Lind, reveals the powerful influence of 'centuries of British precedents' that led the colonists to assume that they should enjoy all the rights and privileges due to British citizens. In the pithy formulation of Louis Hartz, 'the revolutionaries of 1776 had inherited the freest society in the world'. The notion that democracy was an invention of early nineteenth century America is 'plainly wrong', argues John Keane. 'It ignores the long incubation that began during the medieval period – a period that lasted at least five centuries.' Interestingly, Franklin Roosevelt, alone among presidents, emphasized democracy's long historical lineage. This was, however, a time when the Great Depression had weakened confidence in American exceptionalism and boosted the appeal of foreign ideologies.[27]

In the second place, historians of democracy point out that universal suffrage is relative rather than absolute: it is never truly universal. Although the United States was the first nation to achieve an approximation of white manhood suffrage, it did *not*, as Keane notes, 'lead the world in extending the franchise to all men and women'. New Zealand was the first nation to enfranchise adult citizens regardless of race and gender, thereby most closely approaching universal suffrage. In the United States, moreover, suffrage *restriction* accompanied suffrage *extension*. Free blacks who could vote in the 1800s could no longer do so by the 1830s.

Ex-slaves were enfranchised after the Civil War but by 1915 blacks in the South, nine-tenths of the nation's black population, had lost the right to vote. Immigrants were never disfranchised en masse, but they often encountered troublesome registration requirements that were designed to discourage them from casting ballots. In 1900, writes John Keane, neither the United States nor any other nation 'allowed universal suffrage and multi-party elections'.[28]

There is another reason to doubt the idea that the United States has been exceptionally committed to democratic ideals. During the early decades of the nineteenth century when individual states expanded the franchise, the American population was overwhelmingly rural and there was no large industrial working class. Moreover, the white rural population consisted for the most part of farm families that owned their land. The Founding Fathers had dreaded democracy, but by the early nineteenth century James Madison, for one, recognized that universal manhood suffrage posed little threat to private property. The Whig Party, which had feared that numbers would overwhelm property, came to an even stronger conclusion: 'the masses [...] could, if approached correctly, be turned into great defenders of property'. By 1840 the Whigs had abandoned their opposition to universal suffrage and elected their first president – the first chief executive to describe the United States as a 'democracy' in his inaugural address. Nevertheless, constitutional arrangements greatly limited the power of the mass electorate to effect radical changes. America's democracy operated within a constitution that restrained majorities and empowered unelected judges to overrule elected legislatures. As Louis Hartz put it, 'The American majority has been an amiable shepherd dog kept forever on a lion's leash'.[29]

Hence the speed and ease with which America moved toward universal white manhood suffrage reflected the absence of strong opposition from the existing political classes, which saw little to fear from a mass electorate. Unlike Russia or Spain, America had no mass of landless peasants to threaten the owners of large estates. Instead, it had a class of powerless slaves. Wilentz argues that we must discount the exclusion of blacks when judging early nineteenth-century American democracy, accepting that white male suffrage was then the standard. Yet in some states, including North Carolina, free blacks *had* been voters, only to be disfranchised in the 1820s and 1830s. Moreover, it is hard to imagine white male suffrage becoming universal without the existence of slavery. 'The free sector of society could never have achieved its way of life without the support of the unfree', writes J.R. Pole. Unlike Britain, moreover, Jacksonian America had no army of industrial workers to frighten the urban middle class. Alexander Keyssar writes,

> The relatively early broadening of the franchise in the United States was not simply, or even primarily, the consequence of a distinctive American commitment to democracy [...] Rather, the early extension of voting rights occurred – or at least was made possible – because the rights and power of [...] subaltern classes, despised and feared as much as they were in Europe, were not at issue when suffrage reforms were adopted.

Federalists and Whigs had once issued grim warnings that universal suffrage would lead to mob rule. But the mobs that materialized after America's democratic revolution targeted blacks, immigrants, and abolitionists, not capitalists or landlords.[30]

Some historians nevertheless insist that Lincoln's conception of the United States as the 'last best hope of earth' described historical reality. Posing the question, 'Did people in other lands share the belief in America's mission to show them the upward path from autocracy and oppression?', James McPherson answers in the affirmative. The passage of Britain's Second Reform Act in 1867, he argues, was propelled in part by the North's victory. Suffrage reformers like John Bright were ardent admirers of American democracy, while 'anti-Americanism was the hobbyhorse' of English conservatives who expressed contempt for the rule of mere numbers. A Union defeat, McPherson argues, would have confirmed Tory criticisms of democracy, discouraged reformers, and 'the Reform Bill would have been delayed for years'. The American Civil War revived the moribund movement for a democratic franchise and the victory of the North weakened the conservative opposition to it. 'The last best hope of democracy did not perish from the earth', concludes McPherson, 'but experienced a new birth of freedom whose impact was felt abroad with telling effect'. One could hardly find a more explicit endorsement of Lincoln's words as historical fact and accurate prophecy.[31]

As long ago as 1960 Allan Nevins described this argument as 'at some points erroneous, and at a few grossly fallacious'. The notion of a clear divide between pro-Confederate aristocrats and pro-Union democrats is inaccurate. It was William Gladstone, whose call for British mediation in the war betrayed pro-Confederate sympathies, who in 1864 'threw in his lot with the leaders of the hitherto not very convincing reform agitation'. That support, Richard Shannon argues, 'made it inconceivable that a second Reform Act would not eventually emerge from the 1865 Parliament'. Moreover, it was Benjamin Disraeli and the Conservative Party – supposedly aristocratic opponents of democracy – who actually enacted suffrage reform. In order to sustain his thesis that the Civil War polarized British opinion between liberal proponents and conservative opponents of democracy, McPherson has to omit the Tories' role in extending the franchise. He therefore attributes the Second Reform Act to the 'forces of liberalism'. One never learns that a Tory administration engineered Britain's decisive step toward mass democracy.[32]

In short, although the Civil War stirred British public opinion, with supporters of suffrage reform tending to cheer the cause of the Union, it was one event of many that encouraged suffrage reformers. It cannot be said to have been decisive. As D.P. Crook puts it,

> The legislation was shaped by political contingency and expediency, it was engineered by a parliamentary elite within a largely parliamentary context, and it owed its form to hierarchic reasoning rather than to democratic doctrines [...]. The vote might be safely extended to include steady workingmen, likely to be deferential and adhere to current social values [...]. Populations pressures and expanding industrialization rendered some such adjustment inevitable. The significance of American events was as one more sign that the world was going in much the same direction.[33]

European elites discovered – later than American elites but independently of them – that a democratic franchise need not lead to radical consequences. If guided and controlled, manhood suffrage could be tamed. Disraeli ended up promoting a wider franchise because he saw England's working class as 'manageable electoral material' that would redound to the benefit of the Conservative Party. As political theorist John Dunn has argued, the expansion of democracy in Europe owed much to 'deft defensive gambits by audacious conservative politicians'.[34]

It seems clear, then, that the notion of the United States as the inspiration for international democratization is misleading. The history of women's suffrage underlines this point. An international movement from the outset, women's suffrage had been adopted in only a handful of countries, all of them with small populations, before the First World War. At the end of that conflict, however, the floodgates burst open. Between 1918 and 1920 Britain, Canada, Germany, Sweden, the Netherlands, Belgium, the successor states of the Austro-Hungarian Empire and the

United States enfranchised women. There was no question of other nations emulating the United States. Indeed, one historian has suggested that it was the other way round, Britain's enactment of women's suffrage in 1918 influencing the United States: 'Democracy's unsteady dispersion across the world was no testimony to American power, and not much even to the force of American example', writes John Dunn. 'If anything, it testified to the intrinsic power of democracy itself as an idea'.[35]

In *The Irony of American History*, Reinhold Niebuhr pointed out the error of Lincoln's belief that liberty and democracy could only be secured through a republican form of government. In Britain, he pointed out, 'the hated institution of monarchy was gradually brought under control by the rising power of democracy'. In the world at large, neither republicanism nor democracy made much progress after 1865. Of the 48 independent states in 1900 only eight could be characterized as democracies, and only two of the great powers, France and the United States, were republics. As Crook concludes, 'the legacy of the Civil War to European politics was curiously meager'. Europe and the United States moved toward democracy along different paths.[36]

In fact, contrary to Lincoln's belief, democracy proved perfectly compatible with monarchy. Indeed, as Michael Lind points out, 'semidemocratic parliamentary monarchy of the British kind [...] became the dominant form of representative government for most of the new countries created between the American Civil War and World War I'. Moreover, the limited democracy of Europe, whether in republican or monarchical form, went hand-in-glove with imperialism, which, by 1914, had subjected 85 per cent of the earth's land surface to the control of European powers. Pushing his argument to thought-provoking lengths, Lind suggests that

> the principles with which Lincoln identified the Union cause diminished in influence following the Union victory – while the principles of leading Confederates, like the doctrine of nonwhite racial inferiority and a rejection of Enlightenment beliefs in human rights and self-determination, were shared by a majority of the statesmen in London, Paris, Berlin, Vienna, and Moscow.

It took the shattering effects of the Great War to topple the Romanov, Hohenzollern and Habsburg monarchies, and to make republicanism the dominant form of government in Europe. The post-1918 republics, however, quickly became fascist and communist dictatorships, or acquired various types of authoritarian government. Only in Czechoslovakia did democracy take root.[37]

If the United States was *not* actually the 'last best hope of earth', did the Union victory at least bring about a 'new birth of freedom' in America itself? Only to a limited extent. Obviously, the Civil War resulted in the abolition of slavery and the forcible suppression of the Confederacy. However, the democratic promise of Congressional Reconstruction was not fulfilled. The ex-Confederates never accepted the validity of black suffrage, and by 1877, through intimidation and violence, assisted by federal inaction and northern indifference, had regained political power in the southern states. Black southerners found themselves pushed out of the democratic process, first by means of fraud, intimidation and violence, and later, after 1890, through wholesale disfranchisement by state law. McPherson's claim that the Union victory 'left America [...] more democratic' is too unequivocal. The North's attempt to incorporate blacks into the political system failed, and the post-disfranchisement South, with its one-party system and restricted electorate, was less democratic than the antebellum South. The decay of democracy in the South, moreover, weakened the democratic basis of national politics as well.[38]

Conclusion

The disputed presidential election of 2000 revealed that the United States, far from being the exemplar of democracy, did not know how, or was unable, to conduct a free and fair election. The chaotic count in Florida exposed the tip of an iceberg composed of inconsistency, inefficiency and anti-democratic practices. The inefficiency consisted in every city and county in the land conducting the election in its own way, choosing its own technology and following its own rules. More profoundly, the Supreme Court, in deciding the outcome of the election on a 5–4 vote, underlined the remarkable but little noted fact that the federal government has never made the vote an affirmative right. States could not discriminate on the basis of race or gender, but they found any number of other, legal, ways to reduce the electorate. States make it hard to register, insist that voters produce official photo identification, locate polling places inconveniently and deploy too few polling places. States also disenfranchise four million adults, half of them African Americans, on the basis that they are convicted felons. No other democracy has so large a prison population as the United States, and no other democracy denies the right to vote to large numbers of ex-prisoners. Small wonder that voter turnout in America is among the lowest of any democracy.

Michael Lind and Godfrey Hodgson have authored the most trenchant of recent critiques of American exceptionalism. The notion that the United States is a classless society, with equality of opportunity, widespread share ownership, superior public schools and world-beating health care is a myth, Hodgson contends. Lind writes, 'The argument that America is utterly unlike other modern nation-states, whether in its lack of a distinct nationality, its youth, its friendliness to immigrants, its egalitarianism, its idealistic self-conception, or its superior constitution, is chauvinistic mythology'. Insofar as they treat 'last best hope of earth' as an historically accurate insight, historians reinforce civil religion rather than illuminate history. Like 'American exceptionalism', the phrase 'last best hope of earth' connotes moral superiority, not merely difference. Historians should abandon it and, to quote Leo P. Ribuffo, the phrase 'should be buried in a deep hole with nuclear waste'.[39]

Notes

1. Abraham Lincoln, 'Second Annual Message to Congress', 1 December 1862, Miller Center of Public Affairs, online at http://millercenter.org/scripps/archive/speeches/detail/3737 (accessed October 2010).
2. Gary Wills, *Lincoln at Gettysburg: The Words That Remade America* (New York, 1992).
3. Bernard Bailyn, *Ideological Origins of the American Revolution* (Cambridge, MA, 1992), 20; Mark A. Noll, *America's God: From Jonathan Edwards to Abraham Lincoln* (Oxford, 2002), 9.
4. This and all subsequent quotations from inaugural addresses come from the transcripts located in the Presidential Speech Archive, Miller Center of Public Affairs, University of Virginia, online at http://millercenter.org/scripps/archive/speeches (accessed October 2010).
5. Noll, *America's God*, 56; Gentile, *Politics as Religion*, 23; Jean H. Baker, 'Lincoln's Narrative of American Exceptionalism', in James M. McPherson (ed.), *We Cannot Escape History: Lincoln and the Last Best Hope of Earth* (Urbana, IL, 1995), 41.
6. James Truslow Adams, *The Epic of America* (Boston, MA, 1931); Gunnar Myrdal, *An American Dilemma: The Negro Problem and Modern Democracy*, 2 vols (New York, 1944), I, 3–5; Reinhold Niebuhr, *The Irony of American History* (Chicago, IL, 2008 [1952]), 70; Edward McCall Burns, *The American Idea of Mission: Concepts of National Purpose and Destiny* (New Brunswick, NJ, 1957); Robert N. Bellah, 'Civil Religion in America', *Daedalus* 96/1 (1967), 1–21; Melvin B. Endy, 'Abraham Lincoln and American Civil Religion: An Interpretation', *Church History* 44/2 (1975), 229; Sidney E. Mead, 'Abraham Lincoln's "Last, Best Hope of Earth": The American Dream of Destiny and Democracy', *Church History* 23 (1954), 3. See also Orville Vernon Burton, *The Age of Lincoln* (New York, 2007), 115–16.
7. Myrdal, *An American Dilemma*, I, 3–5; Alexis de Tocqueville, *Democracy in America*, 2 vols (New York, 1840–41), II, 238, 426.

8. S.N. Eisenstadt, *Paradoxes of Democracy: Fragility, Continuity, and Change* (Washington DC, 1999), 58–59; Seymour Martin Lipset, *American Exceptionalism: A Double-edged Sword* (New York, 1996), 126.

9. Niebuhr, *Irony of American History*, 24; Burns, *American Idea of Mission*, 91.

10. Charles R. Wilson, *Baptized in Blood: The Religion of the Lost Cause, 1865–1920* (Athens, GA, 1980), 14–15; David W. Blight, *Race and Reunion: The Civil War in American Memory* (Cambridge, MA, 2001), 356; Jamie Malanowski, 'Why Do We Still Name Army Bases after Rebels?', *True/Slant*, 9 November 2009, online at http://trueslant.com/jamiemalanowski/2009/11/09 (accessed February 2012).

11. Adam Fairclough, 'Civil Rights and the Lincoln Memorial: The Censored Speeches of Robert R. Moton (1922), and John Lewis (1963)', *Journal of Negro History* 82/3 (1997), 409–16; Scott A. Sandage, 'A Marble House Divided: The Lincoln Memorial, the Civil Rights Movement, and the Politics of Memory', *Journal of American History* 80/1 (1993), 135–67.

12. The literature on American anti-communism is vast. For two contrasting views, see Ellen Schrecker, *Many Are the Crimes: McCarthyism in America* (Princeton, 1998), and Richard Gid Powers, *Not without Honor: The History of American Anti-Communism* (New Haven, 1998).

13. On King's radicalism, see Adam Fairclough, 'Was Martin Luther King a Marxist?', *History Workshop Journal* 15/1 (1983), 117–25.

14. Harvey Klehr, *The Heyday of American Communism: The Depression Decade* (New York, 1984).

15. Niebuhr, *Irony of American History*, 28; Burns, *American Idea of Mission*, 14.

16. Henry R. Luce, 'The American Century', *Life*, 17 February 1941, online at http://books.google.nl/books; Burns, *American Idea of Mission*, 14; Ronald Reagan, 'We Will Be a City upon a Hill', 23 April 1974, online at http://reagan2020.us/speeches (accessed October 2010).

17. William J. Bennett, *America: The Last Best Hope*, 3 vols (New York, 2011); Joe Scarborough, *The Last Best Hope: Restoring Conservatism and America's Promise* (New York, 2009); William J. Bennett and John Cribb, 'The Last Best Hope of Earth', *Wall Street Journal*, 3 July 2009.

18. Karen Tumulty, 'American Exceptionalism: An Old Idea and a New Political Battle', *Washington Post*, 29 November 2010; Matt Miller, 'Ohhh, America, You're so Strong', *Washington Post*, 18 November 2010; www.newsmax.com/Newsfront/Obama-shirley-american-exceptionalism/2011/12/07. For Obama's comment on 'last best hope of earth', for which conservatives criticized him, see 'Remarks of Senator Barack Obama to Council on Global Affairs', 23 April 2007, online at http://my.barackobama.com/page/content/fpccga/ (accessed October 2010).

19. '51% Say the United States is Last Best Hope of Mankind', *Rasmussen Reports*, 16 May 2010, online at www.rasmussenreports.com/public_content/politics/general_politics/may_2010 (accessed September 2011); Andrew Kohut and Bruce Stokes, *America against the World: How We Are Different and Why We Are Disliked* (New York, 2006), 96.

20. J. Allen Smith, *The Spirit of American Government: A Study of the Constitution, Its Origins, Influence and Relation to Democracy* (London, 1907); Charles A. Beard, *An Economic Interpretation of the Constitution* (New York, 1914); Matthew Josephson, *The Robber Barons* (New York, 1934); idem, *The Politicos* (New York, 1938); idem, *The President Makers* (New York, 1940); C. Vann

Woodward, *Reunion and Reaction: The Compromise of 1877* (New York, 1951); idem, *Origins of the New South, 1877–1913* (Baton Rouge, LA, 1951); idem, *The Burden of Southern History* (Baton Rouge, LA, 1968); Gabriel Kolko, *The Politics of War: The World and United States Foreign Policy, 1943–1945* (New York, 1968); Lloyd C. Gardner, *Architects of Illusion: Men and Ideas in American Foreign Policy, 1941–1949* (Chicago, 1970); Daniel Yergin, *Shattered Peace: The Origins of the Cold War and the National Security State* (Boston, MA, 1977).

21. Conyers Read, 'The Social Responsibilities of the Historian', *American Historical Review* 55/2 (1950), 284; Lillibridge, *Beacon of Freedom*, 123; Susan Jacoby, *The Age of American Unreason* (New York, 2009), 303; McPherson, *We Cannot Escape History*, 4; Eric Foner, 'American Freedom in a Global Age', *American Historical Review* 106/1 (2001), 4–6; Alan G. Guelzo, 'Is America Still the "Last Best Hope of Earth?"', *Christian Science Monitor*, 26 January 2010; Eric Foner, 'The Civil War and the Idea of Freedom', *Art Institute of Chicago Museum Studies* 27/1 (2001), 25; idem, 'American Freedom in the Age of Emancipation', *Journal of American History* 81/2 (1994), 436; idem, 'American Freedom in a Global Age', 4–6; idem, *Reconstruction: America's Unfinished Revolution, 1863–1877* (New York, 1988), xxvii.

22. Mark E. Neely, Jr., *The Last Best Hope of Earth: Abraham Lincoln and the Promise of America* (Cambridge, MA, 1993); Sean Wilentz, *The Rise of American Democracy: From Jefferson to Lincoln* (New York, 2005), 796.

23. G.D. Lillibridge, *Beacon of Freedom: The Impact of American Democracy upon Great Britain, 1830–1870* (Philadelphia, 1955), xiii; William H. Riker, *Democracy in the United States* (London, 1965), 12; McPherson, *We Cannot Escape History*, 1, 4, 10–12.

24. Allen G. Guelzo, 'A War Lost and Found', *American Interest* 7/1 (2011), 14; idem, 'Is America Still the "Last Best Hope of Earth?"'

25. Burns, *American Idea of Mission*, 91; Walter Dean Burnham, 'The Appearance and Disappearance of the American Voter', in Richard Rose (ed.), *Electoral Participation: A Comparative Analysis* (Beverly Hills, 1980), 40; Rosemary O'Kane, *Paths to Democracy: Revolution and Totalitarianism* (London, 2004), 67–81; Gordon Wood, *The Radicalism of the American Revolution* (New York, 1991), 294; John Keane, *The Life and Death of Democracy* (New York, 2009), 294, 359.

26. Wood, *Radicalism of the American Revolution*, 7; Wilentz, *Rise of American Democracy*, 6. The Second Republic also enfranchised newly emancipated slaves in France's colonies.

27. O'Kane, *Paths to Democracy*, 42; Eisenstadt, *Paradoxes of Democracy*, 5–17; Keane, *Life and Death of Democracy*, xvii, 674, 273; M. Lind, *What Lincoln Believed* (New York, 2004), 302; J.R. Pole, *The Pursuit of Equality in American History* (Berkeley, CA, 1978), 14; Louis Hartz, *The Liberal Tradition in America* (New York, 1955), 47.

28. Ivor Crewe, 'Electoral Participation', in David Butler et al. (eds), *Democracy at the Polls: A Comparative Study of Competitive National Elections* (Washington DC, 1981), 219; Keane, *Life and Death of Democracy*, xxiii, 259.

29. John Dunn, *Democracy: A History* (New York, 2005), 154; Wilentz, *Rise of American Democracy*, 485; Hartz, *Liberal Tradition in America*, 128–9.

30. Walter Dean Burnham, 'The Appearance and Disappearance of the American Voter', in Butler et al. (eds), *Democracy at the Polls*, 40–43; Wilentz, *Rise of American Democracy*, xviii, 192–6, 201–2, 431; Pole, *Pursuit of Equality in*

American History, 33; Alexander Keyssar, *The Right to Vote: The Contested History of Democracy in the United States* (New York, 2000), 70.

31. J. McPherson, 'Last Best Hope for What?,' in idem (ed.), *We Cannot Escape History*, 4, 11.

32. Allan Nevins, *The War for the Union: War Becomes Revolution, 1862–1863* (New York, 1960), 242–3; Theodore Hoppen, *The Mid-Victorian Generation, 1846–1886* (Oxford, 1998), 242; Richard Shannon, *The Crisis of Imperialism, 1865–1915* (London, 1974), 54–5; Robert Blake, *Disraeli* (New York, 1967), 463–4; McPherson, 'Last Best Hope for What?', 11. For the impact of the Civil War on British public opinion and politics, see also H.C. Allen, *Great Britain and the United States: A History of Anglo–American Relations, 1783–1952* (London, 1954), 458–9, 493–7; Mary Ellison, *Support for Secession: Lancashire and the American Civil War* (Chicago, 1972); Howard Jones, *Blue and Gray Diplomacy: A History of Union and Confederate Foreign Relations* (Chapel Hill, NC, 2010); idem, *Union in Peril: The Crisis over British Intervention in the Civil War* (Chapel Hill, NC, 1992); R.J.M. Blackett, *Divided Hearts: Britain and the American Civil War* (Baton Rouge, LA, 2001); Amanda Foreman. *A World on Fire: Britain's Crucial Role in the American Civil War* (New York, 2011).

33. Getrude Himmelfarb, 'The Politics of Democracy: The English Reform Act of 1867', *Journal of British Studies* 6/1 (1966), 97–108; Douglas F. Sheppard, 'The Cave of Adullam, Household Suffrage, and the Passage of the Second Reform Act', *Parliamentary History* 14/2 (1995), 149–72; Kristin Zimmerman, 'Liberal Speech, Palmerstonian Delay, and the Passage of the Second Reform Act', *English Historical Review* 118/4 (2003), 1176–1207; Robert Saunders, 'The Politics of Reform and the Making of the Second Reform Act, 1848–1867', *Historical Journal* 50/3 (2007), 571–91; Maurice Cowling, *1867: Disraeli, Gladstone and Revolution* (Cambridge, 1967), 17–44, 242–66; D.P. Crooks, *The North, The South, and the Powers, 1861–1865* (New York, 1974), 379–80.

34. Jean Grugel, *Democratization: A Critical Introduction* (New York, 2002), 32–67; Daron Acemoglu and James A. Robinson, *Economic Origins of Dictatorship and Democracy* (Cambridge, 2006), 63–68, 270–1; L.C.B. Seaman, *Victorian England: Aspects of English and Imperial History, 1837–1901* (London, 1973), 62; John Dunn, *Democracy: A History* (New York, 2005), 153–4.

35. Teri L. Caraway, 'Democratization: Class, Gender, Race, and the Extension of the Suffrage', *Comparative Politics* 36/4 (2004), 447; David Morgan, 'Woman Suffrage in Britain and America', in H.C. Allen and Roger Thompson (eds), *Contrast and Connection: Bicentennial Essays in Anglo-American History* (London, 1976), 281; Dunn, *Democracy*, 91.

36. Niebuhr, *Irony of American History*, 77; Crooks, *The North, The South, and the Powers*, 379.

37. Lind, *What Lincoln Believed*, 304–6.

38. McPherson, 'Last Best Hope for What?', 12.

39. Godfrey Hodgson, *The Myth of American Exceptionalism* (New Haven, NJ, 2009); Michael Lind, *The Next American Nation: The New Nationalism and the Fourth American Revolution* (New York, 1995), 232; Baker, 'Lincoln's Narrative of American Exceptionalism', 41–2; Leo P. Ribuffo, 'Twenty Suggestions for Studying the Right Now That Studying the Right Is Trendy', *Historically Speaking* 12/1 (2011), 6.

Part V
Religion and Revolution

Revolutionary Mystique: Religious Undertones in the Russian Revolution of 1917

Henk Kern

The Russian Revolution was more than just the collapse of a derelict government and the violent introduction of a new dictatorial regime. To those who witnessed and experienced these events, they meant the beginning of an unprecedented new world order in which their wildest dreams – or nightmares for that matter – might come true. It is hard to imagine, but at the same time worthwhile to understand, what impact the revolution had on the thoughts and beliefs of the people who initiated it and lived through it. It is therefore the purpose of this chapter to provide a modest contribution to the exploration of the mental mapping of the revolution.

Concept and Problems

For this purpose, the concept of 'political religion' will be tested for its applicability and relevance as an analytical tool in the study of the Russian Revolution. The idea of political religion as such emerged in the 1930s together with the concept of totalitarianism as specific labels to single out and characterize the new phenomenon of modern mass dictatorships, in the first place exemplified by Stalin and Hitler. One could say that the totalitarian model refers primarily to the hard power of these dictatorships, the coercive instruments and institutions of the system to control society, whereas political religion also draws attention to soft power, the capacity of the system to exercise control over the hearts and minds of its subjects.[1]

Hard and soft power are, of course, complementary and interconnected, but at the same time, the shift in emphasis between the two gained importance in the course of academic enquiries into the actual workings of these modern dictatorships. First, from the 1940s to the

1960s the main effort of scholarly research was devoted to understanding the repressive state apparatus and the mechanisms by which the totalitarian regime successfully subdued and atomized the people into defenceless victimhood. In these circumstances, a group of ideological fanatics armed with a modern organization and technology could keep a society under total control and do whatever harm they wished. But from the 1970s, critical and revisionist researchers argued that on closer look the people under these dictatorships were much better able to withstand the pressures from the regime than previously assumed. Actually, some social groups had willingly cooperated with the regime while using it for their own benefit. The regime had also only partly succeeded in realizing its ambition of total control while being forced to make concessions to the practical constraints of a resistant society. By the 1990s, when the communist dictatorships in Eastern Europe had come to an end as a result of internal reformist developments, the classical totalitarian model had lost much of its attractiveness as an accurate description and explanation for this type of dictatorship. An all too exclusive focus on the hard power of the modern dictatorship had led to a distorted image of reality in which not enough space was given to internal counter-forces and the dynamics of change. Through analysis of its historical examples, the totalitarian model was proven to be simply too rigid. As a result of the demise of Communism, the factors of ideology and mass belief were recognized as being crucial for the effectiveness and sustainability of totalitarian regimes.

The dictatorships in question shared a very specific feature in the way that both their leaders and their adherents showed a single-minded and fanatic devotion towards a certain political ideology. It is on this point that the concept of political religion was rediscovered as a better, more fitting label for this distinctive type of political regime. On the one hand, this concept acknowledges the fact that even with the application of all available modern means of mass mobilization no dictatorship is ever able to achieve complete control of the whole of society. But on the other hand, the concept highlights the fact that certain political movements distinguish themselves by their ability to generate an exceptionally high degree of dedication and motivation on the part of their followers and supporters, in a way that surpasses rational behaviour based on common sense and calculated self-interest. Although the hard power of a political dictatorship might remain imperfect, the soft power of a political religion could still drive people to extreme acts of worship, sacrifice and self-sacrifice. So it is argued by the proponents of the concept of political religion that by means of the so-called 'sacralization of politics' forces are unleashed which will unify and solidify a society into striving for a secular mission of a utopian order. Through the ritualiza-tion and glorification of a political ideology a society could be mobilized towards a holy – if also unattainable – goal in spite of whatever high – not to say inhuman – price it takes. In this sense, the concept of political religion earned its attraction as an explanatory factor behind certain perplexing historical events of mass revolution and mass violence in the twentieth century.[2]

Political religion suits the growing awareness among many contem-porary scholars that ideology was not just an instrument in the hands of a manipulating political elite but that it constituted a fundamental and essential force in the growth and development of certain mass movements. Against the background of the end of the first totalitarian dictatorship ever in 1991, it became fully visible how essential a shared faith and belief had been for the existence of Soviet Communism.[3] This being said, however, the concept of political religion leaves open some important questions of definition and implication.[4] The scholars who make use of this term are not unanimous on what it actually means. Is a political religion just an instrument of propaganda in the guise of a pseudo-religion, or can it be regarded as a true and heart-felt belief system of its own? Is a political religion symptomized by the mere occurrence of outer forms like rituals, symbols and myths similar to established religions, or does it also involve an inner content with the revelation of a higher metaphysical truth? Is a political religion confined to the belief in secular, godless and positive ideas, or does it encompass some belief in transcendental powers as well? And finally, does the initiative for a political religion come from above as part of a top-down effort to mobilize society for the sake of the leaders, or does its impetus come from below through a more dynamic interaction between leaders and society? These questions (and other similar ones) have so far remained unresolved and have led to an impression of vagueness around the con-cept of political religion, despite its undeniable merits as a new way of looking at rather familiar things.

To clarify this controversial concept it will be helpful to put it into practice. By placing the notion of political religion in a specific his-torical context we can see how it actually worked and why, and what implications this has for the further use of the concept. The case of the Russian Revolution seems to be an excellent example of the birth of an organized revolutionary belief system and its attempted implementation into a new socio-political order. So there is good reason to connect this instance to the theory and see what insights this will produce. Moreover, the re-emergence of the concept of political religion coincides with the so-called 'cultural turn' that recently took place in the retrospective study of Soviet history.[5] During most of the last century the focus of historical research on the Russian Revolution was on the political struggle for power by leaders with their organizations and ideologies, on the one hand, and on the influence of the popular masses with their diverse socio-economic interests and aspirations, on the other. The historians of the first category stressed the political authoritarian tendencies in the Russian Revolution, whereas the second category was more open to its popular democratic tendencies. Since the early 1990s a new generation of social historians has entered the scene who are not linked to the preconceived Cold War notions about democracy versus dictatorship and the fundamental opposition between Russia and the West. Since the collapse of the Iron Curtain they can dive deeper than ever before into archives, distant regions and unseen sources. This enables them to place the emphasis of their research on the history of the mentality and cultural experience of individual people and social groups within the context of a rapidly changing and modernizing society. The various meanings of language and symbols in daily life, private feelings, self-image and personal worldviews of Russians are among the more frequently studied subjects in this new approach.[6] It seems fruitful to bring together the results of this new approach with the concept of political religion. What does the cultural perception of the Russian Revolution reveal about the role of political religion?

Revolution as Resurrection

The story goes that shortly after the revolution of 1917, when the Civil War started to unfold, a Red Army patrol entered a Russian Orthodox Church in Riga where at that very moment a service was being held. One of the soldiers stepped to the lectern, opened the Holy Book and read, 'He will wipe away every tear from their eyes, and death shall be no more, neither there shall be mourning, nor crying, nor pain anymore, for the former things have passed away' (Revelation 21:4). Thereupon the soldier closed the book and said, 'Today, this word has come true.' It is not known if this anecdote has any factual basis whatsoever, but as a tableau it contains a historical truth in testifying to the enormous visionary energy in the idea of revolution: old times are over, a new and comforting life begins.[7]

For the large majority of the Russian people religion, in the form of the traditions of the Russian Orthodox Church, was the main frame of reference. In the beginning of the twentieth century Russia tried to present itself outwardly as a great and modern European power, but the inner culture of Russian society remained predominantly rooted in traditional peasant folk culture. Around 1917, peasants made up more than 80 per cent of the total population of the empire, and Russian mass consciousness was largely determined by the Orthodox rituals and beliefs that had been developed in the peasant communities over centuries. Religion provided the meaning and grounding for human existence. The Russian Orthodox faith was intertwined with the daily routines of pastoral life in the villages. It was not so much concerned with texts and dogmas but with forms, rituals and practices such as liturgical ceremonies and choirs, pilgrimages and monasteries, the calendar of saintly festivals and fasts, the icons and prayers, the baptisms and funerals. Together they produced in the mind of the common person many religious images and one religious idiom to make sense of the world around. It has often been contended that in this Russian religious idiom certain peculiar traits of the people's mentality stand out, such as the emphasis on suffering, sacrifice and salvation, or the so-called 'naive monarchism' which implied that the good father tsar was closely connected to God and would personally protect all simple folk against evil oppressors and injustice. Since the sixteenth century, the saintly prince, who sacrificed his life like Jesus Christ for the sake of the people and who was immortalized as an ideal-type lord protector of Russia, had been one of the most persistent themes in traditional Russian political culture and would resurface again after the revolution.

The American historian Mark D. Steinberg studied the ways that religious imagery aided representatives of the Russian uneducated classes in conceptualizing and organizing their strongly emotional and moral impressions during the years of revolution. The main argument of his research is not the endurance of the Christian faith among ordinary Russians but 'the importance of religious symbols, images and feelings in the ways that articulate spokesmen of the lower classes understood and represented the history of their times, especially the coming of revolution'.[8] The focus of his study is on the written testimonials of workers. And while during the revolution these workers turned away from the established church and belief in God, they held on to the visionary vocabulary of the religion of their childhood. They took life as a metaphorical journey through suffering towards salvation. That's why in their imagination the revolution is depicted as an ordeal which required sacred and redemptive sacrifices, such as an early accidental death, but in the end would lead humanity to the establishment of an earthly paradise.

In spite of Lenin's and the Communist Party's condemnation of the use of religious language as 'unproletarian', the proletarian revolution stimulated the spontaneous sacralization of political vision.[9] References to the crucified proletariat, the cross of the great struggle, the building of the new temple of truth on the ruins of the old, are typical expressions of mass mentality in Russia. In the popular imagination secular ideals of emancipation were connected with mystic dreams of a kingdom of heaven after death and winged humans flying to the light of freedom. The hardships and bloodshed of war, revolution and civil strife intensified Russians' feelings of apocalyptic fear and expectation. This is exemplified in many varieties of words by workers, peasants and soldiers who shared their thoughts with the larger public: 'And in agony / We give birth to a new world.'[10] In conclusion, Steinberg states that 'this was religious feeling without religious belief'.[11] The images of crucifixion and resurrection were neither empty forms nor full confessions of Christian faith. They spoke the language of emotion and were a toolkit for the people to make horrible times more understandable and bearable, in a more effective way than any rational ideological theory could hope to do.[12]

But Steinberg's argument can be pushed one step further, as is done by Richard L. Hernandez, an American historian and specialist on the theme of political religion in Russia. He contends that the new revolutionary regime not only derived from the Russian Orthodox tradition its rituals, language and symbols as outward forms of communication, but that on top of that the revolution itself also inspired among its adherents a tremendous inner devotion.[13] Hernandez finds evidence for his idea that Communism generated a true belief in a new metaphysics in a case study of the *Confessions* by Semen Kanatchikov (1879–1940). This memoir and spiritual autobiography of a Bolshevik peasant/worker activist was written in the middle of the 1920s and published for political instruction purposes in several editions between 1929 and 1934. Kanatchikov recounts his personal conversion to 'class consciousness' during the pre-revolutionary years, his coming into a state of virtual ecstasy while reading illegal socialist texts and his sudden grasp of complete knowledge of the mechanics and meaning of existence. He devoted the rest of his life to the preaching and practising of this higher knowledge, in which the salvation of the future working classes through labour and science was central. For him Communism was an authentic eschatology that gave him strength to endure violence and doubts.[14] So judging from this case, it would be misleading to regard Bolshevism as a secular political ideology which was simply sacralized with a veneer of religious words. Instead, Bolshevism contained a mysterious and sacred core of its own.[15]

. From the numerous examples of popular revolutionary imagery collected by scholars such as Steinberg, Hernandez and others[16] it can be deduced that with regard to ordinary people like peasants, workers and soldiers the cultural environment in Russia in the early years of the revolution was at the same time both receptive to political experiments and new ideas but also preconditioned in its perception of these through a traditional religious prism. Whatever the revolutionary socialists, Marxists and Bolsheviks may have had in mind, their initiatives were greeted by the Russian people as apocalyptic signs and hopeful promises of resurrection.

Revolution as God-building

Early on the morning of 25 October 1917, just after Lenin's momentous announcement that the Provisional Government had fallen and that all power had been transferred to the Soviets, Anatoly Lunacharsky, a prominent Marxist thinker and the future People's Commissar of Education (1917–29), wrote a letter from Petrograd to his wife who was staying in Switzerland. He talked about the confusion of the day, the political manoeuvring between parties, the looting and hooliganism in the streets, and about the fear and uncertainty over what would come next. He ended his letter with the words,

> These are really terrible times, on a knife-edge. There's a lot of anxiety and suffering, and perhaps we're threatened with an early death. At the same, I'm happy to be alive at a time of such great events, when history is not half-asleep but is flying like a bird over trackless wastes.[17]

Again, the revolution is imagined as a winged figure on a transcendental journey. But in this instance, it comes from the imagination not of a representative of the uneducated lower classes but of a highbrow Russian intellectual and an ardent supporter of the rational enlightenment and scientific socialism.

At the turn of the century among the educated classes in Russian society, the relatively small segment of roughly ten per cent of the population which received professional training and developed intellectual aspirations, there had occurred a strong upsurge of various spiritual movements, ranging from Christian revivalism to theosophical esotericism. For the Russian intelligentsia, who for a long time had been engaged in explicitly critical ideas and oppositional actions, the decades from the 1890s onward were an era of spiritual crisis. They realized that the early actions of the nihilistic revolutionaries had resulted in sense-less killings and failure. Many thinkers of the next generation sought therefore to regenerate the revolutionary movement by turning towards religion or, as it was called, 'the creative energy of the people' to find a new identity for themselves. Writers such as Nicolai Berdyaev, Andrei Bely and Alexander Blok expressed an apocalyptic mood which was typical for the symbolism in the cultural movement of the Silver Age.[18] 'In no other country in Europe was there such a sweeping literary preoc-cupation with apocalyptic imagery as in Russia under Nicholas II', states Nina Tumarkin in her standard work on the history of the Lenin cult.[19] So it was not just in the lower ranks of the Russian population but also in the higher echelons of society that the cultural environment longed for a new vision combined with eternal religious concepts about life, death and rebirth. As a result, the revolution was welcomed by many educated Russians as the true coming of their wildest eschatological expectations. And even the Bolsheviks, who had a reputation for being the most militant and die-hard realist splinter party of all the socialists, were not immune from this tendency.

The concept that was central to the advocates of a religious inter-pretation of Russian socialism was the philosopher Nikolai Berdyaev's idea of 'Godmanhood'.

> Our religion must be greater than Christianity. It must be the religion of Godmanhood, the religion of the perfect union of the Divinity with humanity, of the complete incarnation of the Spirit in the life of humanity, achieved by adding to and supplementing the truths of Christianity. The phenomenon of Christ was the overcoming of both Godless humanity and manless divinity, but up to the present this overcoming was accomplished only in the person of the Godman. Now it has to be accomplished in humanity, in Godmanhood.[20]

This idea resonated with many members of the intelligentsia in search of spiritual regeneration, and also within Lenin's Bolshevik party. There it crystallized in the submovement of God-building (*bogostroitelstvo*), a loosely connected group of thinkers such as the writer Maxim Gorky, the philosopher Alexander Bogdanov and above all Anatoly Lunacharsky, who tried to turn Bolshevism into a new religion in which God was human. And through 'the miracle of the victory of human reason and will over nature' this new man would create a heavenly future for all humanity.[21] According to Lunacharsky in his book *Religion and Socialism* (1908–11), which contains his main statement of belief, modern science and Marxism had liberated humanity from ignorance and submission but were as mere theories in themselves unable to inspire people with enthusiasm and solidarity. Religion, however, generated the true enthusiasm by which people could create great things. Since the essence of religion was the spiritual bond between people, this could be achieved without reference to an otherworldly god or some form of superstition but instead by the dreams and myths of an unchained humanity. 'Light, hope, poetry, beauty, dignity and enthusiasm were to adorn the struggle of the proletariat.'[22] The God-builders proposed in their writings and teachings that the great men of science and technology would be held up for veneration and imitation, much like Christ and the saints. And next, the people would become God themselves, with a desire for moral and material improvement, master of all things, creator of miracles. In this way, humanity would transcend individualism, create an eternal humanistic community and achieve immortality. That constituted the most attractive element in the God-building movement; it attributed to humanity complete power over fate. In the words of Gorky, 'We are the children of the sun, the bright source of life; we are born of the sun and will vanquish the murky fear of death.'[23] For Lunacharsky human potential could be fully realized only through the building of this new religion of Godmanhood, and the 'greatest and most decisive act' in this process would be the revolution itself.[24]

Lenin was not amused, however, and attacked the God-builders for being reactionaries and posing a threat to the cause of socialism. He regarded religion in any form as a fallacy, hostile to Marx's materialism which was supposed to be absolutely atheistic. Religion could be nothing other than an ideological tool in the hands of the ruling class. Take away its social basis and it will disappear. In his view, God-building played into the hands of the bourgeoisie because it promoted mysticism and daydreaming that could only distract the masses from purposeful action. In two angry letters to Gorky in 1913 Lenin wrote that the belief in any god is like 'necrophilia' and that the belief in God-building was even more dangerous because more difficult to refute. Lenin's objections to the movement were exacerbated by the fact that one of its main spokesmen, Bogdanov, had also been one of his political and philosophical party rivals. Even before 1917 Lenin made sure that this religious current under Bolsheviks was cut-off and that the circle of God-builders was dissolved.[25] Nevertheless, the history of this marginalized minority group within the communist movement indicates that a latent but strong sensitivity towards religion among the future leaders of revolutionary Russia existed, people who belonged to the intelligentsia and who professed their devotion to the principles of secular and rational enlightenment. Lenin and his orthodox Marxist followers might have abhorred it, but the Russian revolutionaries kept on looking for new gods. And although the God-builders were anathematized, their project to deify the human genius would live on in the veneration and immortalization of Lenin himself.

Revolution as Ritual

The personality cult around the leader of the 'Great Socialist October Revolution of 1917' had only slowly and reluctantly been developed during Lenin's lifetime, but during his illness and after his death in 1924, and the events surrounding the mourning and funeral, it reached a rather spectacular height. From that moment on, the central message of the cult was the assertion that Lenin's death was just an illusion; in reality he would keep on living forever. Slogans cried out everywhere: 'Lenin is completely with us', 'He has not died and will never die', 'If Lenin is silent, we the workers hear his voice inside us', 'Lenin is the sun of the future' and finally in the famous poem by Vladimir Mayakovsky: 'Lenin – lived / Lenin – lives / Lenin – will live'.[26]

However, the cult would involve a great deal more than these and similar words on the occasion of his passing. What took place was a compounded effort to ensure the immortalization of Lenin not just in a symbolic and spiritual way but even in a physical sense. The party had already exalted the leader by placing his stylized portrait on posters and banners and with lofty words of praise for the 'prophet' and 'apostle of the socialist revolution'.[27] When Lenin became ill in 1923 the party founded the Lenin Institute to collect his documents and to manage their correct interpretation, which was to become 'Leninism'.[28] The funeral was made into a unique event in which Lenin's body was mummified, put in a glass sarcophagus and displayed in a specially built mausoleum in the shape of, first, a wooden cube, later, in 1929, a red granite pyramid. Like a holy saint, Lenin would never decay. His tomb became a shrine for communist pilgrims and for official memorial ceremonies. The party launched a campaign of oaths, manifestations and publications to pay public homage to the deceased leader. People were spurred on in meetings to join the party ranks as part of the 'Lenin enrolment'. The traditional Orthodox Red Corners of the peasant homes with their icon and candle were transformed into Lenin Corners with banners and a picture of Lenin in the middle. The masses seemed, for the most part, to respond positively to these innovations, probably because they were connected to forms of the Orthodox traditions and naive monarchism of the past.[29] Schools, clubs, factories and cities were renamed after Lenin, of which Russia's second capital city became the prime example in 1924 when it received its new honourable name of Leningrad. Revealingly, this last initiative was a nicely worked-out compromise between the city's residents, who claimed Lenin's burial site for Petrograd, and the party leaders who wanted to keep Lenin in Moscow and gave Petrograd his name in compensation, in order that 'our great proletarian city be forever related to the name of the great leader and beloved teacher of the international working class'.[30] Later, dozens of museums were established, hundreds of statues erected and thousands of medallions, busts and badges produced to commemorate Lenin.

Whereas the other personality cults of party leaders since Lenin always had a temporal character and would expire shortly after the transfer of power into other hands, the Lenin cult always remained the ritual core of the ideological legitimacy of the regime. Lenin symbolized not just the actual Soviet system and its living representatives but also the higher truths about humanity and society behind it. He was the genius of history, the teacher of the people and the promise of future salvation. Lenin personified the deification of humanity. To this central leadership cult many more socialist rituals were added in the course of the revolution. The traditional faith of the Russian Orthodox Church had to be countered by the replacement of its old rituals with new Red ones. That's where the Komsomol carnival Christmas, the Red Wedding, the Octobering or presenting of newborns and the alternative calendar for festive days, such as Harvest Day or the Day of Industry instead of traditional holidays, came from.[31] The desecration of the old regime went hand in hand with the sacralization of the new. So it happened that Communism in Russia took on a ritual and sacred form together with a single-minded and radical mission. Measured by its diagnostic symptoms,[32] it definitely developed into a political religion.

However, in the Soviet Union there would never be any explicit effort to make a formal religion out of Communism. The image is ambivalent and contradictory. The practice of upholding the secular ideology and political system displayed many religious features which were connected to traditional peasant culture or to the modernistic fantasies of the intelligentsia. Since its early inception until the very end of Communism in the late 1980s, the Lenin cult would represent in all its numerous manifestations this peculiar synthesis between secular ideology and religious mysticism. Now the difficult question here is how can this phenomenon be explained? Who took the initiative and for what motive? Did the new regime invent a substitute religion to manipulate and indoctrinate society, or did the society with its pervasive cultural heritage compel the new regime to adjust itself?

On this point historiography diverges. The traditional 'totalitarian' school of historians focuses on the role of Stalin in this process and his monopolizing of the ideology.[33] As a former seminarian and later successor of Lenin as party leader, Stalin is supposed to have planned and organized the Lenin cult as a means to control the party and the public and to legitimize his own power. By deliberately building up a superhuman image of Lenin, he could follow in his predecessor's footsteps and link his own charisma to that of Lenin. In this interpretation, the cult looks more like a clever political scheme and a façade, instead of a truly felt transcendental veneration and devotion. But more recently social and cultural historians, basing their work on new opportunities for archival and local research in Russia and on a demand for a new approach after the Cold War, have challenged this view.[34] They show that the moving spirit behind the Lenin cult originated in various party quarters on both higher and lower levels, partly also in reaction to the wishes and preferences of the wider environment, and that Stalin certainly was not its main architect. The cult had of course a lot to do with the party's concern about the legitimacy and stability of the new regime when it found itself deprived of its great revolutionary leader in such an untimely manner. This situation called for a thoroughly orchestrated cultivation and continuation of Lenin's public image, a task which Felix Dzerzhinsky as head of the state security forces took on.[35] But at the same time, many party members, even at the top where the struggle for succession soon began, sincerely believed that the appearance of Lenin and the revolution represented a Divine Providence for the whole world. The decision not to bury him, as Lenin himself and his wife Krupskaya had wished, but to embalm his body, to display it in a mausoleum on Red Square in Moscow and to make this edifice the ceremonial centre of the Soviet state, was taken by the former God-builders Lunacharsky and Leonid Krasin.[36] The latter, who personally oversaw the mummification of Lenin, had publicly expressed his belief in the resurrection of the dead. 'I am certain that the time will come when science will become all-powerful, that it will be able to recreate a deceased organism.'[37] That's why Lenin should be preserved!

Thus, political calculation and cultural imagination came together in the making of a communist political religion in the Soviet Union.

To draw the balance is a delicate task and depends on one's perspective. A non-Russian expert on this subject, Nina Tumarkin, takes a sceptical position. 'The Lenin cult was less an actual substitute for religion than a party effort to fuse religious and political ritual to mobilize the population [...] If nothing else, the body cult is a show.'[38] In this interpretation the Soviet rituals were primarily determined by politics. A slightly different emphasis is noticeable in the words of the Russian historian Olga Velikanova, a former guide and researcher of the Revolution Museum in Leningrad, who undertook a fascinating in-depth study on the origins of the Lenin cult:

> The death of Lenin revealed powerful trends in society to worship the leader, and the mourning campaign raised this to a mystical plane. That was in line with the mass's feelings. Lenin's authority [...] was keenly used by party top officials [...]. To stay in power, the party needed to channel the existing mass loyalties along a favourable line.[39]

Here the rituals were a reflection of what was present in society, which the political elite skilfully adapted for their own use. Since in Russia Leninism as a theory developed all the powers of a faith, the author suggests we define it as a 'secular religion'.[40] As she put it in the final line of her book, 'The image of Lenin, that cemented the political religion, existed rather in a "faith dimension" than in a rational one.'[41] So was this political religion essentially a show or a faith? Or could it be both at the same time?

Stalin understood this combination very well and knew how to use it. After the more or less spontaneous and contingent inception of the Lenin cult, he hijacked it for his own purposes. He took control of the initiative, firstly during the funeral speeches with a solemn and repetitive vow to 'fulfil the commandments of Lenin', and secondly by supervising the editing and publication of Lenin's work in a concise and dogmatic form, *The Foundations of Leninism* (1924). Referring to this vow, Stalin's biographer observes that 'the style of the *Communist Manifesto* is strangely blended with that of the Orthodox Prayer Book; and Marxist terminology is wedded to the old Slavonic vocabulary. Its invocations sound like litany composed for a church choir.'[42] Leninist doctrine would later be of use to Stalin for excommunicating rival party leaders during the struggle for succession in the late 1920s and to incite a witch-hunt during the Great Purges in the 1930s that would cause terror in society. In the process of unfolding Stalinism, the original

Lenin cult lost much of its enticement, fervour and authenticity. Stalin reduced the ideology to frozen formulas and the rituals to obligatory acts of subservience. This shift marked the reactionary era into which the revolution had degenerated. It is therefore ironic 'how the new Bolshevik order, seeking to impose itself upon Russia, was itself moulded by precisely those elements of old Russian culture that Lenin so desperately sought to destroy'.[43]

Conclusion

This chapter on the cultural perception of the Russian revolution reveals that the concept of political religion is indeed applicable to this case. To the mass of the Russian people the revolution must have been a shocking and life-defining experience. Traditional religious images and beliefs helped many to get a grip on and give meaning to what happened. Through a hidden transcript the revolutionary ideas and actions of the Bolsheviks and others were interpreted in an apocalyptic and messianic way. To the revolutionary intelligentsia with its elite background and sophisticated culture, the revolution meant the possible fulfilment of high, if also very diverse, hopes. Hardcore atheists wanted to get rid of all illusions but the majority of revolutionaries had utopian visions and dreams about the rebirth of humanity on a higher level, up to some sort of deification through a godless religion. The new leaders of revolutionary Russia were not insensitive towards these religious impulses but regarded them with suspicion. Their ambivalence became evident in Lenin's contemptuous comments on any sign of religiosity, on the one hand, and the tendency to glorify him by the party members, on the other. After his death, through a mixture of calculation and devotion, he was made into the living symbol of not just the party but of the revolutionary promise itself. Forces were at work on three levels to transform Communism in Russia into a genuine political religion.

What does this imply about the essence of political religion? The concept was originally put forward as an addition to the analysis and modelling of political systems. It attempts to highlight an instrument of soft power in the hands of a dictatorship by which it can mobilize and manipulate the masses. In the case of the Russian Revolution this is somewhat problematic. The impulses towards a political religion came to a large extent from the social and cultural environment of the new regime. It can even be said that these influences have diverted and perverted the secular Marxist goals that Lenin had in mind. When the cultural heritage of Russia was employed by Stalin to consolidate his personal power, the revolutionary regime reverted to the pre-revolutionary political culture of authoritarian dogmatism and ritualism. So the essence of political religion is not a one-way, top-down political instrument. It looks more like a contested middle ground in which political actors and their cultural environment interact. As such, the concept of political religion has shown its merit less as an explanatory force in the domain of political analysis than as an eye-opener to the pervasive importance of cultural imagery and imagination. Russia proved to be an 'incurably religious' country and its revolutionary leaders had to put up with that reality.

Notes

1. Compare the Introduction to this volume, which refers to the 'religious dimension of totalitarian politics'. Through the 'veneration and sacralization' of political ideology and leadership the masses of the people could be mobilized more effectively than through sheer coercion. The acknowledgement of the importance of this spiritual aspect of politics in addition to its physical powers is reflected in the appearance of the concept of 'political religion'.
2. Gentile, *Politics as Religion*.
3. M. Kula, 'Communism as Religion', *Totalitarian Movements and Political Religion* 6/3 (2005), 371–81.
4. P. Burrin, 'Political Religion: The Relevance of a Concept', *History and Memory* 9/1–2 (1997), 321–49; D.D. Roberts, '"Political Religion" and the Totalitarian Departures of Inter-war Europe: On the Uses and Disadvantages of an Analytical Category', *Contemporary European History* 18/4 (2009), 381–414.
5. R.G. Suny (ed.), *The Structure of Soviet history. Essays and Documents* (New York and Oxford, 2003), 5.
6. See, for example, S. Fitzpatrick (ed.), *Stalinism: New Directions* (London, 2000); O. Figes, *The Whisperers: Private Life in Stalin's Russia* (London, 2007).
7. H. Oosterhuis, *Scheurkalender van de Bijbel* (Amsterdam, 2003), 15 July.
8. M. Steinberg, 'Workers on the Cross: Religious Imagination in the Writings of Russian Workers, 1910–1924', *The Russian Review* 53/2 (1994), 213–39 (214).
9. Steinberg, 'Workers', 221–2.
10. Ibid., 232.
11. Ibid, 223.
12. Ibid., 237–9.
13. R.L. Hernandez, 'The Confessions of Semen Kanatchikov: A Bolshevik Memoir as Spiritual Autobiography', *The Russian Review* 60/1 (2001), 13–35 (13–14).
14. Ibid., 26–32.
15. Ibid., 34–5.
16. See, for example, R. Stites, *Revolutionary Dreams: Utopian Vision and Experimental Life in the Russian Revolution* (New York and Oxford, 1989); O. Figes and B. Kolonitskii, *Interpreting the Russian Revolution: The Language and Symbols of 1917* (New Haven, 1999).

17. Quoted in E. Acton and T. Stableford (eds), *The Soviet Union, a Documentary History: Volume 1: 1917–1940* (Exeter, 2005), 61.
18. From the late nineteenth century until the First World War Russia experienced a second wave of great artistic achievements, coming after the 'golden age' of Russian literature during the middle of the century, which was epitomized by writers such as Gogol, Dostoevsky and Tolstoy. Therefore critics named this era of second flowering the 'silver age' of Russian arts, which distinguishes itself from its predecessor by the shift from realism to idealism. The Russian poets, painters and artists of the silver age such as Bely, Blok and Vrubel shared the eschatological mood of the *fin de siècle*.
19. N. Tumarkin, *Lenin Lives! The Lenin Cult in Soviet Russia* (Cambridge, MA and London, 1983), 18.
20. C. Read, *Religion, Revolution and the Russian Intelligentsia, 1900–1912: The Vekhi Debate and Its Intellectual Background* (London and Basingstoke, 1979), 76.
21. Tumarkin, *Lenin Lives!*, 20–1; R. Sesterhenn, *Das Bogostroitel'stvo bei Gor'kij und Lunačarskij bis 1909. Zur ideologischen und literarischen Vorgeschichte der Parteischule von Capri* (Slavische Beiträge, 158; Munich, 1982).
22. Stites, *Revolutionary Dreams*, 102; Read, *Religion*, 78–84.
23. Quoted in Stites, *Revolutionary Dreams*, 103.
24. Tumarkon, *Lenin Lives!*, 21–2.
25. Read, *Religion*, 92–3; Tumarkin, *Lenin Lives!*, 22–3.
26. N. Tumarkin, 'Religion, Bolshevism, and the Origins of the Lenin Cult', *The Russian Review* 40/1 (1981), 35–46 (37–8); O. Velikanova, *Making of an Idol: On Uses of Lenin* (Zur Kritik der Geschichtsschreibung, 8; Göttingen and Zürich, 1996), 84.
27. Velikanova, *Making*, 30–2.
28. Ibid., 44–5.
29. Tumarkin, *Lenin Lives!*, 126–7; Stites, *Revolutionary Dreams*, 120–1.
30. Velikanova, *Making*, 62–9.
31. Stites, *Revolutionary Dreams*, 109–12.
32. As summarized in the Introduction to this volume, these symptoms of the sacralization of politics are: religious forms, language, myths and rituals, providing meaning, coherence, identity and moral standards, and constituting a belief system which claims to explain the eternal purpose of human existence.
33. I. Deutscher, *Stalin, a Political Biography*, 2nd edn (New York, 1960); R.C. Tucker, *Stalin in Power: The Revolution from Above, 1928–1941* (New York and London, 1992).
34. Tumarkin, *Lenin Lives!*; Velikanova, *Making of an Idol*.
35. Velikanova, *Making*, 92–3.
36. Tumarkin, 'Religion, Bolshevism', 40–1.
37. Ibid., 44.
38. Tumarkin, *Lenin Lives!*, 197.
39. Velikanova, *Making*, 69.
40. Ibid., 145.
41. Ibid., 154.
42. Deutscher, *Stalin*, 270.
43. Tumarkin, *Lenin Lives!*, 3.

The Belief in Disbelief: Anticlericalism and the Sacralization of Politics in Spain (1900–39)

Eric Storm

Undoubtedly the interwar era was the period in European history when the sacralization of politics reached its apex. Totalitarian regimes in the Soviet Union, Italy and Germany perfected their forms of political religion to unprecedented heights, while in most Eastern European countries authoritarian dictators adopted many aspects of it to cement their regimes. In democratic countries in Western Europe, fascist movements, and socialist and communist parties also did their best to gain adherents, causing a fierce ideological competition. One arena where all existing ideologies clashed in an extremely violent manner was Spain during the Civil War (1936–39). A part of the army had rebelled in July 1936 and rapidly succeeded in gaining control over about half the country. The rebels could count on the support of the small but determined Spanish fascist movement, the Falange, the reactionary Carlists – who supported a dissident branch of the House of Bourbon – and most Catholic conservatives and monarchists. Under General Francisco Franco the resulting Civil War was presented as a crusade to reinstate order in Spain. During the war, but more so after his final victory in April 1939, Franco blended the various ideological movements that supported his regime into one eclectic, national-Catholic political religion, which was clearly totalitarian in aspiration and which in various gradations would be characteristic of his semi-fascist dictatorship, which lasted until his death in 1975.[1]

The government of the Second Republic received the support of republicans, the regionalist movements in the Basque Country and Catalonia, socialists, communists and the remarkably strong anarchist movement. Although after the first chaotic phase of the Civil War had passed an unstable compromise was reached between these groups to postpone most far-reaching social reforms until after the war, the various parties and trade unions within the republican camp tried to increase their following during the struggle, while tightening the bonds with their supporters.

The Civil War became a violent clash between left and right with international repercussions. Both camps presented the war as a struggle between good and evil, and many international volunteers flocked to Spain to defend their respective causes. The communists alone succeeded in recruiting more than 30,000 sympathizers from over 50 countries for the International Brigades. And the enthusiasm with which ordinary Spaniards embraced the cause of one of the participating militias or parties was equally overwhelming. However, in order to establish their own land of milk and honey, many obstacles had to be removed. Thus, with almost religious zeal political opponents were killed behind the frontline, creating approximately 50,000 victims in the Republican zone and 180,000 in the Francoist sector.[2] As a consequence, the Spanish Civil War offers a tragic, while intriguing case, not only of the sacralization of politics from above but also of the widely felt need to believe from below.

Within the Republican zone – which will be the focus of this chapter – surprisingly the most widespread, and probably the most deeply felt shared political idea, seems to have been the belief in disbelief, the anticlerical idea that the Catholic Church represented an evil that had to be rooted out. Thus among the radical measures that were implemented on a local level during the first few chaotic months after the outbreak of the war, such as the collectivization of businesses, the occupation of farm land and the formation of revolutionary councils, we find the confiscation of almost all church properties. Ecclesiastical buildings were turned into party headquarters, arsenals or horse stables, but most were simply put to the torch, which only rarely happened with manors, factories or barracks. Moreover, clergymen, more than fascists, monarchists, conservatives or capitalists, were the object of fierce attacks by all kinds of local militias. Whole areas were almost ritually purged of priests, monks and even nuns. This quasi-religious zeal raises the question whether we should understand the anticlericalism in the Republican zone as a political religion that was imposed from below.

Anticlerical attitudes in Spain have been explained in religious terms before. Thus, Gerald Brenan and Eric Hobsbawm have argued that Spanish anticlericalism had strong millenarian undertones. In his classic study of the Spanish Civil War, Brenan even explicitly compares the anticlericalism of the Andalusian anarchists with iconoclast heretical movements from the Middle Ages or the early modern era, such as the Waldenses and the Anabaptists, while the noted British historian Hobsbawm emphasizes the archaic character of their rebelliousness.[3] Other scholars have criticized this focus on the supposed irrational and millenarian character of anticlerical violence by reasoning that the revolutionaries pursued clear political and even rational goals with their supposed primitive means. Although most authors of more recent studies try to be more balanced, they still struggle to find a rationale for this collective outburst of violence.[4] Analysing Spanish anticlericalism in terms of the sacralization of politics could provide an interesting new approach because it sidesteps the dichotomy of rational versus irrational or secular versus religious.

In order to analyse to what extent Spanish anticlericalism can be fruitfully studied as a political religion, we first have to comprehend the origins of this hostility towards the Catholic Church. This chapter will therefore start with a short overview of the development of the transnational conflict between clericalism and anticlericalism since the French Revolution. Then it will address the question why this conflict became so prominent and fierce in Spain. In the last section the outburst of anticlerical violence in the Republican zone will be the object of analysis.

Anticlericalism in Europe, 1789–1905

Modern anticlericalism is primarily the product of the Enlightenment and was therefore not a specifically Spanish phenomenon. Eighteenth-century philosophers such as Voltaire heavily criticized the Catholic Church for its pompous ceremonies, the superstitious worship of saints, the low intellectual level of the clergy and the lack of productivity of the monastic orders. Although some enlightened monarchs initiated reforms, the conflict between church and state would reach a first climax during the French Revolution. On 4 August 1789 the privileges of the Church were nullified by the National Assembly. Shortly afterwards the properties of the Church were 'nationalized'. Since the tithe was also abolished, the Church then had virtually no income, and it was decided that the secular clergy would be paid by the government.[5]

The Revolution thus effectively stripped the Catholic Church of its privileges and most of its possessions. This happened not only in France but also in most of the territories occupied by the French Republic or the subsequent Napoleonic regime. These measures, and particularly the radical anticlerical policy during Robespierre's reign of terror, would continue to frighten many Catholics during the remainder of the nineteenth century. The Church subsequently fiercely opposed all ideas and currents that smacked of Jacobinism and sought cooperation with groups that had also lost their privileges during the Revolution, such as the nobility and the monarchs. The Restoration Era thus witnessed a renewed alliance between throne and altar. Moreover, because the Church more than ever needed donations and bequests, it came to depend more heavily than before on the rich.

As a consequence, in most Catholic countries anticlericalism was clearly on the rise among more progressive groups. Their criticism was directed at the Church, the clergy and sometimes even religion itself, and during the nineteenth century such criticism was generally of a rational and enlightened nature. The underlying argument was that religion belonged to the private sphere and that the Church should play no role in the political debate or public space. The power of the state should prevail and the freedom of conscience of every individual should be respected. In practice, the resulting conflict was often fought out over the control of education. Other areas of conflict included marriages and funerals. In Catholic countries cemeteries generally were administered by the Church or contained a Catholic section. This situation could result in unpleasant conflicts, as the priest could refuse to bury someone – for immoral behaviour – in the Catholic cemetery, even if the family possessed a family tomb there.

Some anticlericals were not satisfied with the removal of the Church from the public domain and also fiercely criticized the clergy. Priests, friars and nuns were often accused of being unproductive and of not living according to the teachings of the Church. They were seen as vain, vindictive, sneaky, fanatical and cruel. Moreover, many did not keep the vow of chastity, which was seen as problematic, particularly for male members of the clergy, as this could lead to sexual intercourse with married and unmarried women, orgies with nuns, unnatural sex and paedophilia. In books, magazines, songs, caricatures and stories such activities were frequently and graphically depicted. Priests were also portrayed as parasites, criminals, perverts and even as infectious diseases. The authors of these tracts did not merely condemn individual behaviour but above all chided the malign influence exerted by the clergy. This criticism could also induce individuals or groups to attack the clergy or to disrupt public expressions of religiosity, such as processions.[6]

A third form of anticlericalism was directed at religion itself. We find examples in satirical writings and parodies but also in word and gesture. Many Catholic dogmas, such as the Trinity and the virgin birth, were ridiculed as absurd, primitive and unscientific. Collecting bones and old rags as relics was denounced as unhygienic and more suitable for primitive tribes. A Frenchman jokingly claimed to have found a tear of Judas in a Swiss glacier. As long as a large part of the people continued to believe in such nonsense, progress based on reason would be impossible, it was argued. Catholic holidays were also desecrated. In 1868, the French literary critic Sainte-Beuve organized a banquet on the occasion of Good Friday. This was a day that Catholics had to refrain from eating meat. So at the banquet there was meat in abundance. For a variety of associations of freethinkers this would even become an annual tradition. Eating lamb at such an occasion was especially popular, as it was a symbol of Christ.[7]

During the second half of the nineteenth century, progressive politicians in most Western European countries succeeded in restricting the influence of the Catholic Church on the public sphere, Spain being the main exception. Developments in Italy, where the relations between the Church and the state began to worsen as a consequence of the wars of Italian unification, would have a particularly strong impact. When in 1848 many Italians called for a war to liberate Lombardy and Venice from Austrian occupation, Pius IX refused to rally the papal state. As a consequence the Pope was briefly driven out of Rome by a popular uprising. When between 1859 and 1861 a new unified Italian kingdom was created, Pius lost most of the papal state, while in 1870 even Rome was conquered by the army of King Victor Emmanuel II. He offered the Pope control over the Vatican and the corresponding part of Rome, but Pius IX turned it down and even refused to recognize the new Italian state or to set foot outside the Vatican.[8]

Responsibility for the deteriorating relationship between the Church and the new authorities could not be fully attributed to the Italian state. After his flight from Rome in 1848, Pius IX repudiated his earlier sympathies for liberalism and began a counteroffensive. In 1854 he declared the popular belief in the Immaculate Conception of Mary an official dogma, while in 1864 he published the Encyclical *Quanta Cura* which rejected various liberal principles, such as religious toleration, freedom of speech and the separation of church and state. As an appendix he included the *Syllabus Errorum* wherein he condemned rationalism, liberalism, socialism, nationalism and secularism. On top of this Pius summoned the first Vatican Council in 1869, which proclaimed Papal infallibility in matters of faith, while he also forbade Catholics to participate actively in the national politics of the new Italian state.[9]

Italy, however, was not the only state that collided head-on with the Catholic Church; conflicts also occurred in the newly unified German

Empire, where Bismarck launched his *Kulturkampf* and in the French Third Republic. In both countries the government limited the political influence of the Church, prohibited a number of monastic orders and particularly curtailed the role of the Church in primary and secondary education. In France, cemeteries were also secularized and crucifixes were removed from schools, hospitals, courts and other public build-ings, while processions in the open air were forbidden.[10]

Pope Leo XIII, who took office in 1878, modified the politics of the Vatican. Instead of confrontation, he sought cooperation with the key European states. So in 1892 he urged French Catholics to accept the republic and to give up their fight for the restoration of the monarchy. Even more influential was his Encyclical *Rerum Novarum* from 1891. In it Leo XIII showed his concern over the fate of the working classes. He called on Catholics to form their own trade unions and other organiza-tions to address the interests of Catholics in general and the workers in particular. This meant in fact that the Pope was no longer looking back nostalgically to the privileged position of the Church under the *ancien régime* but was confronting the modern political realities in Europe, while urging Catholics to accept the rules of the parliamentary system and try to use them for their own benefit.

The Church also attempted to defend its position and influence by increasing its visibility. Thus, pilgrimages to Rome and new pilgrimage sites such as Lourdes were strongly encouraged by the Church. Moreover, new, conspicuous churches were built, such as the Sacré-coeur in Paris, which was meant as atonement for the sins committed during the Commune of 1871. The Jesuits, in particular, promoted the veneration of the Sacred Heart of Jesus, which symbolized God's love for humankind, and Catholics were encouraged to hang a small medallion of the Sacred Heart at the entrance of their house.

This new sacralization or Catholicization of the public sphere and the simultaneous advance of Catholic organizations, trade unions and political parties caused discontent in the progressive, anticlerical camp. In France matters came to a hard confrontation when in 1901 a left-wing government determined that all monastic orders should receive official recognition. The subsequent government refused this recognition based on the argument that the orders were subordinate to a foreign power: the Vatican. It therefore closed down 12,000 Catholic private schools, and 50,000 monks and nuns left the country. In 1905 a law that radically separated church and state was intro-duced, and as a result the government stopped paying the salaries of the secular clergy.[11]

Since in Italy, Germany and France the state thus succeeded in diminishing the public role and influence of the Church as an institution, the urgency to combat clericalism in all its aspects slowly diminished. However, this was not the case in Spain. Here the state failed to diminish the public role of the Church, and as a consequence anticlericals stepped up their efforts.

Anticlericalism in Spain, 1833–1931

In Spain relations between the state and the Church were not free from frictions during most of the nineteenth century. Because the Napoleonic occupation of Spain – which began in 1808 – never succeeded in pacifying the entire country, the first major wave of secularization of church properties would begin only in the 1830s. When King Ferdinand VII died in 1833 he was succeeded by his infant daughter Isabel II. This succession was, however, contested by Ferdinand's younger and extremely reactionary brother Carlos, who received support from those parts of the country, especially Navarre, the Basque Country and Catalonia, where the abolition of feudal rights and privileges during the French occupation had been widely resented. In order to gain the support of her subjects the queen mother had no option but to introduce liberal reforms, while embarking upon a massive scheme of ecclesiastical confiscations to finance the war against the Carlists. Many members of the clergy consequently sided with Don Carlos, and the Church excommunicated those who participated in the confiscations or who bought former church lands.[12]

Relations between the state and the Church settled down only with the Concordat of 1851. The Pope recognized the expropriations, while the state agreed to pay the secular clergy. Moreover, it was recognized that the Catholic religion was, to exclusion of all other faiths, the religion of the Spanish nation and that all education should conform to its doctrines.[13] This new-found balance between a moderate-liberal constitutional monarchy and the Church was shattered with the fall of Isabel II in 1868. A military coup forced her into exile, and the new regime introduced a more progressive constitution in which for the first time freedom of religion was recognized. The new regime even began to anticipate many anticlerical reforms which in the following decades would actually be introduced in the German Empire and France. However, after a short-lived republican experiment ended in total chaos, a new military coup restored the monarchy, thus bringing the so-called *Sexenio Democrático* to an end.

Under the restored Bourbon king, Alfonso XII, a new constitution was to provide broad support for the parliamentary regime of the Restoration (1875–1931). A compromise was found for the religious question, proclaiming that Roman Catholicism would be the religion of the state, while permitting the private practice of other faiths. Although the re-established dominance of the Church in educational matters was fiercely contested by the left, both Pope Pius IX and the Spanish bishops refused to accept this toleration of other religions, which they regarded as a recognition of error and heresy. Nonetheless, under Leo XIII the Vatican took a more moderate stance, urging the Spanish Catholics to accept the political system of the Restoration and even to participate actively in political and social matters.[14]

In general, the Catholic Church prospered under the Restoration regime. There was no separate Catholic political party as in Germany, but the Conservative Party in particular defended the interests of the Church. The state lacked the money to counteract the growing importance of Catholic schools for primary and secondary education, even when moderately anticlerical liberals formed the government. The clergy even taught religion classes at state schools. Moreover, the number of secular clergy, largely dedicated to education, trebled between 1887 and 1900, rising to about 44,000 nuns and 13,000 monks.

The Church also kept a dominant role in the field of private ceremonies, such as weddings and burials, and in many cases received support from the state to impose a virtual monopoly. In 1903, for instance, the Guardia Civil arrested the pall-bearers of a girl who on the expressed wish of her father received a civil burial in the Basque village of Gallarta.[15] Unlike what happened in Italy, Germany and France, the public role of the Church therefore increased after attempts to curb its influence during the Sexenio ended in failure. Furthermore, as the Church now lacked independent sources of income, it became increasingly dependent on wealthy patrons in order to fund its many charitable and educational establishments, while at the same time it failed to develop effective measures to relieve the miserable conditions of the industrial and agricultural working classes.[16]

In this context a new enlightened anticlericalism prospered and at times of crisis could combine with a more popular anticlerical attitude that had much older roots and can be associated with the archaic forms of social protest studied by Hobsbawm. In the Middle Ages dissatisfaction with the Church and the behaviour of the clergy was already widespread. Since the Church claimed to have access to higher powers and that God could bring prosperity, it was also held accountable in times of misfortune or natural disasters, which sometimes led to explosions of violence. Originally these were spontaneous riots, rather than politically motivated revolts, but from the French Revolution onwards anticlericalism would become ever more politically charged, as the Church began to reject all kinds of political innovations, such as parliaments, constitutions, religious tolerance, elections and secular education, while it openly supported reactionary monarchs.

A first outburst of anticlerical violence in the modern era took place in 1834. Traditional elements, such as the belief in the supernatural powers of the clergy that could also be applied for evil purposes, were mixed with more modern political elements. The fight against the Carlist uprising that had received the support of many priests obliged the government to call upon new recruits and raise taxes, both rather unpopular measures. When on top of this a cholera epidemic broke out in Madrid, the situation in the Spanish capital became critical. Rumours that the Jesuits had deliberately poisoned the city's drinking water led to widespread riots. A mob that apparently held the Jesuits responsible both for making common cause with the enemy and for bringing disaster to the city first attacked their convent and lynched those friars that could not escape. Within a few hours other monasteries were sacked as well and their inhabitants killed, ending the day with 78 casualties.[17]

Later in the century, especially in politically unstable times, anticlerical outbursts continued to occur, but most were minor incidents without fatalities. At the same time, a more intellectual, upper- and middle-class anticlericalism developed, which found expression in plays, novels, newspaper articles and caricatures. Anticlericalism, moreover, became the common denominator of the moderate and radical left, and anti-clerical remarks could be found in most progressive periodicals. There were even a few specialized journals whose pages were filled with stories about lascivious priests, greedy monks, lazy nuns and hypocriti-cal Catholics. There were also a few attempts to found private secular schools, while in freethinking societies, republican clubs and freemason lodges inflammatory speeches were given, and, in imitation of Sainte-Beuve, festive banquets were organized on Good Friday.[18]

Nevertheless, the rival positions only radicalized around 1900. This was primarily caused by the fact that both Catholics and progressive groups were increasingly trying to mobilize a mass audience while sacra-lizing their cause. Politics was no longer a matter of closed meetings and preaching to the converted but moved to the streets. Mass manifesta-tions were partly a response to large-scale and well-organized processions and pilgrimages.[19] Two specific developments caused further growth in anticlericalism. In 1898 Spain lost its last major colonies of Cuba, Puerto Rico and the Philippines after a short but disastrous war against the United States. This outcome was at least partly the result of the discontent of the population of these colonies, and as the Church had played a major role in converting, educating and controlling the population, especially in the Philippines, it was seen as one of the culprits for the military defeat. Moreover, progressive Spaniards argued that a drastic modernization of the country was needed in order to escape being overrun and maybe even occupied by one of the Great Powers, and therefore the influence of the Church should finally be curtailed. The separation of state and church in France functioned as another stimulus for the Spanish left. As a consequence of its new anticlerical laws many French clerics had moved to Spain where they hoped to realize their dream of a totally Catholic society, in which the state protected the Church. This influx of large numbers of clerics only served to underline the need for a fresh anticlerical counteroffensive.[20]

This counteroffensive found its first expression when the celebration of the Jubilee of Christ the Redeemer in 1901 was met with the anticlerical Jubilee of Liberty, which commemorated the confiscation of most church properties by the state 65 years earlier. Various other opportunities were seized for public expression during which anticlerical songs were sung. Sometimes these demonstrations turned into riots in which the windows of churches, convents, Catholic schools and seminaries were smashed. Anticlericals also tried to disrupt processions by whistling or yelling, sometimes even resorting to beating up participants with clubs. At other occasions doors were blocked to prevent processions leaving church. In a few cases these actions led to injuries and deaths since the Catholics did not respond passively and sometimes even brought guns to defend themselves. Civil marriages and funerals were also opportunities for anticlericals to express themselves publicly. Increasingly mimicking religious forms, they invented civil ceremonies for the baptism of a child, which sometimes included a parade, preceded by an orchestra, to the Registry Office. Preferably, this took place on a day when there was a Catholic procession that could be disrupted. Children were given names that referred to progressive ideals instead of to biblical personages or saints, like *Paz, Libertad, Aurora, Progreso* or *Emancipación*. Good Friday dinners were opened to the poor, and in some cities during Holy Week an Anticlerical Week was organized, with all kinds of festivities.[21]

In this way an enlightened, intellectual anticlericalism became increasingly connected with its traditional, more popular counterpart.

Around the turn of the century, it was primarily radical republican populist politicians who deliberately tried to link the two movements by sacralizing both their rhetoric and political forms, thus transforming anticlericalism into a broad, progressive mass movement. The best-known and most successful exponent of this new anticlerical populism was Alejandro Lerroux (1864–1949), who succeeded in mobilizing the lower social classes in Barcelona and winning some resounding victories in local elections with a populist, vaguely socialist and strongly anticleri-cal republican programme. Therefore, as shown by the foremost Spanish historian José Álvarez Junco, Lerroux created a Manichaean contrast between a basically good and morally elevated people and a thoroughly corrupt clergy. The Church thus acted as his scapegoat.[22] Apparently a rational plea to remove the Church from the public sphere was not enough anymore, and he resorted to fiercely criticizing the immoral behaviour of the clergy and the detrimental effects of Catholic religious teachings, while converting his own ideals into political absolutes.

The vilifying of the clergy happened in different ways. Among Lerroux's favourite targets were the values promoted by the Church. According to him, clerics were work-shy parasites who wanted to keep the people ignorant. Their activities had ensured that Spaniards had become a lazy and impotent population of beggars and vagrants addicted to the poor relief of the Church. The clerics preached obedience and a slave morality and in this way had converted the Spaniards into a submissive people who could be easily controlled by the government. Progress, rationality, modernity and a functioning democracy in which the people had the power were not possible, according to Lerroux, as long as the Church maintained its leading position.[23]

Another favoured issue was the unnatural attitude of the clergy towards sexuality. The male clerics who dressed as women were expected to abstain from any sexual activity. Opponents argued that this absten-tion was a denial of human nature and could lead only to deviant or unnatural behaviour. Many stories and jokes circulated about priests who lived in concubinage with their housekeeper, confessors who lust-fully touched penitents and chaplains who eagerly took advantage of their free access to convents where they enjoyed all sorts of excesses with nuns and novices. Moreover, priests had intimate interviews with married and unmarried women out of sight of their husbands, fathers and brothers, and they managed almost certainly to get all kinds of sexual favours, which were sometimes even withheld from the spouses. Lerroux and other anticlerical politicians took advantage of these stereo-types by often making explicit or implicit references to them.

A major point of criticism – which was also used against other typical scapegoats such as Jews, ethnic minorities and freemasons – was the mysterious character of the clergy. Everything was done in secret, in the confessional or behind the walls of an enclosed monastery. The Jesuits, in particular, were accused of operating clandestinely. They formed an uncontrolled but extremely powerful and wealthy sect that exerted an enormous influence behind the scenes, especially in the highest circles of society. The Church was thus like a spider or an octopus that stretched its tentacles everywhere. Lerroux also metaphorically compared the Church to an infectious disease that had fatally weakened the people and had to be eradicated.

In this diatribe against the clergy and religion Lerroux often resorted to religious imagery. Science was a magic potion that the people needed to defeat the dragon (the Church) that lived in the cave of darkness or to exorcise the devil. The nation was compared to Christ; she was an innocent lamb sacrificed to save humankind. But one day the people would be resurrected and win the final battle against evil. The people were like Moses, who guided the nation through the Red Sea and the desert and led her to the Promised Land. In the form that Lerroux gave to his political activities religious elements can also be identified, which it can be argued conferred upon his ideology many of the characteristics of a political religion (including the use of violence against political opponents). It is obvious that this was largely done to attract a poorly educated and often even illiterate audience. Therefore, the sacralization of politics seems to be inextricably linked with the emergence of mass politics around 1900.

Lerroux regularly organized mass meetings, which were not meant only to highlight the party ideology, to rationally discuss points of view and proceed with votes on certain issues or candidates. He wanted, above all, to strengthen the unity among his following by appealing more to the heart than to the mind. He positioned himself as a kind of messiah, who was persecuted and misunderstood but who eventually would bring salvation. Supporters killed by police violence were proclaimed martyrs and venerated as secular saints. These martyrs had served as good examples, sacrificing their lives for the republican cause, and this act also charged those left behind with a huge responsibility because these sacrifices could not remain without consequences. Carrying flags and banners and the communal singing of hymns strengthened the feeling of community and made these meetings into surrogate church services, where one went to fortify the soul. Lerroux also came up with an alternative to popular local pilgrimages in the form of 'democratic picnics'. His followers and their families marched to a hill outside Barcelona to eat and drink together, sing revolutionary songs and listen to uplifting speeches. The message was clear in all this: salvation came not from Christ or the Church but only from the revolution.[24]

That revolution seemed to arrive in 1909. This was the consequence of a Spanish defeat in Morocco after which a large number of reservists were forced to re-enlist in the army. They consisted mostly of married workers who now gathered in Barcelona to be transported to Morocco on ships owned by the marquis of Comillas, an arch-conservative Catholic. Patriotic ladies from the wealthy classes distributed medallions of the Sacred Heart to the recruits. Most of them, however, radically opposed the war, and many threw the religious objects into the harbour. On 26 July a general strike was proclaimed to protest this imperialistic war. Riots broke out, the force of which initially was directed against the state as embodied by tax offices, busses and police stations. On the first evening a Catholic school went up in flames, and during the following days 80 monasteries, churches and seminaries followed, destroying half of all church buildings in Barcelona.[25]

The insurgents submerged the city in chaos, while trying to drive the Catholic Church from it. Desecrating churches and monasteries and burning them down was to produce – as had been preached by Lerroux – a catharsis. The rioters also went looking for evidence of clerical debauchery. Thus, tombs in convents were opened to see if there were foetuses or dead bodies of babies – of nuns who had become pregnant – and cells were examined for perfumes, pornographic attributes and titillating lingerie.[26] Apparently, the mob was hoping that demolishing church buildings and providing the clergy with a heavy-handed lesson would be sufficient since only three priests lost their lives during this so-called 'Tragic Week'.

After a week the army restored order with an iron fist. The eruption of popular violence during Tragic Week probably frightened off the more well-to-do anticlericals. Even Lerroux, who for a short time fled the country, moderated his anticlerical rhetoric after he resumed his political career in Madrid. And after a social-liberal government, led by José Canalejas, failed to curtail the influence of the Church, the struggle between Catholics and anticlericals lost its intensity. However, the Church in response tried to increase its presence in the public realm.[27] This Catholic counteroffensive had considerable success after the First World War, especially after the atrocities of the Russian Revolution became clear to the Spanish upper classes.

This became particularly evident when in 1919, at the geographical centre of Spain, on a hill just south of Madrid, a megalomaniac monument of the Sacred Heart of Jesus was unveiled. On this occasion King Alfonso XIII – who until 1914 had given his support to a social-liberal modernization programme – officially dedicated Spain to the Sacred Heart. This gesture once more confirmed that for a growing segment of the political establishment Spain continued to be a Catholic state. The Church would even increase its influence during the military dictatorship of Primo de Rivera, which began in 1923. Although the socialist trade unions would prosper in the new corporatist state, for many supporters of the left the military, the wealthy employers and the Church all seemed to collaborate to exclude them from political influence. A Jesuit who by that time worked in a poor suburb of Madrid recognized that for a labourer society was divided into two: 'rich and religious bourgeois on the one hand, and poor and irreligious workers on the other'.[28]

Second Republic and Civil War (1931–39)

Only after the king and the dictatorship gave way to the Second Republic in 1931 did the government manage to introduce laws that effectively separated church and state. In the new constitution freedom of religion was guaranteed and civil marriage and divorce were introduced. Other measures included the removal of the influence of the Church on public schools, expelling the Jesuits from the country and the proscription of religious manifestations in the open air. Thus about 60 years after Italy, Germany and France, Spain finally succeeded in restricting the influence and presence of the Church in the public realm. However, with the regime change, anticlerical feelings also resurfaced. In May 1931, even before the new constitution was adopted, anti-monarchic riots in Madrid escalated into an attack on churches and monasteries. The wave of anticlerical violence moved to the east and south and reached a climax in Málaga, where all monasteries and churches were set ablaze. A few months later the celebration of our Lady of Victory, commemorating the expulsion of the Moors from Málaga in 1497, was replaced by a parade of local beauties and the election of a Miss Republic.[29] The new legal provisions were also abused by many left-wing municipalities to show their power over the Church. A priest was, for instance, fined for saying mass outside after lightning had destroyed the roof of his church, while another was penalized for monarchist propaganda when churchgoers sang hymns that spoke of the Kingdom of God.[30]

Right-wing parties won the elections of 1933, in which for the first time women were allowed to vote. The new conservative government decided to freeze both the measures against the Church and land reform, thus confirming the close relationship between the political right and the clergy. The turn to the right was best visible in the return of the Catholic Church to the public realm as processions reappeared on the streets. As a consequence anticlerical eruptions became more violent. Thus during the revolutionary strike in Asturias in 1934 about 60 church buildings were destroyed and 34 clergymen were killed.[31]

However, the real explosion of political violence began only after a group of right-wing army officers, including Franco, staged a military coup on 17 July 1936 against the left-wing Popular Front Government that had won the elections a few months earlier. In the following days weapons were handed out to those who supported the legitimate government or were confiscated by workers' and party militias. Thanks to the loyalty of part of the armed forces to the Republic and the enthusiastic support of a considerable section of the population, the military rebels did not succeed in overthrowing the government altogether initially, but they did take control of most of the western and southern half of the country. In the Republican zone, which contained major towns like Madrid, Barcelona, Valencia and Bilbao, the authority of the central government nevertheless largely collapsed, and power fell into the hands of local revolutionary committees and workers' militias. It took the government about six months to restore order and to create a centralized military command in the area it controlled. This first turbulent period, in particular, would witness an unprecedented outburst of anticlerical violence.

Although the strict separation between church and state had by then already been introduced five years before, republicans were apparently still not entirely reassured that legal regulations would be sufficient. Their distrust was fuelled by the fact that the vast majority of the clergy, just like the rest of Spanish conservatives, sympathized with the military rebellion or even openly supported it. Although there was no central coordination, sentiments in almost the entire Republican zone – the main exception being the thoroughly Catholic Basque Country that had remained faithful to the government because it was granted regional autonomy – turned against the clergy and often even against the Catholic faith. Actually, the anticlericalism of the Republic was mirrored by the clericalism of the nationalist camp. Thus, from about October 1936, Franco's uprising to save 'Spain from Marxism at all costs'[32] was baptized a national crusade and received the open support of the overwhelming majority of Spanish bishops and cardinals. The defence of religion became a common denominator for the nationalist camp, even for some rather secular or freethinking generals and Falangists.[33]

However, it was not so much the measures against the Church but the almost religious ardour with which the clergy was persecuted and killed and the ritual forms that were used that linked the anticlerical fury with the sacralization of politics. Virtually everywhere in the Republican zone priests, monks and even nuns were arrested, imprisoned and in many cases murdered. During the Civil War a total of 6832 members of the Catholic clergy were killed, most of them in the first six months, including 13 bishops, 4172 priests, 2364 monks and friars and 283 nuns.[34] In many areas this constituted around 40 per cent of the clergy, while the rest, of which the great majority generally consisted of nuns, were left unharmed, fled or went into hiding. Among the victims of political repression in the Republic the clergy formed the most important professional group representing around 20 per cent of the total.

The actual political sympathies or reputation of individual clergymen – some of whom supported Catalan regionalism or had shown a positive attitude towards working-class demands – did not matter in most cases; they were murdered because they belonged to the clergy. Young novices were in some cases released as they could possibly better their lives, but this was never the case with aged priests. There might be a kind of court hearing, but in most cases the priests and monks were simply shot, and occasionally hanged, drowned, burned or even buried alive. Many were picked up from prison and 'taken for a ride', as it was called euphemistically, and then executed in a remote area. In many cases they were first humiliated and tortured. For example, they had to curse or to undress and sometimes they were castrated or forced to run as bulls to a red rag, after which they were killed like a beast.[35] It seemed a revolutionary duty to exterminate the clergy. In some areas groups of revolutionaries went around villages to verify that the priest had been murdered. Many villagers explained later that they had killed the priest because 'what else could we have done to carry out the revolution'. Or 'what does revolution mean? Had we not agreed to kill them all?'[36] A militia member exclaimed that a priest was detained 'because you [the clerics] are to blame for everything that is happening'.[37]

The destruction of Catholic buildings and symbols was often the most obvious sign that a new era had begun. The only buildings that in many regions were destroyed or set on fire were churches and monasteries. Sometimes the population limited itself to removing the statues of saints and other religious paraphernalia and giving the church buildings a new function as a garage, storage room, hospital, dance hall, barracks or party headquarters. More often, however, it was believed that a real purification could take place only through fire. Desecrating liturgical objects also belonged to the often spontaneously invented rituals. Members of militias trampled on hosts and put on chasubles and other religious garments to celebrate mock masses or processions. The Spanish historian Julio de la Cueva seems to agree with Brenan and Hobsbawm when he refers to the almost millenarian aspects of the anticlerical violence. He concludes that the aggressive behaviour towards sacred images and devotional objects seemed to 'reveal a basic, almost magical belief in their might and the necessity to escape from their influence at any cost'. In the Andalusian village of Lepe, for instance, the inhabitants attacked the formerly adored patroness saint of the village with an unprecedented ferocity, pulling out her eyes, stripping her from clothes and jewels, shooting her, chopping her to pieces and throwing the remains into the river.[38]

The prominent American historian of religion Bruce Lincoln proposes a slightly different and more utilitarian interpretation of these anticlerical atrocities. According to him, they should be seen as acts of iconoclasm, as 'the deliberate and public shattering of sacred symbols with the implicit intent of dissolving all loyalty to the institution which employs those symbols, and, further, of dissipating all respect for the ideology which that institution propagates'. In this he seems to emphasize the atheistic convictions of those who perpetrated these acts, but even for the most radical anticlericals these actions probably also contained an element of breaking the spell that the Catholic religion had cast over the population at large and maybe even over themselves. Lincoln actually gives various examples in which the long-buried corpses of priests, monks and nuns were exhumed and publicly displayed, sometimes for several days. As these bodies were decomposed, it became manifest that even the members of the clergy were subject to death and decay. Many people who went to see the 'spectacle' laughed and jeered at them, as if they experienced 'joy or liberation at the degradation of the mighty'. In this way the anticlericals tried to demonstrate 'the *powerlessness* of the icon'.[39]

Lincoln also acknowledges that these humiliating displays of corpses and other iconoclastic acts had a strong millenarian flavour. By fiercely rejecting the old rules the revolutionaries attempted to 'create a new morality'. He concludes as follows:

> But prior to the attempt at establishing the 'new rules', there was an ominous, violent and profoundly shocking phase of 'no rules' in

the summer of 1936, during which political enemies were ruthlessly murdered, churches burned, and disinterred corpses were placed on public display. In part, these may have been practical steps aimed at demolishing what was left of the *ancien régime*, but they were also the spontaneous dramatization of *absolute* liberation from all bonds of the past, even from those of common decency.[40]

Illustrative of the anticlerical attitude in the Republican zone was the highly symbolic 'execution' on 7 August 1936 of the monument of the Sacred Heart, that 18 years earlier had been inaugurated by King Alfonso XIII with so much pomp. After the fusillade the monument was blown up. Fighting the enemy on the battlefront apparently only made sense if first the republican part of Spain was liberated from the Catholic yoke under which the country had suffered for so long, and for this task some bullets and explosives could certainly be expended.

De la Cueva describes other symbolic acts perpetrated in the first months of the Civil War. Thus, crucifixes and statues of saints along public roads were destroyed. In a graveyard in Aragon a man even tried to remove all religious references from the tombs with a chisel. The common *adiós* as a farewell salute was abolished. Cursing came into fashion and became a way to make clear that one was on the correct side. In some companies blaspheming contests were held. The author also makes clear that this purification was not limited to the public sphere but invaded the private sphere as well. In many villages a large-scale collection of private religious objects was held, including images of saints, devotional pictures, dolls of the child Jesus and medallions of the Sacred Heart. These were lumped together and set on fire.[41]

These events might provide a better understanding of the anticlerical fury of this period. One could argue that the clergy and the Church made easy targets. Rich landowners, right-wing politicians and large employers knew that they could become a victim of the workers' militia and immediately took measures to escape or to defend themselves, but this was much less the case with the Church and its servants. But by attacking clergymen left-wing militants did not so much target the Church's political but its moral and symbolic power. And this 'soft power' was more pervasive and therefore more dangerous than the hard power of the military insurgents, right-wing politicians and their supporters. The latter could conquer only the public space, whereas the Church entered the homes and private lives of the great majority of the population. The totalitarian ambitions of the anticlerical firebrands also aimed to reach into the private sphere and therefore primarily targeted the clergy. They probably did not so much fear the influence of the Church on themselves, but they wanted to protect their children and wives from it. The anticlerical fury thus had a clear gendered aspect as well. Those opponents who could most easily penetrate the female sphere – the priests and confessors – should thus be physically eliminated, while the religious objects should be radically purged from each home. This in a way is confirmed by an old lady from Barcelona who did not want her image of the Virgin Mary to be removed and hoped to protect it (and herself) by attaching an ensign of the Federación Anarquista Ibérica (FAI) to it, exclaiming 'this is the virgin of the FAI! This is one of ours!'[42] Although the lady vainly hoped that a compromise was still possible, she clearly understood that the main issue was the spiritual domination of her own living space and, in the end, of her mind and her heart. In this sense the almost totalitarian anticlericalism that expressed itself in the Republican zone seems to be a political religion that was imposed from below.

However, there are a few aspects that call into question this conclusion. First, it is necessary to take a closer look at the specific anticlerical character of the rear-guard repression. A substantial number of the executions of clerics were in retribution for murderous actions, particularly against civilians, by Franco's troops. For instance, after Gijón was bombed in August 1936, anarchist militias went to the local prison where they killed a large number of supposed sympathizers of the nationalist cause, including 12 clergymen. Similar killings by left-wing militiamen took place in Bilbao between October 1936 and January 1937 as revenge for victims of aerial attacks. Many priests were also among those supposed members of the fifth column – a term introduced by General Mola, who maintained that right-wing supporters of the rebelling army officers would help in the conquest of Madrid – killed just behind the front line, especially when a Nationalist advance was imminent. Thus, when in November 1936 Madrid came under siege and it was decided to evacuate a large number of the prisoners, communist and anarchist militia took matters into their own hands by executing the human cargo of many vans carrying prisoners out of the city, and inevitably many who died were members of the clergy.[43]

It is also doubtful whether most of the other anticlerical killings were totally spontaneous. In many cases it was militias from elsewhere that took the lead in purging the villages, so those who arrested or killed the priests were often not members of their community. Thus, in the Aragonese town of Barbastro, where in the end 88 per cent of the clergy succumbed, workers' militias from Barcelona and other parts of Catalonia – on their way to the nearby front – killed most of the local monks.[44] It is also unclear whether the destruction of church buildings and the killing of members of the local clergy were spontaneous acts, inspired by examples from neighbouring places, or whether militias received instructions to burn down the churches and go after the priests. In general, the incidents were not caused by a mob suddenly going out of control but by a small number of hotheads that took the lead. Nonetheless, in many instances a large number of people participated or looked on more passively.

The Catalan historian Albertí argues that we have to distinguish between the various ideological currents. Most republicans and moderate socialists opposed the anticlerical outbursts, while anticlericalism was not part of the core ideas of the more revolutionary socialists and communists either, which focused on the class struggle against capitalism. For them, dead priests were merely collateral damage that could be justified in the context of the war. This was different for the anarchists, for whom the elimination of the Catholic Church was an integral part of their strategy to bring about a true and lasting social and moral revolution. Demolishing the buildings was not enough, the Catholic religion itself had to be rooted out completely before a new and truly free society could come about. Although in many cases it is difficult to establish exactly who was responsible for the destructions and killings, it is clear, according to Albertí, that the anarchists had the upper hand and that most acts of transgressive behaviour were committed by them.[45]

Conclusion

We can now conclude that the fierce anticlericalism that developed during the first decade of the twentieth century and that came to a dramatic outburst during the Spanish Civil War should be understood – through its use of ritual forms and postulating its own ideals as absolutes – as a form of the sacralization of politics. The realization of progressive political dreams was possible only if the constricting ties of Catholicism were broken, and if that could not be done voluntarily, it had to be realized forcibly by physically eliminating the Church and its representatives. The belief in disbelief also clearly contained a religious element. A brief but thorough purification by ritual, iconoclastic violence would, in the eyes of many, bring a new dawn, a new society and a kind of secular heaven on Earth.

Spanish anticlericalism gained traits of a political religion when in the early twentieth century the earlier enlightened and elitist variant was abandoned and a more populist course was chosen by Alejandro Lerroux. He consciously mixed a rational and secular outlook with elements of an older popular anticlerical tradition, and in order to reach a mass audience he adopted symbols, images and forms taken from Catholicism, with which his audience was still very familiar. Pilgrimages became democratic picnics, saints were replaced by republican martyrs and processions with banners and psalms were turned into demonstrations with republican flags and revolutionary anthems. Moreover, he frequently used terms and concepts derived from the Christian faith, portraying himself in a messianic way while his adversaries were demonized and the revolution was promoted as eventually leading the nation to the Promised Land.

It has also been shown that the Spanish Civil War should not be seen – not even partially – as an archaic religious war. While in other major Catholic countries in Europe the state had succeeded in restricting the influence of the Church in the public sphere during the second half of the nineteenth century, this had not been the case in Spain. As a result, the increasing political polarization between left and right – which happened almost everywhere in Europe during the interwar years – became enmeshed with a maybe even more intense struggle between clericals and anticlericals. What was at stake was not merely the power over the state and the public space but the almost totalitarian dominance over the private sphere and over the hearts and minds of the population.

It is clear that the fierce anticlerical preaching of politicians and intellectuals such as Lerroux had prepared the ground for the anticlerical violence of 1936. Anticlerical rhetoric had proven to be a successful strategy to mobilize the masses and unite all revolutionary forces. However, the outburst of anticlerical violence in 1936 was not coordinated from above but was a spontaneous response by the public to this rhetoric. Apparently, there was a large demand from below for ideologies that gave an all-encompassing and absolute solution to all human problems and sufferings, and this certainly proved to be the case in Spain. As a result the rise and 'success' of political religions cannot be attributed only to irrational but charismatic politicians, such as Mussolini, Hitler and Stalin.

There are, nevertheless, some limits to the applicability of a political religion approach to Spanish anticlericalism. In the first place it was a quite ephemeral phenomenon and did not become an integrated and institutionalized part of a totalitarian regime. When in the spring of 1937 the government regained control over the republican territories public order was more or less restored. As a consequence anticlerical violence subsided and – except for the last days of the war when acts of vengeance became frequent again – rapidly lost its appeal. Furthermore, it is also possible to criticize the presumably spontaneous character of the anticlerical outbursts. Eradicating the Church from Spain seems to have been a primordial element of the anarchist revolutionary strategy, but although most of their anticlerical ideals were shared by at least part of the other left-wing militia and their sympathizers, it is not entirely clear if the violence was produced by a few determined fanatics or radical hotheads who profited from the passive attitude of a large mass of bystanders, or if substantial parts of the public voluntarily decided to participate in the anticlerical violence.

However, by interpreting anticlericalism as a form of the sacralization of politics it has also become clear that Spanish developments were not very exceptional. The anticlerical violence should not be seen as an atavistic outburst of millenarian beliefs or archaic forms of protest, nor as a more rational reaction to centuries of political oppression and economic exploitation, but as a phenomenon that was quite typical of the difficult transition to the age of mass politics that took place all over Europe during the first half of the twentieth century.

Notes

1. See Zira Box, *España Año Zero. La construcción simbólica del franquismo* (Madrid, 2010).
2. The 180,000 victims in the Francoist Zone include about 50,000 executions in the years immediately after the war. Apart from the political adversaries killed, around 250,000 people died directly because of the war, and there were approximately half a million refugees. See Paul Preston, *The Spanish Holocaust: Inquisition and Extermination in Twentieth-century Spain* (New York, 2012).
3. Gerald Brenan, *The Spanish Labyrinth: An Account of the Social and Political Background of the Spanish Civil War* (Cambridge, 1990 [1943]), 188–92, and Eric Hobsbawm, *Primitive Rebels: Studies in Archaic Forms of Social Movement in the Nineteenth and Twentieth Century* (Manchester, 1971 [1959]), 74–93.
4. The main critics were Temma Kaplan, *Anarchists of Andalusia, 1868–1903* (Princeton, NJ, 1977), and Joan Connelly Ullman, *The Tragic Week: A Study of Anticlericalism in Spain, 1875–1912* (Cambridge, 1968). See for the debate, Richard Maddox, 'Revolutionary Anticlericalism and Hegemonic Processes in an Andalusian Town, August 1936', *American Ethnologist* 22/1 (1995), 125–42 (126–8), and Manuel Pérez Ledesma, 'Studies on Anticlericalism in Contemporary Spain', *International Review of Social History* 46/2 (2001), 227–55.
5. See: Hugh McLeod, *Religion and the People of Western Europe, 1789–1989* (Oxford, 1997 [1981]), 1–15.
6. The three different forms of anticlericalism are discussed in Jacqueline Lalouette, 'El anticlericalismo en Francia, 1877–1914', *Ayer* 27 (1997), 15–39 (29–33).

7. Lalouette, 'El anticlericalismo en Francia', 34–6.
8. Martin Papenheim, '*Roma o morte*: Culture Wars in Italy', in Christopher Clark and Wolfram Kaiser (eds), *Culture Wars: Secular–Catholic Conflict in Nineteenth-century Europe* (Cambridge, 2003), 202–27.
9. Christopher Clark, 'The New Catholicism and the European Culture Wars', in Clark and Kaiser (eds), *Culture Wars*, 11–47.
10. See James McMillan, '"Priests Hits Girl": On the Front Line in the "War of the Two Frances"', and Manuel Borutta, 'Enemies at the Gate: The *Moabiter Klostersturm* and the *Kulturkampf*: Germany', both in Clark and Kaiser (eds), *Culture Wars*, 77–101 and 227–55.
11. See also Jacqueline Lalouette, *La libre pensée en France, 1848–1940* (Paris, 1997).
12. William James Callahan, *Church, Politics and Society in Spain, 1750–1874* (Cambridge, 1984), 145–85.
13. Ibid., 190–5.
14. Frances Lannon, *Privilege, Persecution, and Prophecy: The Catholic Church in Spain, 1875–1975* (Oxford, 1987), 119–22.
15. Mary Vincent, *Spain 1833–2002: People and State* (Oxford, 2007), 102.
16. Lannon, *Privilege, Persecution, and Prophecy*, 146–70.
17. Juan Sisinio Pérez Garzón, 'Curas y liberales en la revolución burguesa', *Ayer* 27 (1997), 67–100 (81–3).
18. Julio de la Cueva Merino, 'Los intelectuales, el clero y el pueblo (España, 1900)', *Foro Hispánico* 18 (2000), 31–43; Enrique A. Sanabria, *Republicanism and Anticlerical Nationalism in Spain* (Basingstoke, 2009).
19. Julio de la Cueva Merino, 'Católicos en la calle: la movilización de los católicos españoles, 1899–1923', *Historia y Política* 3 (2000), 55–80.
20. Julio de la Cueva, 'The Assault on the City of the Levites: Spain', in Clark and Kaiser (eds), *Culture Wars*, 181–201.
21. Julio de la Cueva Merino, 'Movilización política e identidad anticlerical, 1898–1910', *Ayer* 27 (1997), 101–26 (111–19).
22. José Álvarez Junco, *El Emperador del Paralelo. Lerroux y la demagogia populista* (Madrid, 1990). See also: Ramiro Reig, 'Entre la realidad y el fenómeno blasquista en Valencia, 1898–1936', in Nigel Townson (ed.), *El republicanismo en España (1830–1977)* (Madrid, 1994), 395–425, and Ferran Archilés i Cardona, *Parlar en nom del poble. Cultura política, discurs i mobilització social al republicanisme de Castelló de la Plana, 1891–1909* (Castellón, 2002).
23. This and the following paragraphs are based on Álvarez Junco, *El Emperador del Paralelo*, 401–14.
24. Ibid., 252–9 and 389–96.
25. Ibid., 375–8. See also Ullman, *The Tragic Week*.
26. Álvarez Junco, *El Emperador del Paralelo*, 403.
27. Julio de la Cueva Merino, 'Democracia liberal y anticlericalismo durante la Restauración', in Manuel Suárez Cortina (ed.), *La Restauración entre el liberalismo y la democracia* (Madrid, 1997), 229–73.
28. Francisco Peiró, as quoted in J. Albertí, *La Iglesia en llamas. La persecución religiosa en España durante la guerra civil* (Barcelona, 2008), 67.
29. Julio de la Cueva Merino, 'El anticlericalismo en la Segunda República y la Guerra Civil', in Emilio La Parra López and Manuel Suárez Cortina (eds), *El anticlericalismo español contemporáneo* (Madrid, 1998), 211–303 (218–19), and Vincent, *Spain*, 120.

30. Manuel Delgado Ruiz, 'Anticlericalismo, espacio y poder. La destrucción de los rituales católicos, 1931–1939', *Ayer* 27 (1997), 149–81 (171).

31. Julián Casanova, *República y guerra civil* (Historia de España, 8; Madrid, 2007), 84–5, 119–20 and 131.

32. Interview by Jay Allen from July 1936, as quoted in Paul Preston, *Franco: A Biography* (London, 1994), 153.

33. Anthony Beevor, *The Battle for Spain: The Spanish Civil War 1936–1939* (London, 2006), 106–7 and 269–70 and Albertí, *La Iglesia en llamas*, 277–86 and 408–14.

34. Figures are originally from Antonio Montero Moreno, *Historia de la persecución religiosa en España, 1936–1939* (Madrid, 1961), 761–4.

35. Julio de la Cueva, 'Religious Persecution, Anticlerical Tradition and Revolution: On Atrocities against the Clergy during the Spanish Civil War', *Journal of Contemporary History* (1998), 355–69 (356); De la Cueva Merino, 'El anticlericalismo en la Segunda República', 260–85 and Mary Vincent, '"The Keys to the Kingdom": Religious Violence in the Spanish Civil War, July–August 1936', in Chris Ealham and Michael Richards (eds), *The Splintering of Spain: Cultural History and the Spanish Civil War, 1936–1939* (Cambridge, 2005), 68–93.

36. Julio de la Cueva Merino, '"Si los frailes y monjes supieran...": La violencia anticlerical', in Santos Juliá (ed.), *Violencia política en la España del siglo XX* (Madrid, 2000), 191–233 (229–30).

37. Quoted in Albertí, *La Iglesia en llamas*, 474.

38. De la Cueva, 'Religious Persecution', 365–6.

39. Bruce Lincoln, 'Revolutionary Exhumation in Spain, July 1936', *Comparative Studies in Society and History* 27/2 (1985), 241–60 (255–8).

40. Ibid., 251–2.

41. De la Cueva, 'Religious Persecution', 362–3.

42. Quoted in Albertí, *La Iglesia en llamas*, 438.

43. Ibid., 300, 304–5 and 272–4.

44. Ibid., 353–6.

45. Ibid., 237–54. See also Gonzalo Álvarez Chillida, 'Movimiento libertario y religión durante la Segunda República (1931–1936)', in Julio de la Cueva and Feliciano Montero (eds), *La izquierda obrera y religión en España (1900–1939)* (Alcalá de Henares, 2012), 99–127.

Concluding Remarks

Joost Augusteijn, Patrick Dassen and Maartje Janse

What do these contributions add to our understanding of the sacralization of politics in democratic systems and the role of ordinary people in it? An important element of this volume has been a re-evaluation of the relationship between politics and religion itself. On a fundamental level Herman Paul has shown that politics constitutes a secular religion if it simply resembles a religion. What is more, he stresses that religion does not function only on a spiritual and symbolic level, but that it also always contains social and political aspects. Most obviously that is the case when political power is based on divine sanction, as with the monarchy in the medieval and early modern periods. However, in the modern era, when political power came to be derived from the people, the connection between politics and religion has also been shown to be very direct. The chapter by Maartje Janse has made clear that political action in a mass democracy was actually in form and content directly based on models stemming from the religious realm, while Eduard van de Bilt has shown that a religious motivation does not necessarily lead to inactivity in the political arena, but neither does it lead to a sacralization of politics. The call upon a higher authority to some extent prevents this from taking place.

The dangers associated with mass politics have often been connected with the rise of socialist parties in the late nineteenth century. Their challenging of the political and social system made them a serious concern for established authority. However, the dangers of mass political action had already been pointed out by commentators in the early nineteenth century, as Janse has shown, when political pressure groups, developed directly out of religious organizations, used moral imperatives and emotional appeals to mobilize the people. Socialism constituted maybe the first secular political movement which possessed

255

all the hallmarks of a religion, as Adriaan van Veldhuizen has shown, including a holy text, a prophet, saints and a Promised Land. Jolijn Groothuizen and Dennis Bos have illustrated how the imagery used by socialists contained many religious elements, while Henk te Velde has shown that the language used was also strongly religious, particularly in relation to the idea of conversion to democratic socialism. Such religious language has continued to be used in a democratic political context, as is particularly apparent in contemporary populism.

The totalitarian regimes of the mid-twentieth century have made the central role of socialism and populism in the sacralization of politics and ultimately in the development of political religions most obvious. However, as Adriaan van Veldhuizen and also Henk Kern have shown, such a sacralization process can largely be a voluntary, even unintentional process initiated by ordinary members looking for meaning. This was the case not only in a democratic context as with Dutch social democrats in the early twentieth century, but was also a fundamental cause of the elevation of Marx, Lenin and Stalin to the pantheon of saints in the Soviet Union. Henk Kern has shown that the creation of a political religion in the case of the Russian Revolution was not only the chosen instrument of power in the hands of a new political elite, but was just as much the result of a compromise with an unavoidable social-cultural reality where the people demanded the re-creation of the communist system in terms of a secular religion.

A similar demand from below lies behind the enthusiastic and inclusive response in German society to the outbreak of the First World War, where a call upon the nation to some extent functioned as a secular religion, mobilizing the people behind the war effort. This can be explained only by an overwhelming desire for unity among large segments of the population in a divided society. However, as Patrick Dassen has shown, this unity was soon broken by the tension caused by the war itself, and the nation could no longer function as a sacralized entity that could rally the people who were absorbed by everyday concerns of survival and confronted by profiteering at the top. Eventually the nation that had signified inclusion and tolerance came to be exclusive, fundamentalist and intolerant. The idea of a *Volksgemeinschaft* common to all, strongly emphasized at the beginning of the war, was nevertheless used again by all kinds of groups after the war, most effectively by the Nazis, to win the hearts and minds of the people.

The ability of nationalism to bring people onto the streets is also a strong current in Ireland from the Enlightenment to the present day, even enabling the formation of a long litany of movements using violence for political ends. Joost Augusteijn has shown that particularly the fusion of cultural and political forms at the end of the nineteenth century turned Irish nationalism from a civil into a political religion, making totalitarian demands on its members. Ironically this merger came to hold sway over the Irish population during a time of war and conflict, while at the same time the German people were losing their belief in the nation as a secular religion. It is apparently not the democratic context in which such a movement functions that determines whether the sacralization of the nation takes on the form of a political religion. Nationalism can take on both forms of sacralized politics. The peculiar form of nationalism created in the United States, which was in principle not based on any ethnic component, has ensured for it the claim to be the prime example of a civil religion. However, as Adam Fairclough has shown, the idea that the United States was not only uniquely fitted to teach liberty and democracy to other peoples but also had a providential mission to do so is itself more a civil religion than a reality, as the system that was instituted excluded many of its own citizens and had clearly coercive and intolerant aspects.

A more unexpected form of the sacralization of politics can be found in the Spanish anticlerical movement in the first half of the twentieth century. Eric Storm has shown how the very practical concern of realizing progressive political goals in Spain necessitated – at least in the eyes of many republicans, socialists and anarchists – the elimination of the Catholic Church and its representatives, which in the end was accomplished by creating an alternative secular religion, a 'belief in disbelief'. In the 1930s the struggle against the Church was increasingly portrayed in religious terms, with symbols, images and forms taken from Catholicism used to mobilize the masses. Just like socialism, anticlericalism had pilgrimages, saints and processions, while the leaders were assigned messianic qualities and were believed to be leading the people to the Promised Land. This sacralization of the movement was again primarily initiated by ordinary activists and not created by its leadership, as we have seen was the case with socialist and communist movements.

In the Introduction we set out two objectives, the first being to reassess the role of the sacralization of politics in democratic systems. What conclusions can we draw in this regard based on the case studies presented in this volume? First of all, that religion or anything resembling a religion has an immense capability of mobilizing people politically. It is difficult to think of anything else that could lend a cause the same degree of urgency and evoke such a strong sense of commitment in so many people at once. What was held sacred was worth fighting for, both in causes that had a strong link to religious beliefs (as in the contributions of Janse and Van de Bilt) and in case studies in which traditional religion did not play a role. Political religions in democratic as well as totalitarian regimes refer to the dreams, beliefs and the faith in redemption that Henk te Velde discusses in his chapter. This volume has once more made clear that these dreams and beliefs are not some naive remnants of a pre-modern era or illogical emotions that need to be addressed when larger groups of uneducated people start to participate in politics. They are essential elements of modern politics because politics entails much more than merely pragmatic administration.

In modern politics, many different elements have been held sacred: the community, the party, the nation, the past, the leader and even a political mission or a struggle could gain a religious character. Such a cause could be very specific; for instance, the abolition of slavery or even fighting the church. Protest movements in support of these causes appropriated the imagery and rhetoric of religious crusades to indicate how much the cause meant to them and how committed they were to it. Causes could also be formulated in more general terms, as in the case of the American mission to bring democracy to the world. In all cases, the sacred nature of these causes indicates that they were more than mere points on the political agenda: they claimed precedence over 'normal' politics.

In the case of attributing sanctity to a group, be it a political faction, party or the nation, implicitly or sometimes even explicitly, the group and its goals come to be seen as more important than other groups but also as more important than its individual members. The threshold for sacrificing individual autonomy and well-being for the greater good – going to war for the fatherland being the prime example – is substantially lowered when the community is considered to be a sacred community. In historiography, this phenomenon has been predominantly linked to totalitarianism. However, it seems to be intrinsically linked to the functioning of modern politics at large.

Mobilization implies motion. What we hold sacred is capable of igniting change and starting a movement. Religious forms of politics have not only been able to shape and channel the participation of the masses in modern politics, but have also initiated political change. The ability of any political agent to mobilize the masses for a new sacred cause, which can then compete with other sacred causes for priority, lies at the heart of the democratic character of modern politics.

Two elements can be discerned in the process of the sacralization of politics, which support each other but are also often at odds: mobilizing and disciplining the masses. Mobilization on behalf of a sacred cause is an essential element of modern mass politics, without which it is impossible to win the hearts and minds of the people. But their hearts and minds were only completely won through participation in political rituals, liturgy, celebration of a shared past and the veneration of charismatic leaders. The religious imagery and discourse in these types of political manifestations are capable of deeply affecting people and transforming their identities. This is the disciplining element. It is important to stress that disciplining in this sense should not be simply understood as forcing ideas on people but rather as the often voluntary submission of people to a leader or cause through these types of experiences. These are the moments people really start believing.

Here we arrive at the second aim of this volume: to reassess the role of ordinary people in the process of the sacralization of politics. As several chapters in this volume show, this role is more important than often assumed. In contrast to the image of a coercive state or of manipulative leaders of totalitarian regimes, many articles demonstrate an authentic need of large segments of the population in any type of political system to fight for a sacred cause, be it abolition of slavery, the emancipation of labourers or the unity of the German nation in the First World War. This striving for a sacred cause or entity was broadly based and found its origin in the genuine need of hope for a better future, desire for national independence or, more widely, the need to give new meaning to the hardships of life; for example, under the conditions of crisis or instability. Therefore, the sacralization of politics often occurs in response to a demand from ordinary people – hence, from below – and is not just forced on them – from above – by political leaders.

Apart from the answers to the questions we posed, the contributions in this volume lead to at least two general conclusions. First, politics and religion are very much interwoven and cannot be clearly separated. The domain of religion is not excluded from power relations or the struggle for authority and legitimacy. The other way around, and more important in this volume, modern mass politics would not function if it did not resemble religion to a certain extent. Religion is not to be found only in totalitarian politics but in all forms of politics, including democratic forms, simply because modern politics does not function without winning the hearts and minds of the people.

This brings us to the second conclusion. Within the era of modern mass politics, for politics to function a certain degree of sacralization is thus necessary, regardless of the regime type. Although this sacralization can take on various distinctive forms which move somewhere between the two ideal types of civil and political religion, the dichotomy between civil religion and political religion can, as the contributions to this volume have shown, in historical reality never fully define the distinction between totalitarian and democratic regimes. This distinction can more fruitfully be found in features such as the rule of law, a functioning constitution, civil liberties and an overall system of checks and balances. The essential connection between religion and politics and the primary role of ordinary people in the process of sacralization, as made clear in this volume, necessitates a fundamental reassessment of the research into the sacralization of politics: one that takes the concept of political religion beyond totalitarianism.

Select Bibliography

Abzug, Robert H., *Cosmos Crumbling: American Reform and the Religious Imagination* (New York and Oxford, 1994).

Álvarez-Junco, José, *The Emergence of Mass Politics in Spain: Populist Demagoguery and Republican Culture, 1890–1910* (Eastborne, 2003).

Aron, Raymond, 'L'avenir des religions séculières' (1944), in idem, *Chroniques de guerre: la France libre, 1940–1945*, ed. Christian Bachelier (Paris, 1990), 925–48.

Augusteijn, Joost, *Patrick Pearse: The Making of a Revolutionary* (Basingstoke, 2010).

Bar-On, Tamir, 'Understanding Political Conversion and Mimetic Rivalry', *Totalitarian Movements and Political Religions* 10/3–4 (2009), 241–64.

Bellah, Robert, 'Civil Religion in America', *Daedalus* 97/1 (1967), 1–21.

Bellah, Robert, *The Broken Covenant: American Civil Religion in Time of Trial* (New York, 1975).

Billington, James H., *Fire in the Minds of Man: Origins of the Revolutionary Faith* (New York, 1980).

Box, Zira, *España Año Zero. La construcción simbólica del franquismo* (Madrid, 2010).

Burleigh, Michael, *Earthly Powers: The Clash of Religion and Politics in Europe from the French Revolution to the Great War* (New York, 2005).

Burleigh, Michael, *Sacred Causes: Religion and Politics from the European Dictators to Al Qaida* (New York, 2007).

Burns, Edward McCall, *The American Idea of Mission: Concepts of National Purpose and Destiny* (New Brunswick, 1957).

Burrin, Philippe, 'Political Religion: The Relevance of a Concept', *History and Memory* 9/1–2 (1997), 321–49.

Canovan, Margaret, 'Trust the People! Populism and the Two Faces of Democracy', *Political Studies* 47/1 (1999), 2–16.

Chickering, Roger, *Imperial Germany and the Great War, 1914–1918*, 2nd edn (Cambridge, 2004).

Clark, Christopher, and Wolfram Kaiser (eds), *Culture Wars: Secular–Catholic Conflict in Nineteenth-Century Europe* (Cambridge, 2003).

Crossman, Richard (ed.), *The God That Failed* (New York, 1954 [1949]).

Cueva, Julio de la, 'Religious Persecution, Anticlerical Tradition and Revolution: On Atrocities against the Clergy during the Spanish Civil War', *Journal of Contemporary History* (1998), 355–69.

Davis, Belinda, *Home Fires Burning. Food, Politics, and Everyday Life in World War I Berlin* (Chapel Hill and London, 2000).

Dietzgen, Joseph, *Die Religion der Sozial-Demokratie. Kanzelreden* (Berlin, 1906).

Dháibhéid Caoimhe, Nic, and Colin Reid (eds), *From Parnell to Paisley: Constitutional and Revolutionary Politics in Modern Ireland* (Dublin, 2010).

Dolan, Anne, *Commemorating the Irish Civil War: History and Memory, 1923–2000* (Cambridge, 2003).

Duvergier, Maurice, *Les partis politiques* (Paris, 1951).

Elliott, Marianne, *Wolfe Tone: Prophet of Irish Independence* (New Haven, 1989).

Evans, Richard, *The Third Reich in Power 1933–1939* (New York, 2005).

Ferriter, Diarmuid, *Judging Dev: A Reassessment of the Life and Legacy of Eamon De Valera* (Dublin, 2007).

Fitzpatrick, Sheila, and Michael Geyer (eds), *Beyond Totalitarianism: Stalinism and Nazism Compared* (Cambridge, 2009).

Fowler, Robert, Allen Hertzke, Laura Olson and Kevin Den Dulk, *Religion and Politics in America: Faith, Culture, and Strategic Choices* (New York, 2010).

Gentile, Emilio, *The Sacralization of Politics in Fascist Italy* (Cambridge, 1996).

Gentile, Emilio, *Politics as Religion*, trans. George Staunton (Princeton, NJ and Oxford, 2006).

Geoghegan, Patrick M., *Daniel O'Connell and the Irish Act of Union, 1800–1829* (Dublin, 2009).

Geoghegan, Patrick M., *Liberator: The Life and Death of Daniel O'Connell 1830–1847* (Dublin, 2010).

Goodwin, Jeff, James M. Jasper and Francesca Polletta, 'Introduction: Why Emotions Matter', in idem (eds), *Passionate Politics: Emotions and Social Movements* (Chicago, 2001), 1–24.

Gregor, Anthony James, *Totalitarianism and Political Religion: An Intellectual History* (Stanford, 2012).

Griffin, Roger (ed.), *Fascism, Totalitarianism and Political Religion* (London and New York, 2005).

Griffin, Roger, '"Religious Politics": A Concept Comes of Age', *Leidschrift Historisch Tijdschrift* 26/2 (2011), 7–18.

Haidt, Jonathan, *The Righteous Mind: Why Good People Are Divided by Politics and Religion* (New York, 2012).

Hardtwig, Wolfgang, 'Political Religion in Modern Germany: Reflections on Nationalism, Socialism, and National Socialism', *Bulletin of the German Historical Institute* NR 28 (2001), 3–36.

Hatch, Nathan O., *The Democratization of American Christianity* (New Haven and London, 1989).

Hobsbawm, Eric, *Primitive Rebels: Studies in Archaic Forms of Social Movement in the Nineteenth and Twentieth Century* (Manchester, 1959).

Hodgson, Godfrey, *The Myth of American Exceptionalism* (New Haven, 2009).

Hoffer, Eric, *The True Believer. Thoughts on the Nature of Mass Movements* (New York et al., 1966 [1951]).

Horne, John (ed.), *State, Society and Mobilization in Europe during the First World War* (Cambridge, 1997).

Juliá, Santos (ed.), *Violencia política en la España del siglo XX* (Madrid, 2000).

Kee, Robert, *The Laurel and the Ivy: The Story of Charles Stewart Parnell and Irish Nationalism* (Hamilton and London, 1993).

Kershaw, Ian, *Hitler 1889–1936: Hubris* (London, 1998).

Kohut, Andrew, and Bruce Stokes, *America against the World: How We Are Different and Why We Are Disliked* (New York, 2006).

Kramer, Alan, *Dynamic of Destruction: Culture and Mass Killing in the First World War* (Oxford, 2007).

Krumeich, Gerd (ed.), *Nationalsozialismus und Erster Weltkrieg* (Essen, 2010).

Lambert, Frank, *Religion in American Politics: A Short History* (Princeton, 2010).

Landsberger, Stefan R., and Marien van der Heijden, *Chinese Posters* (Munich, 2009).

Lane, Christel, *The Rites of Rulers: Rituals in Industrial Society – The Soviet Case* (Cambridge and London, 1981).

Ley, Michael, 'Zur Theorie des politischen Religionen: Der Nationalismus als Paradigma politischer Religiosität', in Michael Ley, Heinrich Neisser and Gilbert Weiss (eds), *Politische Religion? Politik, Religion und Anthropologie im Werk von Eric Voegelin* (Munich, 2003), 77–85.

Lidtke, Vernon L., *The Alternative Culture: Socialist Labor in Imperial Germany* (New York and Oxford, 1985).

Lincoln, Bruce, 'Revolutionary Exhumation in Spain, July 1936', *Comparative Studies in Society and History* 27/2 (1985), 241–60.

Lind, Michael, *What Lincoln Believed: The Values and Convictions of America's Greatest President* (New York, 2004).

Maier, Hans (ed.), *'Totalitarismus' und 'Politische Religionen': Konzepte des Diktatursvergleichs*, 3 vols (Paderborn, 1996–2003).

Man, Hendrik de, *Zur Psychologie des Sozialismus* (Jena, 1926).

Mann, Michael, *The Dark Side of Democracy: Explaining Ethnic Cleansing* (Cambridge, 2005).

Margry, Peter Jan, 'The Murder of Pim Fortuyn and Collective Emotions: Hype, Hysteria and Holiness in the Netherlands?', *Etnofoor. Antropologisch tijdschrift* 16 (2003), 102–27.

McCartney, Donal, *The World of Daniel O'Connell* (Dublin, 1980).

McPherson, James M. (ed.), *'We Cannot Escape History': Lincoln and the Last Best Hope of Earth* (Urbana and Chicago, 1995).

Mead, Sidney E., 'Abraham Lincoln's "Last, Best Hope of Earth": The American Dream of Destiny and Democracy', *Church History* 23 (1954), 3–16.

Michels, Robert, *Zur Soziologie des Parteiwesens in der modernen Demokratie* (Stuttgart, 1989 [1911]).

Mommsen, Wolfgang J. (ed.), *Kultur und Krieg. Die Rolle der Intellektuellen, Künstler und Schriftsteller im Ersten Weltkrieg* (Munich, 1996).

Mosse, George L., *The Nationalization of the Masses: Political Symbolism and Mass Movements in Germany from the Napoleonic Wars through the Third Reich* (New York, 1975).

Mulvey, Helen F., *Thomas Davis and Ireland: A Biographical Study* (Washington DC, 2003).

Niebuhr, Reinhold, *The Irony of American History* (Chicago, 2008 [1952]).

Nipperdey, Thomas, *Deutsche Geschichte 1866–1918. Bd 2. Machtstaat vor der Demokratie* (Munich, 1992).

Ostrogorski, Moseï, *Democracy and the Organization of Political Parties*, 2 vols (New York and London, 1922 [1902]).

Pohl, Klaus-Dieter, *Allegorie und Arbeiter. Bildagitatorische – Didaktikund – Repräsentation der SPD 1890–1914. Studien zum politischen Umgangmitbildender Kunst in der politisch-satirischen Zeitschrift, Der Wahre Jacob'und' Süddeutscher Postillon sowie in den Maifestzeitungen* (Osnabrück, 1986).

Preston, Paul, *The Spanish Holocaust: Inquisition and Extermination in Twentieth-Century Spain* (New York, 2012).

Roberts, David D., '"Political Religion" and the Totalitarian Departures of Inter-War Europe: On the Uses and Disadvantages of an Analytical Category', *Contemporary European History* 18/4 (2009), 381–414.

Schöttler, Peter, 'Das Konzept der politischen Religionen bei Lucie Varga und Franz Borkenau', in Michael Ley and Julius H. Schoeps (eds), *Der Nationalsozialismus als politische Religion* (Bodenheim, 1997), 186–205.

Sironneau, Jean-Pierre, *Sécularisation et religions politiques* (The Hague, 1982).

Stamatov, Peter, 'The Religious Field and the Path-dependent Transformation of Popular Politics in the Anglo-American World, 1770–1840', *Theory and Society* 40/4 (2011), 437–73.

Stibbe, Matthew, *Germany 1914–1933: Politics, Society and Culture* (Harlow et al., 2010).

Stout, Jeffrey, *Democracy and Tradition* (Princeton, NJ and Oxford, 2004).

Stowers, Stanley, 'The Concepts of "Religion", "Political Religion" and the Study of Nazism', *Journal of Contemporary History* 42/1 (2007), 9–24.

Talmon, Jacob L., *The Origins of Totalitarian Democracy* (London, 1961 [1952]).

Unfried, Berthold, and Christine Schindler (eds), *Riten, Mythen und Symbole. Die Arbeiterbewegung zwischen 'Zivilreligion' und Volkskultur* (Leipzig, 1999).

Velde, Henk te, 'Charismatic Leaders, Political Religion and Social Movements: Western Europe at the End of the Nineteenth Century', in Jan Willem Stutje (ed.), *Charismatic Leadership and Social Movements* (New York, 2012).

Verhey, Jeffrey, *The Spirit of 1914: Militarism, Myth and Mobilization in Germany* (Cambridge, 2000).

Vincent, Mary, '"The Keys to the Kingdom": Religious Violence in the Spanish Civil War, July–August 1936', in Chris Ealham and Michael Richards (eds), *The Splintering of Spain: Cultural History and the Spanish Civil War, 1936–1939* (Cambridge, 2005), 68–93.

Voegelin, Eric, 'The Political Religions' (1938), in idem, *The Collected Works of Eric Voegelin*, ed. Manfred Henningsen, vol. 5 (Columbia, MO and London, 2000), 19–75.

Vondung, Klaus, *Magie und Manipulation. Ideologischer Kult und politische Religion des Nationalsozialismus* (Göttingen, 1971).

Wald, Kenneth, and Allison Calhoun-Brown, *Religion and Politics in the United States* (Lanham, 2010).

Walkenhorst, Peter, *Nation – Volk – Rasse. Radikaler Nationalismus im Deutschen Kaiserreich 1890–1914* (Göttingen, 2007).

Wehler, Hans-Ulrich , *Deutsche Gesellschaftsgeschichte. Bd. 4. Vom Beginn des Ersten Weltkrieges bis zur Gründung der beiden deutschen Staaten 1914–1949* (Munich, 2003).

Welch, David, *The Third Reich: Politics and Propaganda*, 2nd edn (London and New York, 2002).

Yeo, Stephen, 'A New Life: The Religion of Socialism in Britain 1883–1896', *History Workshop: A Journal for Socialist Historians* 4 (1977), 5–56.

Young, Michael P., *Bearing Witness against Sin: The Evangelical Birth of the American Social Movement* (Chicago and London, 2006).

Index